WOMEN, EQUALITY,
AND THE FRENCH REVOLUTION

WOMEN, EQUALITY, AND THE FRENCH REVOLUTION

Candice E. Proctor

Contributions in Women's Studies, Number 115

Greenwood Press
New York • Westport, Connecticut • London

Library of Congress Cataloging-in-Publication Data

Proctor, Candice E.
    Women, equality, and the French Revolution / Candice E. Proctor.
        p. cm. — (Contributions in women's studies, ISSN 0147-104X ;
   no. 115)
    Includes bibliographical references.
    ISBN 0–313–27245–X (lib. bdg. : alk. paper)
    1. Women—France—History—18th century. 2. France—History—
Revolution, 1789–1799—Women. 3. Equality—France—History—18th
century. I. Title. II. Series.
HQ1613.P76   1990
305.4′0944′09033—dc20   90–2963

British Library Cataloguing in Publication Data is available.

Library of Congress Catalog Card Number: 90–2963
ISBN: 0–313–27245–X
ISSN: 0147–104X

First published in 1990

Greenwood Press, 88 Post Road West, Westport, CT 06881
An imprint of Greenwood Publishing Group, Inc.

Printed in the United States of America

The paper used in this book complies with the
Permanent Paper Standard issued by the National
Information Standards Organization (Z39.48–1984).

10 9 8 7 6 5 4 3 2 1

For my mother,
and for Samantha and Danielle,
this mother's two
very-much-loved little girls.

Contents

Preface

The present volume is a study of ideas, of attitudes; it is not intended to be either a social or a political history. Nevertheless, in the course of this work it has sometimes been necessary to trespass upon those two preserves, since any discussion of ideas without some look at the social and political realities leaves one with a very incomplete understanding of the significance of the ideas.

Also, because this is a study of ideas, and of a time when a large portion of the population remained illiterate (or at least nonliterary), it might seem important to some to point out that these ideas are for the most part those expressed by the middle or upper classes. These classes are, after all, largely the only ones whose writings and thoughts have come down to us, as well as perhaps the only ones with the leisure time to reflect a great deal upon such matters in the first place. And, as the dominant group, they generally set both the tone and the pattern for the intellectual and emotional tendencies of their age.

A note about sources: the majority of the research for this book was conducted in Paris. Most of the works cited can be found in the Bibliothèque Nationale, the Archives Nationales, the Bibliothèque historique de la Ville de Paris, or the Pompidou Center. A few are in the British Museum. Due to rigid editorial restrictions on manuscript length, the bibliography has been severely reduced. All references to cartons in the Archives Nationales have been eliminated, while the list of secondary sources has been cut to a minimum. Many other secondary sources may be found in the end-of-chapter notes, where relevant.

All translation used are those of the writer, unless otherwise noted.

I would like to express my gratitude, first of all, to Dr. Robert Harris, for providing me with both his guidance and his inspiration. Thanks are due to Kathy Sukhun, to my husband, Ihab Lutfi, and, especially, to my mother, Bernadine Proctor, for their hours of assistance with the typing. I am grateful to Jennifer Bowker, for proofreading the final manuscript, and to my father, Dr. Raymond Proctor, for his help with library sources that were unavailable to me while I was overseas. And my thanks to my children, for allowing me to be their mother and yet to do this, too.

Introduction

The adherents of the French Revolution rationalized their controversial activity in terms of a philosophy of liberty, equality, and what they liked to call the inalienable rights of man. Considering the fact that some one-half the inhabitants of eighteenth-century France were women, it might be expected that even the most haphazard application of those supposedly universal principles would have resulted both in a recognition of the subordinate position of women in French society and in support for the idea of equality between the sexes. The present work investigates to what extent that did or did not happen, and if not, then why not.

To ask such questions is not to indulge in a prolepsis inspired by contemporary events and the modern feminist movement. Modern feminism may trace its origins only as far back as the early nineteenth century, but the debate about the nature of woman and her role in society has been around since at least the Renaissance. Well before the beginning of the Revolution, it was a burning issue; by the eighteenth century it was provoking an unprecedented outpouring of articles, contest entries, essays, and multi-volume publications. Virtually every aspect of a woman's life was being scrutinized and analyzed both by the forces of resistance and by the forces of change. What was a woman's "natural character"? What should it be? Should she be educated? How, and to what extent? What was her proper role in the family? In society? What were her rights? Not merely philosophers and essayists, but novelists, playwrights, journalists, and the man in the street were all asking these questions. And as vital as they are to the understanding of any culture, the answers people give to these questions become particularly revealing in an age that deliberately sets out to remake itself in its own image of the perfect society.

It is important to remember, however, that these questions and the controversy they raised were no more an invention of the French Revolution than they were of nineteenth- and twentieth-century feminism. Both the ideology of sexual equality and the hostility that it provoked predated the French Revolution. The continuity between pre-Revolutionary and Revolutionary thought on the subject is striking.

Also striking, although perhaps less surprising, is the continuity in the age's conceptualization of women. The men and women who frequented the popular societies and took part in the Revolutionary *journées* still conceived of women in essentially the same terms as the men and women who had frequented the salons of the *Ancien Régime*. In the typical eighteenth-century French mind, woman was differentiated from man not merely in terms of gender, but by a presumed discrepancy in relative intellectual strength and by a rigidly enforced division of destinies, duties, characteristics, personalities, and even requisite virtues. The strength and pervasiveness of this traditional eighteenth-century perception of the female sex was obviously a severely limiting factor to the potential of any Revolutionary movement in favor of women's rights and greater equality.

True, the thought of the Enlightenment had made considerable impact, but its immediate effect was questionable. Although the ideas of the perfectability of man suggested to some the possibility of the perfectability of woman, most people were not easily convinced. And the major arguments and techniques of the Enlightenment could just as easily be used to defend the status quo as to attack it. Thus, the subordination of women was hailed as one of the universally binding laws of nature, necessary for both the happiness and the survival of man and society. These and many other arguments supporting the inferior position of women were already "in the air," and the makers of the Revolution would not hesitate to use them.

The development of a Revolutionary movement in favor of greater equality between the sexes was further complicated by the growing popularity in the late eighteenth century of "sentimentalism." Itself in many ways a by-product of the Enlightenment, this cult of sentimentalism, with its emphasis on domestic bliss and its sanctification of the woman as mother, simply added an emotional element to the major intellectual arguments of the day.

It is worthwhile at this point to note that, for the most part, the battle lines in this controversy were not drawn between the sexes. The prejudices of their society were held in common by both the men and the women of eighteenth-century France. Although many women complained about the inferiority of their position, there were many more who defended the status quo and warned against the dangers of any change.

Likewise, although the number of males lining up to defend the patriarchy were legion, some of the best-known champions of equality for women happened to be men.

But the ranks of the supporters of the idea of equality between the sexes did not grow during the Revolution. In the need to reconcile their abstract ideals with the realities of their inherited prejudices and assumptions, the men and women of the French Revolution were presented with a dilemma that few ever managed to surmount. There were indeed some who translated the ideals of the Revolution into a doctrine of equality between the sexes. Nevertheless, it is also true that the traditional eighteenth-century perception of the female sex combined during the Revolution with the evolution of an increasingly stern and puritanical code of republican morality. This, together with the growing belief that the untrammeled power of women under the *Ancien Régime* had enabled them to rule and ruin art, society, and the nation, produced some of the most far-reaching and unhesitating official reaffirmations of female subordination and sexual inequality yet seen.

The French Revolution was responsible for the popularization if not the formulation of many of the ideas of equality and individual rights that have had a lasting impact on the social, moral, and ethical thought of the Western world. A knowledge of the extent to which the adherents of the Revolution did or did not include women in the fullest implications of these principles will contribute to our understanding not only of the French Revolution, but of the ambivalent attitudes towards women that still affect our society today.

WOMEN, EQUALITY,
AND THE FRENCH REVOLUTION

1

Rainbows and Butterfly Wings

> When one wishes to write about women, he must dip his pen into a
> rainbow and sprinkle the line with the dust of butterfly wings.
> [Diderot, *Sur les femmes*]

What is a woman?

A female human being? The answer is rarely that simple in any age or
society, and France in 1789 was no exception. In the mind of the typical
man or woman of late eighteenth-century France, woman was differentiated from man not merely in terms of gender, but by a dichotomy of
carefully apportioned abilities, destinies, virtues, and faults.

This general eighteenth-century perception of womanhood was derived
from a variety of sources, mainly the Judeo-Christian tradition, with its
twin pillars, the Creation and the Fall, and from the teachings of the
Ancients, Aristotle in particular. The Renaissance, seventeenth-century
rationalism, and the Enlightenment had all added to or subtly altered that
perception, but the extent to which they truly had changed it is arguable.
Ideas about women are typically confused and contradictory, and what is
sometimes perceived as a change from one period to the next is often no
more than a mere shift of emphasis.

What does exist, however, is a general pool of thoughts, some arguable, some seemingly so basic that they are taken for granted, into which
each individual in a society dips in order to build his or her own image of
womanhood. And the pool of thought about women that existed in
France in 1789 was essentially the same as had existed in 1788 or even in

1

1750, and which would still exist, with a few significant additions, in 1796 or even in 1815. Changing conditions, events, and intellectual trends can destroy old arguments in favor of the superiority of one sex over the other or create new ones, but their effect on an age's pool of thought about the fundamental nature of woman is usually far less profound and considerably more gradual. And it is, of course, the contents of that pool of thought about the nature of woman that to a large extent determines how receptive a society is to arguments about female equality or inferiority in the first place.

To understand, then, the extent to which Revolutionary thinking about equality did or did not include women, one must first understand the contents of this eighteenth-century pool of thought about the nature of women. It had varied only slightly in the past several hundred years, and it would persist virtually unaltered through revolution, reaction, and restoration.

Some of the most pervasive of the ideas about women that existed in France in 1789 were basically Judeo-Christian in origin. By 1789, France had been a Christian land for over 1,000 years, so that many of the teachings and assumptions of that creed were simply taken for granted, even by those who had ostensibly rejected Christianity as a religion. And according to the Biblical Christian tradition, In the Beginning, God created Man (the male). It was only later that he created Woman, both from and for the Man, to be his companion and aid. In the France of the *Ancien Régime* this tradition was virtually unquestioned, even by self-proclaimed Deists, who often simply replaced the word "God" with "Nature."

The effects of this tradition reverberated even into the language. In French, as in English, the word *homme* was (and still is) used interchangeably to designate both the entire human race or the male half of that species only. Thus, in both the language and religion of eighteenth-century France, the male was seen as the prototype, the absolute; the female was the variation, the "other."[1] This thinking was so dominant that throughout the eighteenth century the female sex was quite commonly known as "*le deuxième sexe*": the second sex, both in order of creation and in hierarchical rank. With equal frequency and even greater artlessness, it was known simply as "*le sexe*"—the Sex—as if the female were the only one with sexual attributes; she was seen as a kind of deviation from the normal, the *male*, man.

This mindset was further reenforced by the teachings of the Ancients, second only to the Bible in influence on eighteenth-century perceptions of the nature of women. Although Plato, in the fifth book of *The Republic*, showed Socrates advocating equality for both sexes, one searches the works of eighteenth-century writers virtually in vain for any significant acknowledgment of his thought on this subject. Instead, it was the teachings of Aristotle that had long held sway and were repeatedly quoted. In his *Generation of Animals*, Aristotle had diagnosed the female as a monster, an "infertile male," an unfortunate but necessary natural deformity. And it was this image of the female as an "*homme manqué*," an imperfect male, which appeared repeatedly throughout the eighteenth century.[2] Nicolas Retif de la Bretonne was particularly attracted to this idea that "the second sex is effectively an *imperfection* of nature, giving to the word the significance not of flaw, or of vice, but that of non-achievement."[3] Even the Faculté de Médecine de Paris posed the question: "Is Woman an imperfect work of Nature?"[4] The idea was so widespread that seventeenth- and eighteenth-century champions of feminine equality repeatedly found it necessary to insist that God (or Nature) had made two different bodies, each perfect in its own way. As François Poullein de la Barre wrote:

It is therefore without reason that some people imagine that women are not as perfect as men, and that they regard in them as a flaw, that which is an essential appanage of their sex, without which it would be useless for the end to which it was formed; which begins and ends with fertility, and which is destined for the most excellent usage in the world, that is to say, to form and nourish us in its breast.[5]

The teachings of the Bible and Aristotle also converged on another point: whether given to him by God or Nature, the female was the vehicle through which man was able to reproduce himself. It was the centrality of this reproductive function to the nature of woman that seemed to dominate virtually everything else and that is significantly lacking in contemporary thought about the nature of man the male. In other words, woman was created to allow man to reproduce himself; man was not there to allow woman to reproduce herself.

As Pierre Roussel put it on the eve of the Revolution: "Man not being able alone to assure the duration of his species, it was necessary that he be united with a being who could aid him to reproduce himself, and this being is Woman."[6] The woman thus became a "being," not quite a separate species, but a supplement, an addition. "I see that woman is uniquely made for man," said another contemporary author; "Her organic form is only a supplement to the organic form of the man, an extension of his organs which doubles them, and thus gives him the ability to reproduce himself."[7]

In this way, the female was essentially deprived of any existence in her own right as an autonomous individual. She became instead a simple means of reproduction: a giant womb, the incubator of the male race. Retif de la Bretonne wrote: "The Woman is a being who, united to the Man, forms a sacred depot, where man, the generative principle, deposits a new existence."[8] In vain did people such as the author of *La Femme n'est pas inférieure à l'homme* complain that men think all creatures are made for them, and that since the male contribution to reproduction is completed in an instant, it might be more logically argued that men were created for women's usage and not the other way around.[9] Despite all evidence to the contrary, an age-old male pride continued to insist on the ultimate application of the image of male as active and female as passive, even in the apparently female-dominated sphere of reproduction.

The exact manner of conception being as yet unknown,[10] it was easy for the male imagination to invent for itself the superior role. "The Man sows, he produces; the Woman receives, and nourishes," explained one late eighteenth-century author.[11] This idea was elaborated in 1791 by Grouber de Groubentall: "The Man appears to be the sole efficient Agent of Procreation, and the Woman, at the moment of conception, has no more influence than does the Earth over the insertion of a seed deposited in its bosom."[12] As was his nature, the Marquis de Sade put the matter even more bluntly:

The fetus owes its existence only to the man's sperm, [although] this latter, by itself unmixed with the woman's would come to naught. But that which [the woman furnishes] has a merely elaborative function; it does not create, it furthers creation without being its cause. Indeed, there are several contemporary naturalists who claim it is useless.[13]

Although known as misogynists, men such as Retif de la Bretonne and the Marquis de Sade were only carrying to its ultimate conclusion an idea that pervaded their society and resulted in the extreme differentiation that characterized their age's perception of the two sexes. Men and women were not "created" for the same purpose. Woman was created to bear man children; man's destiny was something else entirely. Because he was created for other things and woman was created for this one purpose only, she was different. Woman was believed to differ from man not merely in her more obvious physical attributes, but in her character traits, virtues, faults, tastes, and talents as well. Every aspect of human existence and personality was dissected, divided, and allotted. The principles of the division were considered to be self-evident and readily discoverable in a clear understanding of each sex's individual destiny. Each sex had been assigned its unique and immutable destiny at the dawn of existence. Any deviation from that appointed destiny was an unpardonable shock to society, nature, and God.

Although a woman's destiny was believed to begin and end with her reproductive function and its related spheres, man's destiny was far broader. And in an age that came increasingly to place more emphasis on the individual, the "individuality" of the male destiny seemed, if possible, to enhance the man's importance even more. Man was seen as the active, the productive principle. It was for man to go forth into the world, to do great deeds and to think great thoughts. Woman's contribution to society was reduced to the passive continuation of the species; this was what she was created and born for, this was her *raison d'être*. Her value lay not in her individual abilities, talents, or personality; in and of herself she was nothing. Her natural and God-given destiny was both to reproduce and care for the next generation of males.

By extention, because her child-bearing and child-rearing roles were believed to necessarily confine her to the home, woman's "destiny" was also thought to include housekeeping. In the words of the eighteenth century, this was "Natural."[14] As Retif de la Bretonne explained it:

The cares of a household divide naturally into two sorts: those of the exterior and those of the interior of the home. It is in the order of things that the Man, who is the most vigorous, the most free, be charged with the rough work, the affairs that require travel, a long application, etc.; and that the woman, more delicate, encumbered by pregnancies and by children, be domestic, and have only the little details. . . .[15]

In his *Essai sur l'éducation et l'existence civile et politique des femmes, dans la constitution française*, presented in 1790, Charles-Louis Rousseau developed a similar thesis: "Destined to administer the interior of her home, while her husband is occupied out of doors, [a woman] is entirely occupied with the details of the household, and with the care or education of her children."[16]

If a woman's physical destiny was reproduction and housekeeping, her moral destiny was submission.[17] Female submission was ordained by both God and Nature. Man was exalted as the king of the universe; God had placed the sceptre in his hand and all creatures, including woman, were required to bow to his command.[18] "[Women are] born for a perpetual dependence from the first instant of their existence to that of their last passage," wrote the journalist Prudhomme in 1791.[19] Denied a true existence in her own right, a woman could only live as the "complement" of others.

If a woman was considered to be destined for dependence, then she must also be destined for obedience. "When I reduce women to obedience," wrote the young Chevalier d'Artaize, a disciple of Jean-Jacques Rousseau; "I hardly degrade her. She only does what is her primary duty." Submission also implies flexibility, and, according to a popular fantasy, "[A woman] awaits her being and form from those who surround her, her supple and yielding mind receives all that one wishes to engrave there, her character takes on the consistence that one gives it"—somewhat like a slender branch bends between strong hands, wrote Artaize.[20]

Woman was not, however, an entirely passive subject, for her subordinate position carried with it the moral imperative of pleasing her master. All women were considered to have been "destined to please," and, as a result, every little girl was said to be born with a "violent" desire to please. To please was glorified as a woman's "greatest pleasure and obligation," and one from which she was never released. "Nature wished that she should never raise herself above a man, by her behavior or speech," insisted the journalist Mercier; "Nothing exempts her from this eternal subordination, be she on the throne of the world . . . it is not permitted for her to be insolent towards a man, that is to say, to dare to despise her master."[21]

In addition to these physical and moral destinies, tradition also credited woman with a spiritual destiny: woman was given to man to make his life more pleasant. "I see in women those objects made to charm us," said the author of a 1793 pamphlet, *Projet de loi pour les mariages*; "To render our lives agreeable and to give us pleasures that I savor as much as there is a sensitive soul within me."[22] Women were born to delight men, to adorn society, to soften life, to inspire men to valor, to be the guardians of morality, and so on. Although this idea had been around since the days of chivalry and courtly love, the late eighteenth century was particularly infatuated with it. The *philosophe* Paul-Henri Holbach, for example, hailed women as "the most amiable portion of the human species, that which nature seems to have destined to procure the greatest happiness of the other half, to temper his rudeness, to soften his morals and to make his soul more sensitive. . . ."[23] In a 1789 pamphlet entitled *Les Griefs et plaintes des femmes mal mariées*, the women describe themselves as "the amiable half of the human race, created to soften its pains and to make its pleasures. . . ."[24] Although undeniably more flattering to its object, the theme here is the same: the female was created for the male. As one writer succinctly put it:

To raise the man, to nourish him in his childhood, to temper the sharpness of his passion in his torrid youth, to make his happiness in maturity, his consolation and support in old age, such was, without doubt, the destination of the woman.[25]

Once a woman's destiny was clearly understood in these terms, the virtues required of her followed naturally. As housekeeper and mother, her most laudable attributes were obviously fertility and hard work. As a subordinate wife, her goodness implied both patience and meekness, combined with an overwhelming desire to please. But it was in the virtue of chastity that a woman's entire existence as mother, wife, and guardian of morality met and was exalted. Chastity and female virtue became synonymous.

One of the most popular and influential discourses on feminine virtue was to be found in Jean-Jacques Rousseau's *Emile*. After his deification during the Revolution, the work became a virtual bible for female conduct. Rousseau's thesis was simple: woman was dependent upon man for her entire existence; as a result of this, her entire existence must be oriented towards him:

Men depend on women because of their desires; women depend on men both because of their desires and because of their needs; we could subsist without them sooner than they could without us. In order that they have the necessities of life, in order that they be in their proper state, it is necessary that we give it to them, that we wish to give it to them, that we deem them worthy: they depend on our sentiment, on the price that we put on their merit, on our estimation of their charms and their virtues. By the law of nature even, women are at the mercy of the judgments of men. . . . To please them, to be useful to them, to make themselves loved and honored by them. . . . Behold the duties of women.[26]

According to Rousseau, a woman's first obligation was, therefore, to please man: "If woman is made to please and to be subject, she must make herself agreeable to man, instead of provoking him," he said. The sentiment was hardly new with Rousseau. The Art of Pleasing was a much-discussed topic in the eighteenth century. Dependent upon the whims of man, the ability to please was not just a woman's destiny, it was also her only road to power and happiness. "The art of pleasing is the greatest of the arts. When one pleases, all succeeds, all is easy," wrote Mme de Puisieux.[27] Yet, as Mme de Lambert wrote to her daughter, it was difficult to give rules on how to please. As a mother, she advised amiability and "virtue" (although she also acknowledged that men are far more likely to be pleased by a woman's faults than her virtues).[28] The less austere moralists were apt to suggest that a touch of coquetry was helpful, while according to Rousseau's disciple Retif de la Bretonne: "Coquetry is an essential quality in women; it fulfills the end for which they were created, which is to please." But even he was quick to add that indiscriminate coquetry was an "affront."[29]

One of the most traditional ways of pleasing was by means of the *agréments*, or accomplishments: "It is necessary to neglect neither the talents nor the accomplishments," advised Mme de Lambert, "Because women are destined to please."[30] Rousseau carried this dictate even farther, saying: "I would like a young . . . girl to cultivate the agreeable talents to please the husband that she will have with as much care as a young Albanian cultivates them for the Harem of Ispatran."[31] Women were taught to dance, to sing, to play the harp or pianoforte, and to move with grace and beauty. This was the "education" that had been drawing upon itself an increasing barrage of criticism from all directions throughout the eighteenth century, although it continued to be about the only one given to the young lady of leisure (and the one to which her less wealthy contemporaries continued to aspire). Although some learning might be useful to help a woman avoid boring a man, most people considered the more esoteric subjects to be "completely useless" for women.

"The time that women spend learning them would be better employed in acquiring some talents that would make them amiable for everyone," wrote Mme de Puisieux; "Is it not very amusing for a husband . . . that a wife should be capable of occupying a position as an Interpreter? Willingly would I say like M. de *** to his wife, who was racking her brains to study Spanish: 'Eh! Madame! hire a good dancing master, who would teach you to walk and hold yourself with good grace, and don't deafen me with your dozen words of Spanish, which you will never say well.'"[32] In 1790, Roussel expressed a similar sentiment: "The principal destination of women being to please by the agreements of their bodies and by the natural graces, they stray from it in running after the reputation of learning. . . ."[33]

Nevertheless, although accomplishments and beauty were always helpful, the general consensus was that a woman should seek to please by her conduct rather than by her appearance.[34] A good woman, according to Retif de la Bretonne, is "an essentially *agreeable* being: this word says all, because it includes usefulness, meekness, submission. . . ."[35] Here, again, the guiding principle was passivity. A woman's "virtues" were all negative: patience, resignation, complaisance, meekness, and what Mary Wollstonecraft liked to call "spaniel-like affection." The path to glory lay through self-abnegation, self-abasement, and self-renunciation. A good woman bore in silence all the ills with which the world or her men might afflict her and returned only a smile. In *l'Ecole des moeurs*, Jean-Baptiste Blanchard taught that "meekness, patience, indulgence for the faults of their husbands," were all required of women:

They must have the courage to sustain the dislike, the anger, the bad manners, even the contempt of their husbands. A tender, virtuous, and reasonable woman, who, despite all her efforts, finds herself the butt of her husband's bad disposition; a woman who never has the satisfaction to hear herself praised for her better actions, who even is obliged to hide them, and to sometimes appear to be wrong; who, hiding her sorrow from all strange eyes, tries to preserve appearances, and to conceal from the public all that can be; who suffers without complaining and who excuses those things that she was unable to either foresee or prevent the exposure: How that woman is grand! How she is amiable![36]

In the fullest application of this theory, if all women were truly virtuous, then every man would have been provided with a wife who would have indulged his bad tempers and faults without requiring him to correct them.[37] Parents were advised to raise their daughters with the habit of submission, so that it would be easy for them later to submit to a husband.[38] "It is not a question of making her dependence painful," explained Rousseau; "It is sufficient to make her feel it." It was said that daughters should be accustomed to finding themselves interrupted in the midst of play and being turned to other pursuits. "There results from this habitual constraint a docility that women need all their lives," wrote Rousseau; "The first and most important quality in a woman is meekness; made to obey a being as imperfect as man, often so full of vices, and always so full of faults, she must learn early to suffer even injustice, and to support the wrongs of a husband without complaining. . . ."[39]

This insistence on the need for meekness and gentleness in a woman was so great that it was commonly said that an irritated woman "changes her sex," or that an angry woman "forgets herself."[40] A woman "may never impart either insolence or injury to her look," wrote the journalist Mercier, "Without losing her graces, her dignity, and her real *empire*."[41] According to the *philosophe* Denis Diderot, the contrast of any violent emotion with a woman's "natural" tenderness disfigured her and rendered her "hideous."[42]

In the interest of harmony, a good woman was expected to mold her character, opinions, and tastes to conform to those of the men on whom she was dependent (*se plier*, to bend or yield or, literally, "to fold oneself," is the colorful French expression). "Is it a daughter to which you have given birth?" asked Jean-François Saint-Lambert; "Instruct her early to make a sacrifice of her will; you will ensure the tranquility of her life."[43] The need for conformity was carried to the extent that all women were expected to assume the same religion and political beliefs as their fathers or husbands. "When that religion is false, the docility that submits the mother and daughter to the order of nature effaces in God's eyes the sin or error," explained Rousseau.[44]

In addition to meekness, humility, simplicity, and even timidity were all considered female virtues. It was generally held that a young girl should be allowed to speak only when necessary, and then with an air of doubt and deference.[45] Even as an adult, the requirement for self-effacement was no less exacting: "Happy are those women who have known for a long time to hide their merit beneath simplicity and modesty," wrote Mme Necker, while Mme de Grafigny cautioned: "The woman who exchanges modesty for assurance loses half of her charm."[46] In the words of Retif de la Bretonne, God did not make women weak so that they should become imperious or opinionated.[47]

The duty of a good and honest woman in the eighteenth century was to forget both herself and the world, and to think only of her family. She must "live unknown, alone, occupied incessantly with her children, her house, her husband," wrote Charles-Elie Ferrières.[48] A wise mother was told to raise her daughter with the habit of solitude and retirement. "Her happiness is to be ignorant of what the world calls *pleasures*, her glory is to live unknown," said the *Encyclopédie*; "Confined in the duties of wife and mother, she consecrates her days to the practice of the obscure virtues."[49] It was popularly said that the truly virtuous woman was the one of whom people talked the least.

In addition to the type of modesty associated with simplicity and a lack of pretension, the eighteenth-century woman needed another form of modesty, for which the French have a special word: *pudeur*. *Pudeur* was an almost exclusively feminine virtue. It implied bashfulness, shame, and reserve, and it almost always carried with it a sexual connotation. Nature, it was believed, had given women *pudeur* as a restraint for their cardinal desires, and *pudeur*, or the chastity that it protected, was generally seen as the female equivalent of the male virtue valor. "The most indispensable virtue to women, the one that gives them the most influence over [men], is *pudeur*," wrote Mlle Jodin in a 1790 pamphlet; "In it resides the pinnacle of honor for our sex, like bravery in yours."[50]

As a mother, as a wife, and as a daughter, *pudeur* (or chastity) was a woman's ultimate virtue. The association of chastity with virtue was so great that when a woman lost her chastity, she was considered to have lost her "virtue." So important was this one attribute perceived to be that it also engulfed a number of other adjectives. A "wise" woman was hardly the same as a wise man, just as an "honest" woman or an "honorable" one implied something very different from an honest or honorable man. Goodness, purity, wisdom, honesty—all were reduced to the simple, negative, and passive state of chastity. "The dignity of their sex is in its modesty," wrote Rousseau; "Shame and *pudeur* are inseparable in them from honesty."[51] Modesty was considered to be under the safeguard of the "timid sex": "Who will blush if women do not?" asked Diderot.[52] In the sex act, as in all else, it was for the man to be active and to attack, for the woman to defend and to feel shame. In *l'Esprit des lois* the Baron de Montesquieu observed:

All nations are in equal accord in attaching contempt to the inconstancy of women; it is because Nature has spoken to all nations. She established defense, she established attack, and, having placed desire on both sides, she placed in the one temerity, in the other shame.[53]

If chastity equaled wisdom, honesty, honor and virtue, then a woman who had "lost" her chastity must be devoid of all morality. "The violation of *pudeur* supposes in women a renunciation of all virtues," wrote Montesquieu.[54] Boudier de Villement agreed: "When once they give up that discretion which is the primary merit of their sex, there is hardly any excess of which they do not become capable."[55] According to Rousseau: "The audacity of a woman is the sure sign of her shame; it is for having too much for which to blush that she blushes not."[56]

Why was something so shameful in a woman not equally so in a man? "Why should what one of the two sexes believes himself permitted be a crime in the other?" asked one of the authors of *Encyclopédie*; "I respond . . . that the consequences are not the same for the two. . . . I add, finally, that thus nature wished it, and it is a crime to smother her voice."[57]

Since chastity was a woman's ultimate virtue, its violation was her ultimate vice. "*Pudeur*, modesty, must be above all their virtues," warned Blanchard:

The more one respects their sex, the more one despises those who dishonor it. Chastity is for them what honor is for men, their most beautiful ornament. . . . The world, as corrupted, as lax as it is with regard to this vice of which we speak, never fails to scorn those women who forget themselves, and to make them the butt of its mockery.[58]

The fate of a fallen woman was dire. In his essay *Sur les femmes* Diderot describes the consequences of one moment of forbidden love:

[You will] sacrifice your innocence and your morality, lose the respect that you have for yourself and that you obtain from others; walk with your eyes downcast in society, at least until by the habit of libertinage you have acquired effrontery, surrender all claims to any state of honesty, make your parents die of sorrow. . . .[59]

It was a discouraging picture indeed. For many, the only retreat and asylum left open for a fallen woman was the convent. "She must hide herself completely and make herself forgotten, if possible," wrote Blanchard.[60]

With such a price to be paid for infamy, it is not surprising that a woman's reputation was almost more important to her than chastity itself. Women were constantly warned to guard their reputation: it was not enough merely to *be* chaste. "It is not sufficient for them to be wise, it is necessary for them to be known as such," wrote Rousseau. "Their honor is not only in their conduct but in their reputation, and it is not possible that she who passes as infamous could ever be pure . . . what one thinks of her is no less important to her than what she is in fact."[61] The most frequently presented role model was none other than Lucretia, the famous Roman matron who actually sacrificed her chastity to protect her reputation (and then expiated the sin of her rape by committing suicide). A woman's tranquility depended upon society's opinion of her conduct, and if a woman was not *truly* virtuous she was advised to endeavor to at least *pretend* to be so. "Reputation is more precious than life," wrote Mme de Puisieux. "One cannot be happy without at least the appearance of virtue; the study of a woman who has ceased to be virtuous must be to appear so."[62]

What was a woman's reward for all these virtues? Simultaneous beatification, deification, and coronation. She became an angel, a saint, a goddess, a queen. "She raises in her own heart a throne to which all come to render homage," panegyrized Rousseau.[63] Woman had been placed far from the tumult of the world in the temple of Hymen, and, according to Saint-Lambert at least, her bed was her throne: "It is there that she must reign, and this instant of *empire* consoles her for a long dependence."[64] As a spokesman for the Jacobins in the dark days of 1793, the deputy Pierre-Gaspard Chaumette tried to reconcile the female sex to their lack of a civil or political existence by promising them: "You will be the divinity of the domestic sanctuary; you will reign over all that surrounds it, by the invincible charm of beauty, grace, and virtue."[65]

A woman's power lay in her virtue. This was the source of her *empire*, that illusive eighteenth-century concept of female influence or even dominance. It was the tyranny of the weak over the strong. "Her orders are caresses, her menaces are tears," said Rousseau. Grace, modesty, and shame were the weapons with which nature had armed the weak to subject the strong. This was woman's only permitted avenue to "equality," and she "governed" man "by obeying him."[66] There was, however, a clear message here: woman reigned only so long as she stayed in her proper place; any attempt to aspire to the active "male" virtues, to compete with men on their own level, and she was lost.

Yet, however hard she tried, could any mortal woman live up to what was expected of her? "It seems that an image of woman, full of grace and dignity, floats unceasingly before man's eyes," wrote Mme Necker; "It seduces him, it misleads him in his youth and finishes by inspiring him with aversion for all that deviates from the perfect model that seems destined to enchant him."[67] There was little doubt that the men of eighteenth-century France found the women in their lives very different beings from the goddesses and angels they eulogized. Some of them blamed the discrepancy on women's failure to understand or faithfully fulfill their proper destinies and duties, but the general tendency was to consider the deficiency as somehow inherent in the female character.

"What is woman?" asked one of the Marquis de Sade's characters. "A puny creature, always inferior to man, infinitely less attractive than he, less ingenious, less wise . . . of a sharp turn of humor, shrill, shrewish, bitter, and thwart; a tyrant if you allow her privileges, mean, vile, and a sneak in bondage; always false, forever mischievous, constantly dangerous. . . ."[68] The passage might simply be dismissed as an example of de Sade's misogyny, had not the *Encyclopédie* also described women as "vindictive" and "cruel," or François Fénelon called them vain, jealous, and artificial, or the Prince de Ligne characterized them as envious, capricious, and childlike. If de Sade was a misogynist, he had a lot of company.

It was a common adage that there was little variety in women's characters. "There is less differentiation in your characters than ours," wrote Saint-Lambert; "One woman differs from another less by her soul than by her face." In fact, continued Saint-Lambert, women are distinguished mainly by the differences in their ways of pleasing men.[69] Actually, two distinct female types emerge from the literature of this period: a foolish capricious butterfly, full of excess sensibility, frivolity, and indiscreet chatter, and her opposite, a passionate, malicious, and always ambitious Jade.

Although some have seen the eighteenth century as a period of transition, when early modern stereotypes of a powerful, dangerous, sinful sex were giving way to the modern stereotypes of a frail, submissive, virtuous sex, it is probably more correct to see this rather as a shift of emphasis. Both images had been, and would remain, in the general "pool of thought."[70]

In 1788, there appeared a work by Pierre Roussel entitled *De la Femme, considérée au physique et au moral*. It was produced as part of the Bibliothèque Universelle des Dames, a library of books geared specifically toward the female reading public, and it contains a typical eighteenth-century analysis of the female character. Roussel begins by emphasizing the inherent differences between the sexes. In the male, "his lofty height, his proud step, his novel tastes, his original ideas, in a word, everything retraces in him the image of force, and carries the imprint of the sex that must master and protect the other." The female, by contrast, is "delicate and tender, she always retains something of the temperament characteristic of children." According to Roussel, the primary principle underlying a woman's nature is her weakness: she is weak not only in body, but in mind and spirit as well. From this inescapable and overriding weakness emanate all of her distinguishing characteristics. A woman's organs are "weak and mobile"; as a result, she lacks perserverance, although she is capable of rapid thoughts and sensations. But lest this be thought an advantage, Roussel is quick to point out that although it might give women tact and the ability to discern subtle nuances and details, it also renders them incapable of either reflection or the loftiness of generalized conceptions. Their exquisite sensibility, and the distraction of all those rapid impressions striking them incessantly, is what makes women indecisive and capricious. In contrast, says Roussel: "A man is always himself, and whatever he wanted one time he wishes always." The combination of their weakness and this extreme sensibility also makes women fearful and overly imaginative. Constantly overborne by their senses, explains Roussel, women are incapable of cold reason.[71]

These stereotypes appear and reappear constantly throughout the second half of the eighteenth century. "Oh women, you are very extraordinary children!" wrote Diderot in his *Essai sur les femmes*.[72] Voltaire was so fond of comparing a woman's caprices to the flutters of a weathervane that the image appears some half-dozen times in his works. Women were artificial, they were false, they would mislead you with insidious flattery. They were indiscreet. "It is difficult for children and for women to keep a secret," wrote Blanchard; "It is often an indiscretion to confide anything important to them."[73] Women were, in a word, weak and very foolish.

But there was also a darker, more manacing, side to the female character, one that excited more male fear than contempt. The Chevalier d'Artaize was a very passionate young man who had suffered a severe disillusionment and disappointment in love. In revenge he sat down and wrote *Reflections of a young man: degradation of man in society or, Essay on the decadence of taste in the arts and the sciences* (this was quickly followed by *New Reflections of a young man . . .*). The reason for all the decadence and degradation in the world was, according to Artaize, purely and simply: women. From the time they are little girls, says Artaize, women are ruled by "pride, jealousy, hate, fury . . ." (unlike men, who are naturally good, generous, and friendly). Being weaker than men, explains Artaize, women are also "more mistrustful, more suspicious, more egotistical, more interested in themselves." Not only are they eternally false in their feelings, speech, and conduct, they are also "proud, intractable in their excesses, uncontrollable in their passions, ingenious in crime, fierce, implacable in their hate. . . ." Vain, vindictive, ruthlessly ambitious . . . Artaize managed to run on in that vein for over two hundred pages.[74]

Although he may have been an extreme case, there is little in Artaize's works that does not appear elsewhere. Diderot, who was in many ways sympathetic to the plight of women in his society, once wrote that "pride is more their vice than ours," and he characterized women as "impenetrable in dissimulation, cruel in vengeance, constant in their projects, without scruple in methods of succeeding. . . ."[75] Blanchard wrote that "women . . . are born passionate and fiery. . . . There is scarcely any wrath greater or more terrible than theirs, and there is no excess of which they are not capable." Better to live with a lion or a dragon, he decided, than such a woman.[76]

These characterizations of women are even more revealing when contrasted with their complimentary portraits of the male temperament. One is left with the impression that all of these faults are the exclusive preserve of the female sex. The male is portrayed as steady, firm, naturally sincere, reasonable, generous, prudent, in every way majestic. His virtues are bravery, courage, and friendship, and no one seems to question how well the average man lives up to these requirements. By definition of being male, all men seem to have received them as a birthright. We are told that

To fulfill well the duties [of friendship] it is necessary to be capable of speaking and understanding the male and austere language of truth. It is necessary to possess a courage that is startled by neither sacrifices nor dangers; it is necessary above all to have that unity of character that women, by the variety and eternal mobility of their passions, rarely possess. . . .[77]

Not only were women considered to be incapable of friendship, they were also denied the capacity for true self-sacrifice, which was said to require "masculine" force, courage, and reason.[78]

Even when men granted women what at first appeared to be a favorable characteristic, it often carried with it a hidden insult. Women were allowed to be more gay than men, but perhaps that was because women did not reflect as much as men do. Women were also known as the "devout sex"; they were more religious than men. Or were they? Lacking the force required to reason, examine, or meditate, women were said to have a greater need to believe. Religion was therefore seen as a refuge for their weakness, an asylum for their sorrow, their hope for greater happiness in another world. "Hence, it seems by a consequence even of the character of women that their religion must be more tender and that of men stronger," wrote Antoine-Leonard Thomas; "The one tends more to practices, and the other to principles." Furthermore, their well-publicized tendency towards extremes could be said to make women preys to superstition.[79]

Despite all this abuse, the women of the eighteenth century worked hard to please; they practiced their "accomplishments," they hid their talents and intelligence, and they lived out their lives, unknown, in the depths of their domestic sanctuaries. Yet they obviously still had failed in their objective. With unusual insight, Mme Necker once wrote: "One must agree: in all times men have slandered the objects of their cult; their vanity is revenged for an involuntary homage, they wish to debase what they adore, and it is thus that they have dishonored both sexes at the same time."[80]

NOTES

1. See Simone de Beauvoir's discussion in *Le Deuxième Sexe*, 2 vols. (Paris: Gallimard, 1949).

2. See, for example, the article "Femme" in D. Diderot and J. d'Alembert, eds., *Encyclopédie ou dictionnaire raisonné des sciences, des arts, et des metiers, par une société de gens de lettres*. (Paris: 1751–1780), Vol. 6, p. 468.

3. Nicolas Retif de la Bretonne, *Le Gynographe ou idées de deux honnêtes femmes sur un projet de règlement pour mettre les femmes à leur place et opérer le bonheur des deux sexes* (Le Haye: Godd & Pinet, 1776), p. 369.

4. "La femme est-elle un ouvrage imparfait de la nature?" Reynier believes the topic was introduced as a joke; whether or not this is true, it is nonetheless significant. G. Reynier, *La Femme au XVIIᵉ Siècle* (Paris: 1933), p. 41.

5. François Poullain de la Barre, *De l'Egalité des deux sexes, discours phy-sique et moral où l'on voit l'importance de se défaire des préjugés* (Paris: chez Jean du Puis, 1673), p. 191.

6. Pierre Roussel, *De la Femme, considérée au physique et au moral*, 2 vols. (Paris: 1788–1789), Vol. 1, p. 4.

7. [Charles Elie de Ferrières], *La Femme et les voeux* (Paris: Poincot, 1788), p. 45. See also Mlle Archambault, *Dissertation sur la question: Lequel de l'homme ou de la femme est plus capable de constance? Ou la Cause des Dames* (Paris: Pissot et J. Bullot, 1750), p. 110.

8. Retif de la Bretonne, *Le Gynographe*, p. 178.

9. [Philippe Florent de la Puisieux], *La femme n'est pas inferieure à l'homme* (London: 1750), p. 70. This work is listed as a translation from an English work, which itself appears to have been a translation or at least an adaptation of an earlier French work by Poullain de la Barre, although it is written as though the author were feminine.

10. See, for example, Voltaire, the article "Femme" in his *Dictionnaire phi-losophique*, in *Oeuvres complètes de Voltaire* (Paris: Garnier frères, Libraires-Editeurs, 1883), Vol. 17, p. 95.

11. Retif de la Bretonne, *Le Gynographe*, p. 369.

12. Grouber de Groubentall, *Discours sur l'autorité paternelle et le devoir filial, considérés d'après la Nature, la Civilisation, et le Pacte social* (Paris: chez l'auteur, 1791), p. 29.

13. Marquis de Sade, *The Complete Justine, Philosophy in the Bedroom, and Other Writings*, tr. Richard Seaver and Austryn Wainhouse (New York: Grove Press, 1965), p. 206.

14. Although much of the eighteenth-century insistence on the virtues of dom-esticity can be seen as a product of growing sentimentality and a reaction to the *precieuses*, its origins are much older. The idea of dividing duties between the sexes was already old when Aristotle wrote about it. During the seventeenth-century revival of the *dévots*, for example, Jansenists, Jesuits, and the laity alike condemned worldliness and luxury and thunderously consigned women to domes-tic duties. Historically, the more women have been perceived as escaping from the home to other areas, the more an age seems to insist that they belong nowhere else besides the kitchen. This growing insistence on domesticity has recently been addressed by many writers, although most overestimate its novelty. See, for instance, Elizabeth Fox-Genovese, "Women and the Enlightenment," in Renate Bridenthal and Claudia Koonz, eds., *Becoming Visible: Women in Euro-pean History* (Boston: Houghton Mifflin, 1977); Elizabeth Fox-Genovese and Eugene D. Genovese, "The Ideological Bases of Domestic Economy," in *Fruits of Merchant Capital* (New York: Oxford University Press, 1983); Margaret Dar-row, "French Noblewomen and the New Domesticisty, 1750–1850," *Feminist Studies 5*, no. 1 (Spring, 1979), pp. 41–65; Cissie Fairchild's "Women and Fam-ily," in Samia Spencer, ed., *French Women and the Age of Enlightenment* (Indi-ana University Press: 1984).

15. Retif de la Bretonne, *Le Gynographe*, p. 58.

16. Charles-Louis Rousseau, deputé de Tonnerre, *Essai sur l'éducation et l'ex-istence civile et politique des femmes, dans la constitution française . . . lu au Waux-Hall le 13 décembre, 1790* (Paris: Imprimerie de Girouard, n.d.), p. 29.

17. See, for instance, Retif de la Bretonne, *Le Gynographe*, p. 208.

18. See, for instance, the anonymous pamphlet *Les Concitoyennes, ou Arrêté des Dames composant l'ordre de la Vraie Noblesse de Brest en Bretagne, du samedi, 24 janvier 1789* (n.p., n.d.).

19. [par Prudhomme], Révolutions de Paris, Vol. 7, No. 83, 5–12 February 1791, p. 231.

20. Feucher d'Artaize, *Réfexions d'un jeune homme. Dégradation de l'homme en société, ou Essai sur la décadence du goût des arts et des sciences* (Paris: chez Royez, 1786), pp. 10–11.

21. Louis-Sebastian Mercier, *Tableau de Paris*, Vol. II (Hamburg: chez Virchaux & Co., 1781), p. 24. See also Retif de la Bretonne, *Le Gynographe*; Ann Thérèse Lambert, *Avis d'une mère à sa fille* (Paris: chez Etienne Ganeau, 1734); and Mlle Archambault, *Dissertation sur la question*.

22. Pierre le Noble, *Projet de Loi pour les Mariages, présenté à l'assemblée nationale* (Paris: Garnéry, year II), p. 9.

23. Holbach finished his sentence by saying that instead of doing all that, they "often cause the greatest ravages in society." Paul-Henri-Dietrch Holbach, *Système Social, ou Principes naturels de la morale et de la politique* (Paris: Niogret, 1822), p. 347. The juxtaposing of women's "potential" contributions to society vs. their "actual" one was a popular strategem: cf. "Companion given to lighten my woes, why have you increased them?" Jacques-Henri-Bernardin de Saint-Pierre, *Discours sur cette question: Comment l'éducation des femmes pourrait contribuer à rendre les hommes meilleurs,* in *Oeuvres complètes de Saint-Pierre* (Paris: Méquignon-Marvis, 1818), p. 155.

24. [Cailly], *Les Griefs et plaintes des femmes mal mariées* (Paris: Boulard, 1789), p. 4. This was a popular literary device. cf.: "Charming sex, made to add to the pleasures of men's lives and to soften their troubles. . . ." *Adresse au beau sexe, relativement à la révolution présente, par M.L.C.D.V.* (n.p. 1790), p. 3; or "Great, precious and amiable sex that forms the destiny of our life and the charm of our society. . . ." Benedetto Toselli, *Apologie des femmes ou Vérités qui font triompher le beau sexe* (Milan: Soffietti, 1792), pp. 10–11.

25. d'Artaize, *Réflexions d'un jeune homme*, pp. 5–6.

26. Jean-Jacques Rousseau, *Emile,* in *Oeuvres complètes* (Dijon: Imprimerie Darantiere, 1969), Vol. 4, pp. 702–703.

27. Puisieux, *Conseils à une amie* (n.p., 1749), p. 36.

28. Lambert, *Avis d'une mère à sa fille*, pp. 120–121.

29. Retif de la Bretonne, *Le Gynographe*, p. 503.

30. Lambert, *Avis d'une mère à sa fille*, p. 120.

31. Jean-Jacques Rousseau, *Emile*, p. 716.

32. Mme de Puisieux, née Madeleine d'Arsant, *Conseils à une amie*, p. 24.

33. Roussel, *De la Femme*, p. 145.

34. See, for instance, the teachings of Mme de Maintenon, who maintained a faithful following throughout the eighteenth century. She believed that a woman who sought to please and attract by her appearance was culpable for any sin which a man might commit against her. Françoise d'Aubigné de Maintenon, *Conseils et Instructions aux demoiselles pour le conduite dans le monde*, 2 vols. (Paris: Charpentier, 1857), Vol. 1, p. 101.

35. Retif de la Bretonne, *Le Gynographe*, p. 32.

36. Jean-Baptiste Blanchard, *l'Ecole des Moeurs ou Réflexions morales et historiques sur les maxims de la Sagesse*, 3 vols. (Lyon: J. M. Bruyset, 1782), Vol. 1, pp. 355–356.

37. "Je veux, Madame, une femme indulgente. Dont la beauté douce et compatissante, à mes defauts facile à plier. . . ." explained one of Voltaire's characters in *Nanine*, in *Oeuvres*, Vol. 5, p. 16.

38. Blanchard, *L'Ecole des moeurs*, p. 42.

39. Jean-Jacques Rousseau, *Emile*, pp. 710–711.

40. See, for instance, Puisieux, *Conseils à une amie*, p. 38.

41. Mercier, *Tableau de Paris*, Vol. 2, 1781, p. 24.

42. Denis Diderot, *Sur les femmes*, in *Oeuvres complètes* (Paris: Le Club français du livre, 1971), Vol. 10, p. 32.

43. Jean-François Saint-Lambert, *Le Catèchisme universel*, in *Oeuvres philosophiques de Saint-Lambert* (Paris: H. Agasse, year IX), Vol. 1, p. 70.

44. Jean-Jacques Rousseau, *Emile*, p. 721. "It is not so much a question of explaining to them the reasons one has for believing, as revealing to them clearly what one believes."

45. This insistence on crushing a girl's self-confidence was widespread. See François de Salignac Fénelon, *De l'Éducation et des devoirs des filles* (Paris: Vve Hérissant, 1776); and F. Maintenon, *Conseils et Instructions aux Demoiselles*.

46. Suzanne Curchod Necker, *Mélanges extraits des manuscripts de Mme Necker*, 3 vols. (Paris: C. Pougens, 1798), Vol. 3, p. 377, and L. J. Larcher and P. J. Martin, *Les Femmes peintes par elles-mêmes* (Paris: Edition Hetzel, Librairie Magnin, Blanchard & Co., 1858), p. 189.

47. Retif de la Bretonne, *Le Gynographe*, p. 205.

48. [Ferrières], *La Femme et les voeux*, p. 135.

49. Desmahis, "Femme, morale," *Encyclopédie*, Vol. 6, p. 475.

50. Mlle Jodin, *Vues legislatives pour les femmes, adressées à l'assemblée nationale (1790)*, p. 28.

51. Jean-Jacques Rousseau, "*Lettre à d'Alembert, sur les spectacles*," in *Oeuvres complètes de J. J.Rousseau* (Paris: chez P. Dupont, 1824), Vol. 2, p. 115.

52. Diderot, *Sur les femmes*, p. 51.

53. Charles de Socandat, Baron de la Brede et de Montesquieu, *L'Esprit des Lois*, in *Oeuvres complètes de Montesquieu*, 3 vols. (Paris: Librairie Hachette et C^{le}, 1874), Vol. 1, p. 347.

54. Ibid., Vol. 2, Book 26, Chapter 8, p. 134.

55. Boudier de Villement, *L'Ami des femmes ou Morale du sexe* (Paris: Royes, 1788), p. 225.

56. Jean-Jacques Rousseau, *Lettre à d'Alembert*, p. 126.

57. *Encyclopédie*, Vol. 13, p. 549.

58. Blanchard, *L'Ecole des moeurs*, p. 163–164.

59. Diderot, *Sur les femmes*, p. 49.

60. Blanchard, *L'Ecole des moeurs*, p. 167. True, notions of chastity are not necessarily uniform throughout a society. Nevertheless, seduction and unwed pregnancies were still a shame for lower-class women. Without the cloister as a refuge, many of these "fallen women" found no recourse but a career in prostitution.

61. Jean-Jacques Rousseau, *Emile*, p. 702.

62. Puisieux, *Conseils à une amie*, pp. 81 and 94.

63. Jean-Jacques Rousseau, *Emile*, p. 743.

64. Saint-Lambert, *Le Catéchisme universel*, Vol. 3, p. 40. See also Saint-Pierre, *Discours sur cette question*, p. 156.

65. *Journal de la Montagne*, No. 6, 29th day of the 2nd month of the year II, p. 43.

66. Jean-Jacques Rousseau, *Emile*, pp. 766 and 712.

67. Larcher and Martin, *Les Femmes peintes par elles-mêmes*, pp. 68–69.

68. Marquis de Sade, "The Complete Justine, or Good Conduct Well Chastised," in *Philosophy in the Bedroom*, p. 647.

69. Saint-Lambert, *L'Analyse de l'homme et de la femme*, in *Oeuvres philosophiques de Saint-Lambert* (Paris: chez H. Agasse, the year IX), Vol. 1, pp. 207–209.

70. As H. R. Hays has observed: "The male tends to project his fears and antagonisms in terms of derogatory attributes by insisting that women are evil, inferior and valueless (because different) and hence should be made to obey, be kept in their place, or fulfill some unreal role which neutralizes them and removes them from the sphere of competition . . . traditions and stereotypes are born which can always be called upon to justify the inherent tendencies in male behavior." H. R. Hays, *The Dangerous Sex: The Myth of Feminine Evil* (New York: G. P. Putnam's Sons, 1964), p. 281. For other views see Madelyn Gutwirth, "The Representation of Women in the Revolutionary Period: The Goddess of Reason and the Queen of the Night," *Proceedings of the Consortium on Revolutionary Europe, 1983* (1985), 224–241, and Marlene LeGates, "The Cult of Womanhood in Eighteenth-Century France," *Eighteenth-Century Studies*, 10 (Fall, 1976), 21–39.

71. Roussel, *De la Femme*, Vol. 1, pp. 11, 36, 45, 51, 63.

72. Diderot, *Essai sur les femmes*, p. 33.

73. Blanchard, *l'Ecole des moeurs*, Vol. 2, p. 37.

74. d'Artaize, *Réflexions d'un jeune homme*, pp. 24, 25, and 29.

75. Diderot, *Essai sur les femmes*, pp. 39–40.

76. Blanchard, *l'Ecole des moeurs*, p. 110.

77. Antoine-Leonard Thomas, *Essai sur le caractère, les moeurs, et l'esprit des femmes dans les différents siècles*, in *Oeuvres complètes de Thomas* (Paris: Desessarts, the year X), Vol. 4, p. 266.

78. Saint-Lambert, *l'Analyse de l'Homme et de la Femme*, p. 235.

79. Thomas, *Essai sur le caractère*, pp. 259–260, and Saint-Lambert, *L'Analyse de l'homme et de la Femme*, p. 227.

80. Necker, *Mèlanges*, Vol. 3, p. 430.

2

The Enlightenment
and the Question of Sexual Equality

The problem with this century is that
it is not enlightened enough. . . .

[d'Alembert, *Lettre à J.-J. Rousseau*]

When a society perceives the dichotomy between the two sexes to be so
vast and fundamental as to go beyond differences in mere reproductive
functions and relative physical strength, and to extend to differences in
mental capacity, personalities, and individual destinies, then it is difficult
to even begin talking about "equality." Nevertheless, the pool of thought
about the nature of women that existed in France in 1789 was not held in
its entirety by all members of the population. Although most people
probably agreed on most points, it is also true that they disagreed sharply
on some others, and that there were certain rare individuals who disagreed with the general concensus almost entirely. It was this disagree-
ment that had given rise to, and continued to fuel, the Woman
Question—or Quarrel, as it was often called.

The Woman Question predated the Enlightenment by hundreds of
years.[1] At its inception, the Quarrel had been concerned less with equality than with superiority—the sublime superiority of one or the other
sex's character and destiny—and consequently apathetic to such banal
considerations as rights or justice. It had been largely (although not
entirely) a mock combat, fought for the amusement of pundits and scholars, who armed themselves with a battery of quotations, citations, and

examples to "prove" their various points. The Ancients and modern scholars alike were both quoted to some extent, but it was the Bible, predictably enough, that was the most popular source for both sides of the conflict.

Both the supporters of female "superiority" and their opponents amassed impressive arrays of sophistic arguments from the stories of the Creation and Fall, as well as from the New Testament. The champions of the "fairer sex" generally emerged victorious on the subject of the Creation. Adam may have been created first, went the argument, but Eve was God's last and greatest masterpiece—his *chef-d'oeuvre*. Likewise, man was made from earth, whereas woman was formed in heaven and therefore more noble. The defenders of feminine superiority did tend to suffer a setback over the issue of the Fall, but they carried the challenge on, undaunted, into the New Testament: i.e., Christ was the son of a woman, not the "son of man"; three Marys cried at the foot of the cross but only one disciple, while the risen Christ showed his preference for the gentler sex by appearing first to a group of women. Unfortunately, this last argument could be rather maliciously countered with the contention that since Christ wished to broadcast the news of his resurrection as quickly as possible, he very wisely chose to make his first appearance before a sex well known for talking too much.[2]

Even seventeenth-century rationalism failed to discredit the citation method entirely, although it had begun to fall into disuse toward the end of the eighteenth century. But another popular method, the cataloguing tradition, continued strong well into the nineteenth century. Practitioners of the cataloguing method apparently believed that one need only accumulate a sufficiently large number of appropriate examples in order to effectively prove or disprove the existence of any inherent tendency in the female psyche. The catalogue of women assembled by both defenders and detractors alike was culled broadly (and without any apparent recognition of incongruity) from the Bible, ancient mythology, history, and modern literature. The Muses, Messalina, Clotilda, Aphrodite, Joan of Arc, Delilah, and a cast of thousands could all be trotted out to show that women were treacherous and vain—or faithful and modest, depending upon the women chosen and the inclinations of the author.

Despite the tenacity of the citation and cataloguing traditions, however, by the late eighteenth century the Quarrel had altered significantly from the days of its origins as an academic debate, begun half in jest. The coming of the Enlightenment had brought with it new techniques and arguments, as well as an increasing sense of earnestness that affected the partisans of both sides. While the traditionalists clung stubbornly to a fortified vision of male supremacy, the defenders of the feminine cause turned away from the championship of a concept of sublime feminine superiority and fought instead for the acceptance of simple equality. As Mlle Jodin noted in 1790:

One sex was not established the oppressor of the other, and these ridiculous debates of superiority are an injustice to nature. You are born our friends, and not our rivals; we are your equals, [whom] you reduce to slavery.[3]

Furthermore, by the late eighteenth century, the Quarrel was not only increasingly concerned with the question of equality rather than sublime superiority, but the circles in which the debate took place had also broadened. Major texts on the subject were now written in French, not Latin. No longer confined to the academic melieu, the topic was discussed in the salons, in letters between friends, in essays and journals, and in general works on related topics. It was also a discussion in which women themselves increasingly came to play a part. Although dissatisfaction with the traditional conceptualization of their sex had existed among women at least since the days of the Renaissance and the writings of women such as Christine de Pisan and Mlle de Gournay, the increase of literacy among women and the growing number of female authors meant that their voice was being heard more than ever before. And although it was true that in recent years the major theorists of sexual equality, from Poullain de la Barre to the *philosophe* Jean-Antonine Condorcet, had all been men, almost every feminine writer of the eighteenth century expressed varying degress of frustration and discontent with her society's view of women. Sometimes angry and inflammatory, frequently veiled and resigned, their protests were less often demands for rights or even unhesitating avowals of equality as they were attempts to end what they saw as a general contempt and lack of respect for their sex.

As women became more vocal, one of the primary targets of their rancor was the entrenched assumption that the male is the *raison d'être* for the female sex. "I do not believe that we are any more made for [men] than they are made for us," declared Mme de Puisieux, for example.[4] Women began to demand a recognition of their existence as autonomous human beings and to question the tradition that insisted on emphasizing the differences between the sexes to the extent of making women almost alien beings. "We are scarcely a different species on this earth than you," wrote Mlle Jodin in 1790; "The spirit has no sex, any more than the virtues."[5]

Not surprisingly, it was the relegation to the status of ornamental plaything that provoked some of the most indignant outbursts from women writers. "How insensitive men are to the moral laws of Nature," cried the author of the pamhlet *Motions adressés à l'assemblée nationale en faveur du sexe*; "[They act like] barbarians towards a sex that they consider only as a frivolous object, taken by chance, uniquely placed on earth to satisfy a momentary frenzy."[6] The author of the pamphlet *Remontrances, plaintes, et doléances des dames françaises* was equally bitter:

What are we in the world and civil society with regard to men? Idols of flesh, vile instruments in men's hands, who exist only to the extent that we know how to obey, who are in the world only to live under their laws, who only breathe as long as their happiness, their love, even their jealousy has need of us, who can have no lot but submission, no other soul but their will, no other hopes but their bliss.[7]

These women, and others like them, had begun to ask out loud: "Are men really so superior?" The author of *La Femme n'est pas inférieure à l'homme* observed that men seemed to think themselves exempt from all the imperfections they attributed to women; yet, she said, look at all of their excesses. Where is this profound judgment they attribute to themselves? If men cannot even control themselves, why would nature make them the masters of women? Men say we are incapable of defending ourselves; but, she asked, just exactly from *whom* do they protect us?[8]

Yet, as widespread as these feminine grumblings about society's conceptualization of their sex were, there were only a few people—either male or female—in eighteenth-century France who actually went so far as to launch systematic attacks on their society's assumptions about women. None of the "leading lights" of the Enlightenment—with the notable exception of Condorcet—ever took up the problem of the suppression of women and made it their own, although they did sometimes touch upon it. Nevertheless, there were some lesser-known thinkers who did devote considerable time to the subject, and although the idea of equality between the sexes never became an integral part of Enlightenment thought, the influence of the Enlightenment on these writers' arguments and thought patterns is readily discernible.[9] Eventually, these arguments entered the general "pool of thought" and became so common—although by no means accepted by all—that they even can be found in the works of writers such as Mme Necker, who were basically hostile to the idea of equality between the sexes.

One of the major tenets of the Enlightenment was the belief that the differences in the "manners and abilities" of men were, in the words of Locke, formed more by their society and education than by anything else. If this was true of the differences between men, argued some, could it not also be true of the differences between men and women? Were women really innately inferior, or were they made to seem so by their upbringing? If women were educated and treated like men, would not all of the apparent differences between the sexes disappear? These were heady thoughts, but although they sounded logical to those who advanced them, the proponents of sexual equality would have to argue long and hard to convince their society that what was true for man the male must also be true for man the human being.

The most obvious differences between the sexes were physical. And because the extreme differentiation of the sexes was based first and foremost on an exaggeration of these physical differences, it was there that the defenders of equality between the sexes often began their attack on society's prejudices. The *Défense du beau sexe*, written by Don P. J. Caffiaux in mid-century, contains arguments typical of this type of literature. According to Caffiaux, men and women are equal, and the only difference between them is one of sex—which is, he noted, only an animal characteristic. For Caffiaux, the soul, the *esprit*, is sexless: "The *esprit* of woman is not made any differently from that of man," he said; "The woman's *esprit* is united to a body; that of a man is as well. The same sentiments, the same passions, the same wishes form and maintain this union in one sex as in the other."[10] Men may be stronger than women, he conceded, but what kind of basis is that for a claim to superiority? If strength is the only foundation for man's claim to dominion, then, suggested Caffiaux, he must be content to submit himself to the rule of apes and elephants, for they are surely stronger than he.

What raises man above the animals, argued Caffiaux, is his reason. He asked how, as a human being, can woman have less reason than man? "The most exact anatomy has not yet noticed any difference between the head of man and woman," he observed; "Her brain is exactly the same as ours. Impressions are received from the senses and assembled there in the same fashion, and retained there in the same manner. . . ."[11] Like men, said Caffiaux, women hear with their ears and see with their eyes. They have the same ability to know truth and, added the *philosophe* Condorcet, the same right to know it.

The problem was, if women had been born free and equal to men, then how was it that they were everywhere in chains? The Enlightenment had found an answer for the degradation of man in the existence of a conspiracy between kings and priests, and many advocates of equality between the sexes had a similar answer for the degradation of women: it was all a male conspiracy.

"It is us who have smothered the génie of the *Beau sexe*, by confining it within a circle of puerile occupations," wrote Benedetto Toselli in *l'Apologie des femmes*. "We are the only ones to blame."[12] It was a popular idea. Spurred to anger and honesty by one of J.-J. Rousseaus's tirades against the female sex, the *philosophe* Jean d'Alembert found the cause for their apparently inferior condition in:

The slavery and type of disparagement where we have put women; the impediments which we give to their *esprit*, and to their soul; the jargon to which we reduce our commerce with them, [which is] futile and humiliating for them and for us, as if they lack a reason to cultivate, or are not worthy of it; in the disastrous education, I should say almost murderous, that we prescribe for them, without permitting them to have any other.[13]

Women were seen to have been treated like a conquered but nonetheless redoubtable nation, which the conquerors had found it necessary to disarm to prevent any future revolt. Not only were men found guilty of passive neglect or unconscious discrimination, but they also seemed to be actively engaged in trying to keep women down in the subservient position to which they had been relegated. "This sex is too interested in stupifying in us the gifts of nature . . ." complained *le Courrier de l'hymen* in 1791.[14] Mme Grafigny observed: "It seems to me that women are born . . . with all the dispositions necessary to equal men in merit and virtue. But, as if they admit it in the depths of their heart, and their pride is not able to support this equality, they contribute in every way to make them despicable."[15] Self-interest and male pride were both blamed for the refusal of the male sex to open its eyes and see women as equally respectable beings. The masculine sense of self was seen as too dependent on this image of the male as a superior being to enable the individual man to comfortably question it.

Some writers went one step further and blamed not only male pride, but male jealousy and fear as well. "I may be wrong," wrote d'Alembert, "But it seems to me that [considering] the way we keep women at a distance from all that could enlighten them and elevate their soul . . . one might say that we sense their advantages, and that we want to prevent them from profiting from them."[16] Despite the lack of education, the lack of political or economic opportunity, and all the other evil effects of their subordinant position in society, it was recognized that women had still managed to acquire a considerable amount of influence and power. Many people accused men of harboring a latent fear of female superiority. What would happen if women were allowed to compete with men on an equal basis? In the *Prince philosophe*, by Olympe de Gouges, one of the characters says: "If one gave women the means to add to their charms both courage and learning that was profound and useful to the State, they could one day seize superiority for themselves, and make men, in their turn, weak and timid."[17]

In addition to the conspiracy theory, the defenders of the second sex also borrowed the contradiction theory from the Englightenment. According to this hypothesis, there was a direct contradiction between women's natural character and the one that society expected from them. The resulting need to assume a false character left women open to derisory charges of artificiality. When Mme Grafigny sought the cause for her society's contempt for women, she believed she had discovered it in "the little rapport that exists between what they are and what people imagine they must be."[18] Forced from childhood to conform to a traditional imagery that visualized them more as females than as human beings, the women of eighteenth-century France grew up with little sense of self. In his *Lettre à J.-J. Rousseau*, d'Alembert complained of "the education where [women] learn almost uniquely to dissemble, to have not a sentiment that they do not suppress, an opinion that they do not hide, or a thought that they do not disguise. We treat nature in them like we treat it in our gardens, we seek to embellish it by smothering it."[19] The result was that dissimulation, which the *Encyclopédie* described as a woman's "duty of State," was said to have made the female soul "so secret" that neither men nor perhaps even women themselves could know or understand it.[20]

In their search for an answer to the problem of the degradation of women, the eighteenth-century advocates of sexual equality also turned to history and nature. They looked at nature, and saw the sexes living together in a peaceful companionship. In 1790, Olympe de Gouges demanded:

Who gave you the sovereign authority to oppress my sex? . . . observe . . . look at nature, in all its grandeur, to which you seem to want to draw nearer, and give me, if you dare, an example of this tyrannical authority. Go back to the animals, consult the elements, study the plants . . . search, investigate and distinguish, if you can, the sexes in the administration of nature. Everywhere you find them intermingled, everywhere they cooperate together harmoniously. . . . Only man has dressed himself up as an exception to this principle, bizarre, blind. . . .[21]

If the sexes were equal in nature, then it must have been when man "entered into society" that the female sex was oppressed. The supremacy of men was denounced as an excercise of the *loi du plus fort*, the law of the strongest. The stronger male suppressed the weaker female, it was said, because men abused their force. "Men usurped authority over women by force, rather than by natural right," wrote Mme Lambert.[22] Having once seized power by force, explained the advocates of sexual equality, men later forgot their injustice and sought to rationalize their supremacy. "One searches in vain for grounds to justify [this usurpation] by the difference in [the sexes'] physical organization, by what one would like to find in the force of their intelligence or in their moral sensibility," wrote the *philosophe* Condorcet. "This inequality had no other origin than the abuse of force, and it is to no purpose that one has tried ever since to excuse it by sophisms."[23]

Here was an unjust usurpation of power, and the champions of sexual equality did not fail to make full use of the linguistic opportunities it provided: men were described as "tyrants": they had exercised "a tyranny through the ages"; women had been "enslaved" and were treated like a "second class." The coming of the Revolution only expanded the supply of emotional catch-words: the male sex became a "privileged order" and, most infamous of all, a "male aristocracy."

Having once seized power, these early sociologists contended, the male sex then passed laws to maintain and fortify its dominance. "When the legislators established the rights of men and women," wrote Mme Necker, "they certainly did not consult the common good of both sexes."[24] Women were now powerless under the law because, accused a 1789 pamphlet, "the secret, the truth, is that the strongest made the law."[25]

The suppression of women was believed to be complete only among savages, who lacked moral force to soften their physical force. The progress of civilization was seen to have brought with it an amelioration of the plight of women and an increasing state of equality between the sexes. But sexual equality was considered more than just an effect of civilization: some identified it as one of the prerequisites for the ultimate perfection of humanity. "Among the progresses of the human spirit the most important for the general happiness," wrote Condorcet, "We must count the entire destruction of the prejudices that have established between the two sexes an inequality of rights disastrous even to the one it favors."[26]

Far from being for the common good, the suppression of women was recognized as having had an undesirable effect on the character of both sexes. It had made men vain, overweeningly proud of a false superiority, and sensuously contemptuous of the sex they ought to have respected as companions and equals; women, in contrast, had been enervated and corrupted by the state of nonentity to which they had been reduced, and were condemned to the use of subterfuge and ruse to escape their slavery and to triumph. "The slave only dreams of breaking its chains," wrote Etta Palm d'Aelders, "Of vengeance for its servitude."[27] Diderot actually envisioned a secret conspiracy of all women to seduce and rule over men: "Armed with a profound and secret hatred against male despotism," he wrote, "it seems as if there exists among them a tacit plot of dominance, a sort of league such as the one that exists among priests of all nations; they understand the articles without them being communicated."[28] The weapons women used were their beauty, sex, and that greatest of all feminine *agréments*, coquetry. This humiliating need to play on their sex was seen to have only degraded women further. "Can they lower themselves without shame and without pain to the methods employed with the same success by the most vile slaves?" asked a Revolutionary pamphlet.[29] Diderot predicted that, when times are more enlightened,

We will cease to keep women beneath the yoke and in ignorance, and they to seduce, cheat and govern their masters. Love will be then between the two sexes what the gentlest and truest friendship is between virtuous men; or rather it will be an even more delicious sentiment, which, in nature's intention, must make us happy, and which, to our sorrow, we have altered and corrupted.[30]

The awkward thing about the suppression of women, its opponents realized, was that both men and women were so used to seeing it that they could not imagine their world any different. Women had been born and raised as dependent, and though they might complain about a lack of respect and recognition, or use their charms to increase their influence, most continued to accept their condition as natural. "Habit can familiarize men with the violation of their natural rights," observed Condorcet, "to the point that among those that have lost them, no one dreams of reclaiming them, nor believes that he has suffered an injustice."[31] One of the women in Pierre Marivaux's comedy, *La Nouvelle Colonie, ou la ligue des Femmes*, at one point complains: "They yell at us from the cradle: "You aren't capable of anything, don't mix in anything. . . .' They said it to our mothers who believed it, and who repeated it to us; we have our ears deafened by these foul remarks; we are gentle, idleness mingles in, they lead us like sheep!"[32]

Even those women who recognized and/or objected to the miserable existence of women in their society still tended to advise their own sex to submit: "Our sex is even more exposed to suffering because it is always dependent. Do not be angry or ashamed of this dependence . . . but sanctify it in submitting yourself good-naturedly for the love of [God]," wrote Mme de Maintenon in her *Conseils et Instruction aux demoiselles;* "They are the masters; one can only suffer with good grace."[33] Even Mme de Puisieux wrote: "I do not know if my heart cheats me, but it tells me that they were not destined to impose the law on us . . . yet the yoke is given, one must submit to it."[34] At the end of the masterful *La Femme n'est pas inférieure à l'homme*, the author explained that her purpose was not to incite women to revolt or to change the existing order; she only wanted to end men's contempt for her sex.[35] The Comtesse de Miremont also counseled a certain amount of resignation: "It is often necessary, despite oneself, to cede to the times, circumstances, and customs; he who wishes to brave them all, obtains nothing."[36]

In fact, women were hampered not only by their own reluctance to brave popular opinion and custom, but also by the repressive teachings of a number of men who were respected as among the wisest of their day. Far from seeking to destroy them, the philosophers and moralists of the eighteenth century were more likely to refurbish and reinforce the sex stereotypes so dear to the vulgar. "Even philosophers," complained Mme Necker, "those enemies of prejudice, preserve those of their sex and, to hear them, men are the unique object of women's virtues. These wise men . . . want to divide men into two very distinct classes."[37]

The only *philosophe* of any stature who consistently and indefatigably defended both the integrity and the rights of the female sex was the Marquis de Condorcet. In a variety of works written from 1788 until his death in 1794, Condorcet continuously questioned the presumption of a sex that insisted on finding itself the *cause finale* for the existence of the other. In obvious derision of his fellow *philosophes*, Condorcet wrote:

Some philosophers seem to have taken pleasure in exaggerating these differences [between the sexes]: in consequence they have assigned to each sex its rights, its prerogatives, its occupations, its duties, and practically its tastes, its opinions, its sentiments, its pleasures; they take the dreams of a romantic imagination as the will of nature, they have dogmatically pronounced that all is *the best possible* for the common good; but this optimism, which consists in wondrously finding in nature everything as one invented it . . . must be banished from philosophy.[38]

The truth was that if the defenders of sexual equality could use Enlightenment theory and technique, so, too, could their opponents. If there had ever been a time when reminders of the Fall had sufficed to justify the subordination of women, those days were in the past. Erasmus and the humanists had long ago challenged the prejudices of the church fathers, and the secular eighteenth century found the need to invent new, more "naturalistic" reasons for the inequality between the sexes that characterized their society.

The opponents' greatest weapon in this struggle against the notion of equality for women was the popular idea that "What is, is good, and any general law is not bad."[39] In true Enlightenment tradition, the champions of the suppression of women looked about them, cast their eyes through history, and found that in all times and in all places women had been subjected to the rule of man. The suppression of women must therefore be one of the "constant and universal principles of human nature" and consequently not only natural, but also necessary.[40]

Beginning with the state of nature, the opponents of sexual equality studied the animal kingdom and (apparently looking at different animals than Mme de Gouges) found that everywhere the male reigned supreme. "Equality is not found in any species of animal," wrote Retif de la Bretonne; "In all, the male commands." Reason, he deduced, says that it must be the same among men.[41] In the state of nature, explained a number of different writers, all women belonged to all men (this concept of a common pool of women available on demand to every male was a marvelously attractive idea, and one upon which the sensualists tended to dwell wistfully). With the coming of society, however, the theory went, men divided up their property and women—being property—were divided up too. This was the reason, they explained, that women are not normally allowed to own property, since they are property themselves.[42]

Among those peoples who continued to live closest to nature, it was observed that the sex roles remained clearly defined, and women were kept in their place. In vain did some people protest that savages oppress women because they *are* savages and not because they are closer to nature. Throughout history, throughout the world, the situation was the same. As one author saw it:

People debate over [women's] most proper place in the social order, and one has

in front of his eyes that which nature truly assigned. Is it not true that among all
the nations of the world, women are the same? . . . that they have the same
duties? . . . that they have the same generic character? It seems that [one must]
close his eyes to keep from seeing what nature and providence have wished
women to be. . . .[43]

The defenders of the status quo had a number of other naturalistic
rationalizations for maintaining the subordinate position of women. One
of the most popular rested on women's presumed intellectual weakness.
Women were intellectually inferior to men not because of a lack of education, went the argument, but because nature had made them that way.
Therefore, it was considered natural that the sex with the most judgment
govern the one with the least. With their supposedly delicate mental
organs, their extreme sentimentalism and vivid imaginations, women
were seen as in constant need of superior male guidance. "Let us only use
our authority to preserve them from those mistakes which could be disastrous for them," advised Saint-Lambert paternalistically; "And even then
our orders should be preceded by tender lessons and polite councils."[44]

Another argument used by the opponents of sexual equality was based
on women's physical weakness. Here was one difference that no one
could deny was a product of nature rather than of society. And in an age
that was everywhere decrying the *loi du plus fort*, most people still saw no
contradiction in saying that it was "natural" that the weaker sex, the one
in need of aid, should be dependent and subservient to the stronger sex
that aids it. "All submits woman to man," wrote one author; "Her weakness, her needs, her timidity. . . ."[45] This argument was carried to its
extreme and logical conclusion by the Marquis de Sade, who said: "It
cannot be denied that we have the right to decree laws that compel
women to yield to the flames of him who would have her. . . . Indeed!
has nature not proven that we have that right, by bestowing upon us the
strength needed to bend women to our own will?"[46] Or again: "Why,
were it not nature's intention that one of the sexes tyrannize the other,
would she not have created them equally strong? . . . has she not ade-
quately indicated that she wills the mightier to exploit the rights she has
given him?"[47]

Woman's dependent state, her character, and the differences between
the sexes could all be comfortably demonstrated as existing not as a result
of education or society, but as a product of nature. It was seen as the
order of nature that man command and woman obey. Therefore, when a
woman complained of injustice, she was considered wrong. "This inequality is hardly a human institution," wrote J.-J. Rousseau; "Or at
least it is not the product of prejudice but of Reason."[48]

It is important to realize that these arguments supporting the suppression of women produced during the Enlightenment did not replace those

based on the Christian tradition; the Enlightenment notwithstanding, France in the eighteenth century remained a predominantly Catholic nation, and these new ideas were only added to and used to strengthen the existing Christian tradition of male preponderance, which still rested firmly on its twin foundations of the Creation and the Fall. Although only a few fanatical abbots might still have agreed with Tertullian that women ought to walk about draped in mourning and ashes in repentance for the murder of mankind and the son of God, the teachings of St. Paul were well entrenched. "There does not exist a reasonable woman," wrote Mlle de Archambault, "however superior that she might be to her husband, who aspires to shaking off a yoke imposed by divine law, that she must even regard as forming part of her penitence."[49] By a curious line of reasoning, one author was very careful to emphasize the fact that the Fall destroyed neither a woman's "equality" nor her "independence"; it did, however, destroy her *civil* equality and independence. He explained: "It subordinated her by giving to the man a legal and civil superiority; that is to say, that the man has the right to govern and to command in the social order, and that the woman is inferior to him in this measure."[50]

To these arguments of natural and pentitential subordination could also be added those of utility. Whether it was right or wrong, the suppression of women was considered necessary for society. For man to go forth into the world and do his great deeds, argued the adherents of the old order, woman *must* stay home to keep his house clean and raise his children. Familial harmony was said to require that the male voice predominate, and very few men wanted to find in their wives a rival. Moreover, said many, morality would suffer if women left the retreat of their homes and mixed freely with men: virtue, modesty, all would be lost.

The utility theories were closely related to the idea that the greatest good is what produces the greatest happiness for the greatest number, and, according to this theory, women are really *happy* subordinated. Men, it was said, must be proud, active, productive; in contrast, not only a woman's honor but also her happiness were considered to reside in her meekness, modesty, and retirement. According to the popular adage, little pleasures suffice for women; what amuses them satisfies them, and only men were believed to be tormented and inspired towards great works and ideas. Men, it was said, are vain and want glory, but a woman prefers to please, and her only real happiness lies in sacrifice.[51] It followed from this that although some women might *think* they want more authority, they really did not. "Let us make women the judges in this case," suggested Retif de la Bretonne, "and ask them if they want us to cede to them authority and all its accompaniments. The cry of nature will rise in the depths of their hearts, to beg us to hold on to the reins."[52] Women were said to be naturally attracted to the "pleasures of dependence" and to have a "delicious love of submission." All women, ran the theory, love to be dominated. "However imperious a Parisian woman might be," wrote Mercier, "she will always recognize the ascendancy of the man over her, if he knows how to be firm and prudent."[53] The haughtiest woman, it was commonly said, is always the first one subdued.

If a woman's true happiness lay in submission and dependence, then it followed that any creed that promised to give her equality actually only threatened her happiness. Happiness, harmony, equilibrium—they were very emotionally appealing words, and they were used by many writers to combat the dangerous currents they perceived in the society around them. According to men such as Boudier de Villement, neither sex was inferior or superior; men and women were "naturally" *equal*—but their roles and destinies were, of course, *different*. It was from this necessary but complementary difference that came harmony, balance, and happiness. Any attempt to confound the roles, any suggestion that women should try to assume a masculine posture in society, and the result would be disharmony, chaos, and, ultimately, misery for women. It therefore followed that if women wanted to be truly happy, they should resist these dangerous new teachings and concentrate instead on becoming good wives and mothers.[54]

These ideas joined with and became a part of the cult of sentimentalism that was sweeping France in the second half of the eighteenth century. The late eighteenth century had seen an increase in the popularity of a number of different tendencies and attitudes that, taken together, are labeled as "sentimentalism." The reasons given for this so-called rise of sentimentalism vary. Some see it as a reaction against the seventeenth-century *precieuses* and the worldliness, idleness, frivolity, immorality, and pursuit of fashion that were believed to have characterized the upper classes earlier in the century. Others point to the late eighteenth-century emergence of the modern nuclear family, with its resulting new view of love and marriage, while some see it as just another manifestation of the Enlightenment itself, with its belief in happiness on earth as a valid and viable goal.[55]

Whatever its causes, this increase in sentimentalism, with its emphasis on romantic love and domestic bliss, could only be counterproductive to a movement for greater equality between the sexes. For one thing, romantic love tended to exaggerate the differences society had always imagined between the sexes. The romantic feminine ideal was soft, gentle, and pure. Untainted by ambition, she provided her male with a quiet refuge from the competition and pressures of his world; she did not clamor to be allowed to play an equal part in that world, nor did she threaten to present him with a rival and competitor capable of undermining his sense of masculinity. Instead, she devoted herself to the care of her home and children, a task that the sentimentalists glorified as never before.

As part of the sentimentalist creed, these images held a seductive lure for many women, for they promised women respect—of a sort.[56] And it was respect that women could acquire not by challenging tradition and transforming society, but simply by transforming themselves. True happiness for women lay not in seeking an education or demanding a place in politics or the professions, but simply in becoming virtuous wives and good mothers. It was a goal that any woman was capable of achieving.[57]

Partially as a result of this growth of sentimentalism, there were few things for which the eighteenth century held more contempt than the masculine female. Everything had to be feminine in a woman. "One does not like to encounter the exterior qualities of the man in a woman," said the *Encyclopédie*; "Experience has caused us to attribute to each sex a tone, a step, the movements, the features that are proper for it, and we are shocked to find them displaced."[58] Nature was said to have made woman to be soft and modest; the air of the chevalier, a man's muscles and hardiness, all made her a monster. Women were supposed to be different from men, and from the opposites would be born not only harmony, but also mutual attraction. Men were described as both surprised and repelled to find a woman with their own inclinations. "We live in a country where the women want to make themselves men . . .," wrote one writer; "What madness to introduce a rivalry between those beings that must please each other by their differences."[59]

It was not only in their physical attributes that the difference between the sexes had to be preserved; neither a man's interests, nor his intelligence, nor even the "masculine virtues" were considered proper for a female. Any woman who tried to become a man was told that she could only hope to lose the virtues of her own sex, without ever being able to attain those of men. "Woman has more merit as woman and less as man," wrote Rousseau; "Wherever she asserts her rights she has the advantage; wherever she wants to usurp ours she remains below us."[60]

The greatest scorn of all was reserved for the woman who tried to compete with men in their own sphere, particularly in the area of learning: such a woman was out of her place, and, like all things out of place, she was despised as ridiculous. "It is only gauche women without accomplishments who want to establish a rivalry between themselves and men," wrote Saint-Lambert.[61] According to the popular belief, the only woman who would ever want to try to "act like a man" must be one who was incapable of acting like a woman.

The reaction of these shocked moralists to any idea of further change or even greater sexual equality was predictably one of dismay and anger, born of fear. "To maintain vaguely that the two sexes are equal and that their duties are the same is to lose oneself in vain declarations . . .," wrote J.-J. Rousseau defensively.[62] Retif de la Bretonne reacted even more violently: "Dangerous maxims of equality of the sexes!" he cried; "Maxims seductive at first glance, but which, well considered, are the overthrow of all order and common happiness."[63] Women were warned that any attempt towards equality would only mean the loss of their "real" *empire*. They were warned that these so-called "rights" were only "chimerical," and contrary to women's best interests. "Oh, women!" encouraged one author; "Beware of any man who wants to make you assume our occupations; he is a Seducer, who is trying to tear you away from the restraints where your *pudeur* is safe, to lay you bare and to expose you to all blows. Do not listen to him. Do not follow the allure of a dangerous curiosity and a presumptuous vanity."[64]

It is important to note here that although they seem so in retrospect, Rousseau and his ilk did not see themselves as conservative reactionaries, desperately shoring up the embattled status quo. On the contrary, they saw themselves as reformers, out to destroy the evil effects of what they saw as female dominance and improper behavior.

One of the rationales often given for the suppression of women was actually the widespread belief that women already had too much power and influence as it was. "They are strong enough with their ascendancy over us," wrote Pierre-Joseph Roussel; "Let us leave them with the *empire* of grace and beauty."[65] The Chevalier d'Artaize put it more forcefully: "Reason and the facts prove that it is a thousand times less dangerous to reduce women to the most severe slavery, rather than to let her take the least part in government."[66]

There was a growing conviction that women had somehow managed to gain tremendous power and influence in society, and that most of it was for the worst. Part of this animosity had been aroused by the important role played in society by the salons and the women who ran them. The Chevalier d'Artaize was not the only one who held women responsible for the degradation of the arts and sciences. As supposedly frivolous, shallow, and lazy beings, women were depreciated as being unable to either understand or appreciate the truly serious and sublime. Women were accused of being attracted by glitter and superficiality, and of favoring only the most worthless men with their patronage. As long as men of letters continued to fawn over women and sought only to please them, said the disgruntled, mediocrity would reign.

If commerce with women was blamed for having degraded the arts and sciences, it was held to have had an even worse effect on men themselves. It was said that men were beginning to act like women: weak, petty—in a word, effeminate. "Not being able to attain our grandeur, they try to make us share their smallness," wrote one author; "Not being able to raise themselves to our genius, they have been forced to pull us down to their level."[67]

Nor were women content to confine their interference to the arts and science: women were accused of having sought influence and domination in the governmental sphere as well.[68] Participants on both sides of the Quarrel were likely to agree that male attempts to keep women suppressed had never been completely successful. "Free like the air, even when we oppress them, they know how to escape from slavery; it only costs them a sigh," wrote one author in 1791; "You use force, they use their tears. Women's independence is located in their very weakness; a smile restores them to the liberty that you wish to rob from them."[69] With all male roads to authority and glory closed to them, women were required to find their own devious routes. The path lay through ruse and seduction. "What has the impotence and inferiority of woman produced?" asked Olympe de Gouges; "Contradictions of every kind. What she had lost by force, she recovered by address. You refused her the art of war, while you taught her the art of inflaming it. . . ."[70] Lacking the power to act openly, it was said that women observed and carefully perfected their knowledge of society and men. According to Thomas, women could play society like a musical instrument: they knew even before they touched it what sound it would make.[71] After having learned men's weaknesses and vices, accused Thomas, women then used that knowledge to corrupt men and to dominate them. As a result of this theory, although women were formally excluded from the throne and government of France, they were said to rule the nation.

The most famous protest against the influence of women at court is probably that of Montesquieu. In his *Persian Letters*, he finds France entirely governed by women:

I heard one day a woman who said: "One must do something for that young colonel; his worth is not known: I will speak to the minister about it." Another might say: "It is surprising that this young abbot has been forgotten; he must be a bishop; he is a well-born man, and I can answer for his morals." One must not imagine that the women holding these conversations were favorites of the prince; they perhaps had only spoken to him twice in their life. . . . But there is no one who has any kind of position at court, in Paris, or in the provinces, who does not have a woman through whose hands pass all the favors and sometimes the unjustice that he can do. These women all have relations with each other, and form a sort of Republic of which the ever-active members mutually help and serve one another: it is like a new State within a State, and someone who is at court, at Paris, or in the provinces, who sees the ministers, magistrates and prelates acting, if he does not know the women who govern them, is like a man who sees clearly a machine which works, but who does not know how it works.[72]

Montesquieu's opinion was shared by many. The Marquis d'Artaize was so repelled by the spread of female power in France that he devoted the entire volume of his *New Reflections of a Young Man* to the per-fidious influence of women at court.

This myth of a government and nation corrupted and ruled by women continued to grow until by the time of the Revolution, women would be held responsible for the entire ruin of France and the general decadence that made revolution necessary. In 1791, Prudhomme wrote:

What took place at Versailles during three reigns does not weigh in favor of the happy influence of women on liberty; its sway would date from a much earlier period without them. . . . They reigned despotically in the circles and even in the diplomatic cabinets. The scepter of beauty pressed almost as heavily as that of the kings; it was necessary to present oneself in the boudoirs, like at court, in order to be happy. . . .

The reign of the courtesans precipitated the ruin of the nation. The influence of the Queens consummated it. . . .

The women of the rich bourgeois class modeled themselves on the dames of the court. First frivolity seized ahold of all spirits. Then corruption gained the hearts; and that is all one could wish. One does all with a nation that does not reflect and that has no morals; and thanks to the women, we had come to that point, despite several good books for which the women showed a decided aversion, more pen-etrating than us, they foresaw from a distance that the fall of their dominance would be the immediate result of the reign of thought, and that they would be put back in their place from the moment that men reassumed their rank.[73]

There already existed in France a long tradition that somehow man-aged to find a woman to blame for everything that had ever "gone wrong" in history, from the destruction of Greece to St. Bartholomew's Day.[74] "Almost all the bloodiest wars, and the destructions of Empires, of Kingdoms, and of the most prosperous States, had no other origin but the ambition or the jealousy and the secret intrigues of women," wrote one author; "Their passions, which had aroused the wars, perpetuated them, and could only be satiated in the blood and ruin of the people."[75] Montesquieu and a number of others held women entirely responsible for the wide-spread, debilitating effects of luxury, while the Chevalier d'Ar-taize was only one of many who blamed women for the spread of im-morality: "Shall I say it? The horrible, incredible cause of the precocious libertinage, and of the general corruption of men? I shudder at it, but I cannot keep silent; women, it is once more you!"[76] It was observed that among strong, robust, and virtuous peoples, women lived obscure, dom-estic lives; their emergence from seclusion and their growing influence was seen to coincide exactly with the coming of corruption and decadence and to spell the ultimate doom of a state. The warning was obvious: wise and long-lived societies keep women in their place. "Fear the secret ambition of women," cried Artaize; "Their authority announces your doom!"[77]

Yet everywhere they looked, the alarmed moralists of the late eighteenth century saw their own society in decay. The journals, essays, and letters of the period resound with Boissi's cry: "Oh century! Oh times! Oh morality! What indecence!"[79] Instead of modest, timid, and retiring women, everywhere they looked, these men saw licentiousness and lasciviousness. "They were the object of a cult," wept one; "Now they are only the occasion of a passing desire."[79] If women attack, what will become of us, asked another man, faced with their charms and their audacious passions?[80] "Oh happy times . . . of our fathers," sighed Diderot, "when there were only honest or dishonest women; when all those who were not honest were dishonest." Nowadays, it was impossible to tell them apart; all were sinking together in one systematic morass of depravity.[81]

Women were accused of having ceased to want to be good wives and mothers; good housewifery, it was said, was despised as a bourgeois virtue. "Women must be formed to please," complained one man, "but the women of our day do not please; on the contrary, they displease."[82] Women were believed to be losing the most touching characteristics of their sex: their timidity, their simplicity, their naive innocence. Instead of being meek and submissive, it was said, women were becoming haughty and imperious. In fact, women had become so insupportable and corrupt that they were blamed for increasing the number of bachelors: "In a nation without morals," wrote Holbach, "men fear to enter into marriages that religion and the law prevent ever being broken."[83]

There seemed to still exist only two classes of respectable females. One was the second order of the Bourgeoisie. "Attached to their husbands and to their children . . . they offer a model of wisdom and hard work," praised Mercier; "One does not notice them and, nevertheless, at Paris they are the honor of their sex."[84] The conduct of the women of the countryside and mountains was also held to be commendable. "In our mountains, the women are timid and modest; one word makes them blush; they dare not raise their eyes to men, and keep silent before them," noted Rousseau approvingly. In contrast, the women of Paris and the aristocracy were undoubtedly the worst of all. "In our big cities, *pudeur* is ignoble and base; it is the only thing of which a well-bred woman is ashamed," said Rousseau.[95] These women were told that they had gone too far to return to their own sex; they could only try to make themselves men, said their detractors.

It is difficult to say with any degree of certainty to what extent these moralists' alarms and accusations were actually grounded in fact. True, the late eighteenth century saw a dramatic rise in the number of illegitimate and abandoned children, as well as an increase in prostitution, but social historians have been inclined to view this not as a sign of declining morality, but as the product of a declining economy, which forced large segments of the society to either postpone marriage, or abandon it entirely.[86]

Men of all ages have complained that the women of their day were not acting like women "should"—which, considering the nature of the traditionally idealized and unrealistic image of the perfect woman, is not at all surprising. Nor was the late eighteenth century the first age to complain about what it perceived as the "immorality" of its age in general and the female sex in particular. Since the virtuous woman was visualized as a basically desexed being, the normal desires of any woman with a healthy sex drive would naturally be viewed as shocking and corrupt. Similarly, since the burden of maintaining both morality and chastity was placed squarely on the shoulders of the female sex, any loosening of sexual mores was likely to be hailed as the fault of that sex alone.

Nevertheless, the role of women in eighteenth-century French society had in fact altered. In a changing and expanding economy,[87] more and more women were becoming wage earners in their own right, and money means power, even within the restricted sphere of the family. A rising female literacy rate was exposing women to the world that existed outside the narrow confines of the home, and both expanding and redefining their self-awareness. But at the time of the Revolution, this evolution was more potential than realized and would not reach its full development until the nineteenth or even the twentieth century. The majority of the women of late eighteenth-century France, as well as their men, still conceived of themselves along the general outlines laid down by the traditional society of which they were all a part.

Male-dominated societies have traditionally been covetous of all male perogatives, and proportionally afraid of losing them. The constant need to protect this male superiority from feminine assault leads to fear and an exaggerated perception of the power and influence of the female sex. That some women in eighteenth-century France exercised enormous sway is undeniable; nor can it be doubted that a number of strong and intelligent wives dominated the lives of their weaker husbands. But the women of the eighteenth century were politically, legally, and morally hamstrung; the importance of the role that they still somehow managed to play was in spite of and not because of the attitudes of their society. It was a tribute to their basic human intelligence, talent, and ingenuity, and should not be overestimated. It loomed large in the minds of their contemporaries only in proportion to the state of complete feminine nonentity that was held up as the ideal.

What is important, however, is that a growing segment of French society believed that the women of the *Ancien Régime* had both ruled and ruined their nation. In an atmosphere of traditional and fanatical moralism, the makers of the French Revolution were determined not to increase the influence of women in their government and society, but to destroy it.

NOTES

1. For a brief overview of the history of the Woman Question from the sixteenth century to the Revolution, see George Ascoli, "Essai sur l'histoire des idées féministes en France du XVIe siècle à la Révolution," in *Revue de synthèse historique* 13 (1906), pp. 25–27, 161–184. See also Leon Abensour, *La Femme et le féminisme avant la révolution* (Paris: E. Leroux, 1923).

2. Arguments of this type may be found in Cornelius Henricus Agrippa, *De la Précellence du sexe féminin*, translated by Gueudenville (Leiden: 1726); Mlle Archambault, *Dissertation sur la question*; and Abbé Joseph-Antoine Toissant Dinouart, *Le Triomphe du sexe, ouvrage dans lequell on démontre que les femmes sont en tout égales aux hommes* (Amsterdam: I Racon, 1749).

3. Jodin, *Vues législatives pour les femmes,* p. 22.

4. Mme de Puisieux, *Conseils à une amie,* p. 119.

5. Jodin, *Vues législatives pour les femmes,* p. 19.

6. Anonyme, *Motions adressés à l'Assemblée Nationale en faveur du sexe* (Paris: Imprimerie de la Vve Delaquette, 1789), p. 2.

7. Anonyme, *Remontrances, plaintes et doléances des dames françaises, à l'occasion de l'assemblée des Etats Généraux, par M.L.P.P.D. St. L., 25 mars 1789* (n.p., n.d.), p. 11.

8. [Puisieux], *La Femme n'est pas inférieure à l'homme.*

9. For Enlightenment thought in general, see Carl Becker, *The Heavenly City of the Eighteenth-Century Philosophers* (New Haven, CT: Yale University Press, 1947), and Peter Grey, *The Enlightenment: An Interpretation*, 2 vols. (New York: Alfred Knopf, 1966 and 1969), among others. On women and the Enlightenment, see Samia Spencer, ed., *French Women and the Age of Enlightenment* (Bloomington, IN: University of Indiana Press, 1985), Paul Hoffmann, *La Femme dans la pensée des lumières* (Paris: Editions Orphys, 1977), and a host of others, including Elizabeth Fox-Genovese, "Women and the Enlightenment," in Renate Bridenthal and Claudia Koonz, *Becoming Visible: Women in European History* (Boston, MA: Houghton Mifflin, 1977); K. B. Clinton, "Femme et Philosophe: Enlightenment Origins of Feminism," *Eighteenth-Century Studies* 8 (Spring, 1975), 283–299; Terry S. Dock, "The Encyclopedists' Woman," *Proceedings of the Tenth Annual Meeting of the Western Society for French History, Oct. 1984* (Lawrence, KS: University of Kansas, 1984), pp. 255–263; A. P. Humphreys, "The Rights of Women in the Age of Reason," *Modern Language Review*, 41 (1946), pp. 257–263; M. R. Raaphorst, "Voltaire et le féminisme, un examen du theatre et des conts," *Studies on Voltaire and the Eighteenth Century*, 89 (1972), 1325–1335; D. J. Adams, *La Femme dans les contes et les romans de Voltaire* (Paris: Nizet, 1974); and J.-G. Rosso, *Montesquieu et la féminité*, (Pisa: Libraire Goliardica Editrice, 1977).

10. Don Philippe-Joseph Caffiaux, *Défenses du beau sexe, ou Mémoires historiques, philosophiques et critiques pour servir d'apologie aux femmes*, 3 vols. (Amsterdam: 1753), Vol. 1, p. 90.

11. Ibid.

12. Benedetto Toselli, *L'Apologie des femmes*, p. 19.

13. Jean Le Rond d'Alembert, "Lettre à J.-J. Rousseau, citoyen de Genève, sur les spectacles," in *Oeuvres complètes d'Alembert* (Paris: A. Belin, 1822), Vol. 4, p. 450.

14. *Le Courrier de l'hymen, Journal des Dames*, No. 19, 24 April 1791, p. 73.

15. Mme de Grafigny, *Lettres Péruviennes* (Paris: 1749), Vol. 2, p. 67.

16. d'Alembert, "Lettre à J.-J. Rousseau," p. 450.

17. Olympe de Gouges, *Le Prince philosophe* (n.p., n.d.).

18. Grafigny, *Lettres Péruviennes*, Vol. 2, p. 54.

19. d'Alembert, "Lettre à J.-J. Rousseau," p. 450.

20. *Encyclopédie*, Vol. 6, p. 472.

21. Olympe de Gouges, *Droits de la femme* (n.p., n.d.), p. 5.

22. Ann Thérèse Lambert, *Réflexions nouvelles sur les femmes* (London: chez J. P. Codère, 1730), p. 7.

23. Jean-Antoine-Nicolas Condorcet, *Esquisse des progrès de l'esprit humain*, in *Oeuvres complètes*, Vol. 8, p. 359.

24. Necker, *Mélanges*, p. 430.

25. *Offre genereuse des dames françaises du Tiers Etat ou Moyen de rétablir les finances en 24 heures* (n.p., 1789), p. 2.

26. Condorcet, *Esquisse*, p. 359.

27. Etta Palm née d'Aelders, "Addresse des citoyennes françoises à l'assemblée nationale," in *Appel aux Françaises sur la régénération des moeur et nécéssité de l'influence des femmes dans un gouvernement libre* (Paris: Imprimerie du Cercle Social, 1791), p. 40.

28. Diderot, *Essai sur les femmes*, p. 39.

29. *Les Griefs et plaintes des femmes mal mariées* (Paris: Boulard, 1789), p. 22.

30. Diderot, *Essai sur les femmes*, p. 451.

31. Jean-Antoine-Nicolas Condorcet, "l'Essai sur l'admission des femmes au droit de la cité," *Le Journal de la Société de 1789*, No. 5, 3 July 1790, p. 1.

32. Pierre Cralet de Chamblain de Marivaux, *La Nouvelle Colonie, ou la ligue des femmes* (Paris: Libraire Hatier, n.d.), p. 19; cf. Mary [Godwin] Wollstonecraft: "Considering the length of time that women have been dependent, is it surprising that some of them hug their chains, and fawn like the spaniel?" *A Vindication of the Rights of Women* (London: J. Johnson, 1796), p. 182.

33. Maintenon, *Conseils et Instructions*, pp. 162, 164.

34. Puisieux, *Conseils à une amie*, p. 131.

35. [Puisieux], *La Femme n'est pas inférieure à l'homme*, p. 140.

36. Anne d'Aubourg de la Bove, Comtesse de Miremont, *Traité de l'éducation des femmes*, 7 Vols. (Paris: P.-D. Pierres, 1779), p. xxx.

37. Necker, *Mélanges*, p. 430.

38. Condorcet, *Esquisse*, pp. 559–560.

39. Jean-Jacques Rousseau, *Emile*, p. 712.

40. See Carl L. Becker, *The Heavenly City of the Eighteenth-Century Philosophers* (New Haven, CT: Yale University Press, 1947).

41. Retif de la Bretonne, *Le Gynographe*, p. 58.

42. This theory was a very popular one; see, for instance, [Ferrières], *La Femme et les voeux*.

43. Ibid., p. 44. The most famous practitioner of this art was, of course, Montesquieu. The advocates of this historical/sociological approach were particularly fond of dwelling on the seraglios of the east and the institution of polygamy, which held obvious appeal. They were also simultaneously repelled and attracted by the story of the Amazons.

44. Saint-Lambert, *l'Analyse de l'homme et de la femme*, in *Oeuvres*, Vol. I, p. 257.

45. d'Artaize, *Réflexions d'un jeune homme*, p. 10.

46. Marquis de Sade, *Philosophy in the Bedroom*, p. 319.

47. Marquis de Sade, "Justine, or Good Conduct Well Chastised," p. 647.

48. Jean-Jacques Rousseau, *Emile*, p. 697.

49. Archambault, *Dissertation sur la question*, p. 159.

50. Dinouart, *Le Triomphe du sexe*, p. 12.

51. See, for instance, the anonymous pamphlet, *Les Concitoyennes ou Arrêté des dames* (n.p., n.d.); Thomas, *Essai sur le caractère, les moeurs et l'esprit des femmes;* and Saint-Lambert, *L'Analyse de l'homme et de la femme*.

52. Retif de la Bretonne, *Le Gynographe*, p. 216.

53. Mercier, *Tableau de Paris*, Vol. 2, 1781, p. 23.

54. Pierre Joseph Boudier de Villement, *l'Ami des femmes, ou Morale du sexe* (Paris: Royez, 1788).

55. See, for example, Cissie Fairchilds, "Women and Family," in Samia Spencer, ed., *French Women and the Age of Enlightenment*; Elizabeth Fox-Genovese, "Women and the Enlightenment," in *Becoming Visible*; or Barbara Corrado Pope, "Revolution and Retreat: Upper-Class French Women After 1789," in Carol Berkin and Clara Lovett, eds., *Women, War, and Revolution* (New York: Holmes and Meier, 1980).

56. For the peculiar attraction Rousseau held for a woman such as Mme de Staël, see Madelyn Gutwirth, "Madame de Staël, Rousseau, and the Woman Question," *Publications of the Modern Language Association*, 86 (1971), pp. 100–109.

57. This idealization of the woman as wife and mother is one that is generally associated with Rousseau and his popularizers, but its origins were much older. It was already current at least as early as the late seventeenth century, when Fenelon and Maintenon advanced the need to train young women to be virtuous wives and devoted, industrious mothers as their justification for the moral education of women.

58. "Effeminé," *Encyclopédie*, Vol. 5, p. 404.

59. Saint-Lambert, *Le Catéchisme universal*, p. 43.

60. Jean-Jacques Rousseau, *Emile*, p. 700.

61. Saint-Lambert, *L'Analyse de l'homme et de la femme*, Vol. 1, p. 204.

62. Jean-Jacques Rousseau, *Emile*, p. 698.

63. Retif de la Bretonne, *Le Gynographe*, p. 232.

64. Ibid., p. 203.

65. Pierre-Joseph Alexis Roussel, *Le Château des Tuileries* (Paris: Lerouge, 1802), p. 45.

66. d'Artaize, *Réflexions*, pp. 10–11.

67. [Ferrières], *La Femme et les voeux*, p. 166.

68. For examples of the power of individual women in politics, see Susan P.

Conner, "Sexual Politics and Citizenship: Women in Eighteenth-Century France," *Proceedings of the Tenth Annual Meeting of the Western Society for French History, October 1982* (Lawrence, KS: University of Kansas Press, 1984), pp. 264–273, or Conner, "Women and Politics," in Samia Spencer, ed., *French Women and the Age of Enlightenment*.

69. *Le Journal des droits de l'homme*, No. 14, 10 August, 1791 (Paris: Imprimerie de Feret), pp. 3–4.

70. Gouges, *Le Prince philosophe*.

71. Thomas, *Essai sur le caractère*, p. 255.

72. Montesquieu, *Lettres Persanes*, in *Oeuvres complètes*, Letter 108, p. 127.

73. [Prudhomme], *Révolutions de Paris*, Vol. 7, No. 83, 5–12 February 1791, pp. 227–228. Even before the Revolution began, there was a widespread belief that under the "austere morality" of a republic, women would be denied the "corrupting influence" that they could exercise in a monarchy. See, for instance, [Ferrières], *La Femme*, pp. 110–111, and Montesquieu, *l'Esprit des lois*, Book 7, Chapter 9, p. 213.

74. I.e.: Agis' wife let herself be seduced by Alcibiades, who was then forced to flee to Persia; Cleopatra started the fall of the Roman Empire and Livia finished it, etc. One of the best of these "look at what women have wrought" histories can be found in the anonymous, *De l'Influence des femmes dans l'ordre civil et politique* (à Eleuthéropolis, 1789).

75. Archembault, *Dissertation sur la question*, p. 124.

76. d'Artaize, *Réflexions d'un jeune homme*, p. 183.

77. Ibid., p. 198.

78. Abbé Reyre, *Ecole des jeunes demoiselles ou lettres d'une mère vertueuse à sa fille avec les réponses*, 2 vols. (Paris: Varin, 1786), Vol. 1, p. 301.

79. [Ferrières], *La Femme et les voeux*, p. 164.

80. Mercier, *Tableau de Paris*, Vol. 2, 1781, p. 4.

81. Diderot, *Sur les femmes*, p. 52.

82. Retif de la Bretonne, *Le Gynographe*, p. 43.

83. Holbach, *Système social*, p. 358.

84. Mercier, *Tableau de Paris*, Vol. 2, 1781, p. 25.

85. Jean-Jacques Rousseau, "Lettre à d'Alembert," p. 120.

86. See, for instance, Olwen Hufton, "Women and the Family Economy in Eighteenth-Century France," *French Historical Studies*, Vol. 9, 1 (Spring 1975), pp. 1–23. Also see Colin Jones, "Prostitution and the Ruling Class in eighteenth-century Montpellier," *Hist. Workshop*, 6 (autumn 1978), pp. 7–28.

87. Although the economy was contracting in the years immediately prior to the Revolution, the eighteenth century had nevertheless witnessed an end to the great killing famines of the past and the beginning of a steady increase in population, as well as general economic growth and a rise in prices in the years following 1730. See, for instance, Elizabeth Fox-Genovese, "Women and Work," in Spencer, ed., *French Women and the Age of Enlightenment*, or Olwen Hufton, *The Poor of Eighteenth-Century France* (London: Oxford University Press, 1974).

3

A New Dawn Is Breaking

> Open your eyes, adorable sex, charming sex, sex too long degraded;
> open your eyes, your chains are broken, your impudent oppressors
> have disappeared, the reign of august liberty shines forth in all its
> brilliance . . . you were, according to all accounts, slaves; now,
> behold, you are citizens!
>
> [Anonymous, *Adresse au beau sexe,
> rélativement à la révolution présente*]

The coming of the Revolution in 1789 brought with it optimistic visions of
change and improvement. A new dawn was breaking; the shadows of
ignorance, tyranny, and prejudice would soon be dispelled, and the light
of liberty would shine forth for all. "France has broken its chains,"
exclaimed the author of *Les Griefs et plaintes des femmes mal mariées;*
"Liberty is coming. . . . Will the most amiable sex, the gentlest and
weakest sex, continue to sigh in captivity, among a people who pride
themselves on acting gallantly toward women?"[1]

There was a kind of naive confidence in the power of the Revolution to
correct all the wrongs of an infamous past. Discrimination, injustice,
repression—all were to be expected in centuries of darkness and corrupting despotism. But now? "All is possible in this century of light and philosophers," exclaimed Mme de Gouges.[2] The Revolution was the vehicle
through which enlightened visions of equality and liberty would be realized. Women had been suppressed in the past, but who could imagine
that they would not now be free? It would be the honor of France to be

43

the first to correct those ancient and widespread abuses that had kept women subjugated. "The glory was reserved for you, Sirs," Etta Palm d'Aelders told the French, "To be the first to overcome the odious ramparts with which prejudices oppose the recognition of those imprescriptible rights of nature, of which the weakest but most precious half of humanity has been defrauded for so many centuries."[3]

In pamphlets, speeches, and letters to newspapers, women heralded the coming of the new order. It was noted that the Negro slaves were to be freed, and the common people of France were to come into their rights: "It is to the philosophy that is enlightening the nation to which one will be indebted for these benefits," wrote the author of *Cahier des doléances et reclámations des femmes*; "Could it be possible that it be mute with respect to us? Or, rather, that, deaf to its voice, and insensible to its wisdom, men should persist in wanting to make us the victims of their pride or of their injustice?"[4] It did not seem possible. "Break the ignoble chains that crush us," invited Etta Palm; "Would that *couronnes civiques* might replace on these interesting heads those miserable pompoms, symbols of frivolity and shameful signs of our servitude."[5]

This was the spirit of optimism that reverberated through the first days of the Revolution, but if some women were hopeful that they would be able to contribute officially to the regeneration of the nation, they were doomed to disappointment. The female sex was allowed little input into the long and complicated process that led to the election of the delegates to the Estates General and to the compilation of the *cahiers*, or lists of grievances and recommendations, that they carried with them. In times past, female religious orders, widows, and unmarried women who were owners of fiefs had been allowed to vote for the deputies of the first and second estates, while women's corporations had been admitted to the deliberations of the Third Estate. Under the *règlement royal* of 24 January 1789, however, the feudal rights of these women were still recognized, but now they were allowed to vote only through the agency of male *procureurs*, and not for themselves as before.[6]

Whether or not it resulted from this omission, the *cahiers* of 1789 included few concerns of special interest to women. Only one general *cahier*, that of the Third Estate of Chaterault, seems to have included women in its demands for a broader suffrage. This *cahier* asked that "the assembly be formed on an equitable basis; in consequence, that all citizens of both sexes and of all ages have the right equally to concur in the deliberation and the nomination of deputies."[7] Among the numerous general *cahiers* that expressed demands for national education, some 33 also extended their recommendations to include education for girls, although the nature or extent of this education was not specified.[8] Other demands that seem at first to be directly concerned with women are actually more closely related to an intense national desire to increase the

French population and birthrate. As a result, there are a number of suggestions for the establishment of maternity hospitals and requests for the training and regulation of midwives. The same motivation was also the inspiration behind requests for more equitable dowry arrangements and the general encouragement of marriage. Of even greater importance was the widespread desire to improve standards of public morality, an interest that appears in 119 of the extant general *cahiers*.[9] This last request was the natural product of prevailing alarms over what was seen as an increasing state of decadence and immorality and tended to be directed against women in general and prostitutes in particular.

To be properly recognized as true *cahiers*, these lists of suggestions and complaints are required to have come from legally recognized electoral assemblies or they are not, by definition, "legal" *cahiers*.[10] As a result, the lists of grievances and suggestions drawn up by several corporations of female workers in Paris are not considered "legal" *cahiers*. In a vain attempt to be heard, these corporations sent their *cahiers* successively to the electors of their district, the Bureau de la Ville, to Necker, and, finally, to the Estates General itself. Although never officially recognized, they are distinctly different from the wide variety of pamphlets that also appeared under the title of *"cahiers"* or *"doléances"* but usually came from the pen of one author. One such *cahier* from a woman's corporation, the *Cahier des voeux et doléances de la communauté des marchandes de modes, plumassières fleuristes de Paris*, begins with the following observation:

The community, out of respect for the orders of the King, did not wish to protest against the convocation which was done by *quartier* for the Estates General, when according to the terms of the *Règlements* it should be done by corporation. But this numerous community, paying annually to the King a considerable sum as much in taxes as in mistress fees and other dues, could hope to be represented.

Although they were "hopeful," the women of this corporation were obviously fully aware that, far from expanding the rights of their sex, the current march of events actually seemed to be eroding the political rights they had enjoyed in the past. They were, in fact, being subjected to "taxation without representation."

Another of the *cahiers* from a women's corporation, the *Doléances particulières des marchandes bouquetières fleuristes chapelières en fleurs de la ville et faubourgs de Paris*, likewise began by saying hopefully:

The liberty given to all citizens to denounce to the representatives of the nation the abuses which press them from all directions is, without doubt, a sure presage of an approaching reform.

In this confidence, the flower merchants . . . dare to address themselves to you, our seigneurs.[11]

The contents of both of these *cahiers* are almost uniquely concerned with the special needs of these particular communities; nevertheless, their introductions as well as their authors' repeated attempts to have them recognized are rare insights into what must have been a widespread feminine frustration over a woman's inability officially to express either her hopes or her needs.

Despite these inauspicious beginnings, however, a number of French women, like French men, maintained their enthusiasm for the Revolution and their confidence in its ultimate success. In fact, all of the women of the Revolution who were to become famous as champions of women's rights—Olympe de Gouges, Etta Palm d'Aelders, Théroigne de Méricourt, and the two presidents of the *Club des Citoyennes Républicaines Révolutionnaires,* Claire Lacombe, and Pauline Léon—were revolutionaries first and women second. Their primary enthusiasm was for the Revolution itself, and most did not even seem to realize that their belief in women's rights deviated from the mainstream of revolutionary thought. It was only later—after their eager contributions had been ridiculed and rebuffed—that these women began to articulate both their sense of frustration and their belief that the rhetoric of the Revolution must be applied to both sexes equally or risk accusations of hypocrisy and ultimate failure.

These active women of the French Revolution, whose names and personalities have come down to us, were each unique individuals in their own right, yet all tended to reveal a certain number of common characteristics.[12] To begin with, most were what in another age would be called "emancipated women." Rejecting contemporary ideas that a woman is born to live dependent and with her destiny bounded by marriage or the cloister, these women chose an independent course and supported themselves as best they could in the economic system of their day. As mature but still young women, living under their own roofs, their behavior often deviated widely from eighteenth-century prescribed standards of feminine conduct, and although the image has certainly been exaggerated by the accusations of their enemies, it is undeniable that most of these women also personally rejected contemporary ideas governing the sexual activity of an unmarried woman.

Olympe de Gouges, for example, had been married at a young age to a man whom she disliked. After a few years she either had been widowed or else had simply taken her young son and escaped to the metropolis, where she seems to have made a living as an actress—generally not considered a respectable occupation—and as a playwright (one of her plays, the *Esclavage des Négres*, was produced by the Maison de Molière in December 1789). Whether or not she found other means to supplement her income is open to conjecture; accusations of immorality against prominent or outspoken women were a typical way of discrediting them, and Olympe de Gouges had many enemies: Retif de la Bretonne wrote against her in his 1794 *l'Année des dames nationales*, as did l'abbé de Bouyon in *Folies d'un mois, 8ᵉ nᵒ 3*. Nevertheless, her writings do show that she was an outspoken critic of her age's extreme double standard for sexual morality, and when she was sentenced to death in 1793, she did claim to be pregnant (a not uncommon claim by women desperate to postpone death even for a few more days).

Théroigne de Méricourt, likewise, was a singer by profession, although she was also said to be the mistress of a marquis. Less is known about the personal life of Etta Palm d'Aelders, who seems to have been a less flamboyant and more intellectual character, but she, too, appears as a young, single female acting independently. Pauline Léon and Claire Lacombe, prominent members of the *Club des Citoyennes Républicaines Révolutionnaires*, were also young, single women. Although Léon was a chocolate maker who supported her widowed mother and younger brothers and sisters, Lacombe practiced the disreputable profession of acting, and first Lacombe, and later Léon, engaged in love affairs with the *enragé* Théophile Leclerc.[13]

In other ways, however, these women differed considerably. Olympe de Gouges rarely spoke in public and tended to confine her revolutionary energy to the production of a deluge of ardent pamphlets, on the publication of which she expended a small fortune. Although several times she urged women to unite together, she appears neither to have organized a club herself nor to have joined any of those already in existence in Paris.

Théroigne de Méricourt, on the other hand, was an active revolutionary in every sense of the word. Although she was apparently absent from the storming of the Bastille, she was publicly awarded a *couronne civique* for her part in the 10 August 1792 attack on the Tuileries, and she gave a speech at the Société Fraternelle asking to be allowed to form a "legion of Amazons." In 1790 she had helped to organize a club, the *"Amis de la loi,"* which included members of both sexes, and in the same year she was either sent as a Jacobin agent, or traveled on her own initiative (depending upon the version of the tale) to Belgium, where she was arrested for inciting revolution and incarcerated in an Austrian prison. After her release in 1791, she returned to Paris, where she was greeted with honor and acclaim.

Etta Palm d'Aelders, however, is best known for her speeches, although she was arrested after the Champ de Mars. She first attracted attention in late 1790, when she created a small sensation in the *cercle social* by her outspoken support of women's rights. Throughout 1791 and 1792 she delivered a number of speeches on the same subject and also founded a women's club known as the *"Société patriotique et bienfaissance des amies de la vérité,"* intended mainly to assist the needy.

In contrast to the "bourgeois" background of the others, Claire Lacombe and Pauline Léon, the two most prominent members of the *Citoyennes Républicaines Révolutionnaires*, were both *"sans-culotte* women,"

more given to action than making speeches. Pauline Léon helped to
throw up the barricades in July 1789 and was arrested (along with her
mother) at the Champ de Mars in July 1791. Like Théroigne de
Méricourt, she went with her pike on 10 August 1792, and she and Lacombe were willing to bear arms for the Revolution, both petitioning
the Legislative Assembly and leading a delegation to the Jacobins to
announce their intentions. Claire Lacombe, like Théroigne, was awarded
a *couronne civique* for her part in the August attack on the Tuileries.
She was also acknowledged even by her enemies to be a powerful and
provocative orator, perhaps because of her theatrical training.

It is interesting to note that, despite the fact that these women all
shared, to some extent, the belief in the need for greater equality
between the sexes as well as a fervent enthusiasm for the Revolution
itself, their political allegiances nevertheless differed considerably.
Although the flight of the King converted Olympe de Gouges to a
Republican, she nevertheless maintained a sympathy for Louis XVI and
was brave (or foolhardy) enough to defend him in public. Théroigne and
Etta Palm, on the other hand, were Girondins and members of the *Société fraternelle des patriotes de l'un et l'autre sexe*, whereas Claire Lacombe and Pauline Léon were personally active in the overthrow of the
Girondins in mid-1793 and then later veered off in the direction of the
enragés. Their shared belief in equality between the sexes never brought
these various women to work together. Nor did the lack of support for
the idea of equality between the sexes on the part of their particular
chosen fellow-revolutionaries (with the possible exception of Leclerc and
the *enragés*) seem in any way to have affected these women's allegiance
to them. The fact was that these women saw themselves as Revolutionaries who also believed in equality between the sexes; they did not see
themselves as women's rights advocates.

These five individuals are, of course, only a handful of the numerous
women who were active in the Revolution. They stand out from the
others both because they were articulate enough to leave behind them
speeches and pamphlets that explain and clarify their beliefs and actions
and because their unhesitating belief in the principles for which they
fought led them to extend the application of those principles to their own
sex.

None of these women seems to have found her sex inconsistent with
her chosen role of revolutionary. It simply seemed inconceivable to them
that women should remain passive and silent at such a moment. Mlle
Jodin, the otherwise unknown author of the pamphlet *Vues législatives
pour les femmes*, explained:

When the French show their zeal to regenerate the State, and to build its happiness and glory on the eternal basis of virtue and law, I thought that my sex . . .
could also claim the honor and even the right to contribute to the public

prosperity; and that in breaking the silence to which the public seems to have condemned us, we could usefully say: "And we, too, are citizens."[14]

These women thought it obvious that the success of the Revolution would depend upon the devotion of *all* citizens: "Can we exist in a culpable state of indifference, when the alarmed *Patrie* calls all its children to its aid?" asked the author of *Lettres d'une citoyenne à son amie sur les avantages que procurerait à la nation le patriotisme des dames.*[15] These women all wanted to be "useful": they believed that they, too, had something worthwhile and necessary to add to the task at hand. "At this moment, when the happiest of revolutions is preparing itself," wrote Mlle Jodin, ". . . we hope that you will call us to contribute with you to the great work of the restoration of the public good."[16] Many even believed that there were some problems that only women were capable of correcting: "The destruction of a certain number [of abuses] depends on us, yes, Madame, on us alone," wrote the author of *Lettres d'une citoyenne.*[17] These women found it difficult to understand why their male counterparts would not welcome their aid. "In order to favor the destruction of aristocracy and despotism, why not employ all the resources of good citizenship and the most pure zeal . . .?" asked Théroigne. "Yes, Sirs," Etta Palm told the French. "Nature created us to be the companion of your labors and of your glory."[19]

The passive role normally assigned to women in society was obviously a severe handicap to the aspirations of any woman anxious to associate her sex with the work of revolution. "Woman is in [men's] eyes a being useless in society . . .," complained Olympe de Gouges.[19] In another work she wrote: "It seems that [the female sex] only has the right to raise its voice in great crises."[20] Etta Palm also raged against a prejudice that "keeps us in an idle and humiliating state of nullity."[21] But opposition only seems to have made these women more determined to prove the worth of their sex. There appears a repeated desire to inspire women to do something—anything—in order to "show" men that women are worthy both to contribute to the glorious revolution and to benefit from it as well. "Imitate me," Olympe de Gouges advised her sex; "Make yourself useful, and you will have forced them to restore the rights which the presumptious have usurped from you."[22] In another work she wrote: "All right! I must prove to the Public that there are more noble means, if women still want someday to become essential."[23] Etta Palm also sought "a means to prove that [women] are worthy of the justice which the august representatives of the nation are going to give to them."[24] Théroigne de Méricourt likewise urged: "Let us show Europe that Frenchwomen know their rights and are at the height of the enlightenment of the eighteenth century, in despising those prejudices which, simply because they are prejudices, are absurd, and often immoral in that they make for us a crime of virtue." Let us show men, she wrote, "that we are their inferiors neither in virtue nor in courage."[25]

Women had traditionally been the central force in the bread riots that periodically rocked France, which is perhaps why the initial involvement of women in the Revolution seemed natural to so many. But women were not only involved in the *journées*, they were also attending Revolutionary ceremonies and meetings, writing political pamphlets, and wearing the Revolutionary symbols. One of the more unorthodox ways in which women could further the cause of the Revolution would be to form some sort of a "Legion of Amazons," an armed corps of women that would guard against the forces of despotism and aristocracy at home, while their men marched forth to do battle with the same foes in the Vendee or on the frontiers. "Let us arm ourselves," urged Théroigne; "We have the right by nature and even by the law."[26] Pauline Léon, a veteran of the taking of the Bastille and a future member of the *Club des Citoyennes Républicaines Révolutionnaires*, led a delegation of women to the legislature in 1792, where she declared: "[These] women patriots present themselves before you to claim the right of every individual to be able to defend his life and his liberty. . . . We are citizens, and the fate of the *patrie* cannot be a matter of indifference to us. Your predecessors deposited . . . the Constitution in our hands as well as in yours. . . ." In their demand for arms and training, the women promised: "Our weakness will not be an obstacle; courage and intrepidity will supplement it, and both the love of the *patrie* and the hatred of tyrants will make us easily brave dangers." It is important to note, however, that this delegation very carefully stressed the fact that they were not proposing to abandon the care of their homes and families to go running off after the enemy—their purpose was purely and simply self-defence. "You cannot refuse us," they added confidently, "Nor can society deprive us of this right that nature gives us, unless one claims that the Declaration of Rights has no application for women, and that they must let themselves be slaughtered like lambs without having the right to defend themselves. . . ."[27] Similar requests also came from Olympe de Gouges, Claire Lacombe, and others.

With a revolution to be made, patriotism and courage could no longer be considered exclusively male virtues. Mlle Jodin complained:

A modern writer dared to assert that women scarcely comprehend any political idea . . . and he adds, that [they are] strangers to patriotism. . . . Who then gave this writer the measure of our faculties, to trace so impudently their boundary? This opinion could only gain credit by means of prejudices that were the natural result of despotism, and of the dependence to which we were subjected by an imperious sex which, surprised to find itself, at the dawn of nature, stronger than the companion she gave him in her bounty, thought that he was superior in everything.[28]

Before the Revolution there had indeed existed an ongoing debate over whether or not a woman was capable of true patriotism. The general concensus had tended to be "no." To begin with, women were credited with a complete lack of love for humanity: it was simply too abstract of a concept for their simple minds, occupied as they always are with the present and the particular.[29] Nor did it seem more possible that a woman could sustain any true love for her country. According to Thomas, patriotism in men "is always a mixture of pride, interest, ownership, hope, and the memory of actions or sacrifices. . . ." Since women are excluded from virtually all participation in public life, he said, "It is easy to see that almost none of these sentiments are applicable to women.[30] According to Saint-Lambert, most women "fear disorder in the State less than in their coiffure. . . ." In fact, he decided, a woman is rather like a slave; she has no *patrie*; it must always remain for her nothing more than the domain of her masters. As a result, said Saint-Lambert, the particular form of legislation is a matter of supreme indifference to women.[31]

The coming of the Revolution obviously showed that these confident assumptions were wrong. Women *were* interested (some would say that women were *too* interested), and were displaying both patriotism and that so-called male virtue, courage. "Honor to the most interesting half of humanity," exclaimed the journalist Louise Robert; "Up until today one counted few female patriots, but now, Behold. . . ."[32] When she courageously offered herself as Louis XVI's defender, Olympe de Gouges wrote: "Heroism and generosity are also the lot of women, and the revolution offers more than one example."[33]

Some of the tributes to the courage and patriotism currently being displayed by the female sex were worded in such a way, however, that they suggested greater praise of the Revolution itself than of the particular women involved—as when Jacques Roux said:

In what other part of the globe have you seen persons of a sex that is naturally timid out of doors and cowardly in their own homes, exchange, in the rapture of patriotism, the distaff and spindle for the glory and danger of combat, the myrtles of love for the laurels of Mars? It was necessary, Sirs, that nature have made some prodigious efforts to cause force suddenly to succeed to weakness, and violence to tenderness . . . it was necessary that liberty have worked a miracle. . . .[34]

Although the men of the Revolution could not help but be grateful for the assistance given them by their female counterparts at the storming of the Bastille and more especially in the October Days, the idea persisted that this kind of activity was somehow neither normal nor proper in a woman. In the disintegration and confusion that characterized the beginning of the Revolution, some women might have managed to escape from the traditional restraints of their sex and assume a more masculine course, but the transformation was regarded not so much as a vindication of the sex's natural inclinations and abilities as simply a "miracle." The "Amazons" were exceptions, and it was expected that they would remain so. These women had "made themselves men to fight for the Revolution," and although Frenchmen might at this point be forced to be grudgingly thankful for their support, there were few who wanted their wives, sisters, and daughters to emulate them.[35]

NOTES

1. *Les Griefs et plaintes des femmes mal mariées* (Paris: Boulard, 1789), p. 40.

2. Olympe de Gouges, *Sera-t-il Roi, ou ne le sera-t-il pas?* (n.p., n.d.), p. 15.

3. Etta Palm d'Aelders, "Réponse de Etta Palm, née d'Aelders, à la municipalité, et les citoyennes de Creil-sur-Oise, le 15 fév. 1791," in *Appel aux Françaises*, p. 14.

4. *Cahier des doléances et réclamations des femmes, par Mme B. . . B. . .* (1789), p. 3.

5. Etta Palm d'Aelders, "Discours sur l'injustice des lois en faveur des Hommes, au dépend des Femmes, lu à l'Assemblée Fédérative des Amis de la Verité, le 30 décembre 1790," in *Appel aux Françaises, sur la régénération des moeurs et nécessité de l'influence des femmes dans un gouvernement libre* (Paris: Imprimerie du Cercle Social, 1791), pp. 6 and 9.

6. Articles XI and XX; see also Alfred Dessens, *Revendications des droits de la femme au point de vue politique, civil, économique pendant la Révolution* (Toulouse: Imprimerie Ch. Marques, 1905), p. 24. In the Valley of the Baréges, the old custom allowing women to vote evidently continued throughout the Revolution. See Abensour, *La Femme et le féminisme avant la Révolution*, p. 337. According to Cordier, in his *Le Doit de la famille aux Pyrénées*, they even took part in the 1793 Plebiscite over the Constitution. There are other indications that a few women, generally of the Third Estate, did manage to participate in the primary assemblies in some areas. See Paul-Mariet Duhet, *Les Femmes et la Révolution, 1789–1794* (Paris: 1971), p. 25. These were, however, exceptions. In Paris, women were specifically excluded, which is why several women's corporations later complained that they had been deprived of their ancient right both to be represented in the assemblies and to make their complaints heard.

7. *Archives parlementaires* (AP), Vol. 2, p. 691, Col. 1; see also Beatrice Fry Hyslop, *French Nationalism in 1789 according to the General Cahiers* (New York: Columbia University Press, 1934), p. 74.

8. Of these 33 *cahiers*, 16 were from the clergy, 9 from the nobility, and 8 from the Third Estate; see Hyslop, *French Nationalism*, p. 50.

9. Ibid., pp. 37 and 106.

10. Beatrice Fry Hyslop, *A Guide to the General Cahiers of 1789* (New York: Columbia University Press, 1936), p. 14.

11. C.H.-L. Chassin, *Les Elections et les cahiers de Paris en 1789*, 4 vols. (Paris: Quantin, 1888), Vol. 2, pp. 531–536.

12. Numerous short bibliographies of these women exist, most with varying degrees of inaccuracy. In addition to general works such as Scott and Rothaus, *Historical Dictionary of the French Revolution*, see: Marie Cerati, *Le Club des*

citoyennes républicaines révolutionnaries (Paris: Editions Sociales, 1966), for Pauline Léon and Claire Lacombe; Francoise Kermina, "Guillotinée pour féminisme," *Historia, 397* (Sept. 1979), 5–56, for Olympe de Gouges; and O. Ernst, *Théroigne de Méricourt, d'après les Archives de la Cour de Vienne* (1935). The accounts given of these women and the others by Leopold Lacour, *Les Origines du féminisme contemporain; Trois femmes de la Révolution: Olympe de Gouges, Théroigne de Méricourt, Rose Lacombe* (Paris: Plon-Nourrit, 1900); E. Lairtullier, *Les Femmes célèbres de 1789 à 1795, et leur influence dans la Révolution* (1840); A. Lasserre, *La Participation collective des femmes à la Révolution Française* (Paris: 1906); J. Michelet, *The Women of the French Revolution* (Philadelphia, PA: Henry Carey Baird, 1855); G. Sokolnikova, *Nine Women, Drawn from the Epoch of the French Revolution* (1932); W. Stephens, *Women of the French Revolution* (London: 1922); A. Thomas-Latour, *Femmes pendant la Révolution* (Toulouse: Imprimerie de A. Henault, 1851); R. M. Wilson, *Women of the French Revolution* (1936); and Alfred Dessens, *Revendications des droits de la femme*, and many like them, tend to be somewhat patronizing in tone and rather too quick to accept the slanders of these women's enemies. Errors abound. Claire Lacombe is frequently referred to as "Rose," while one recent historian, David Williams, in his article "The Politics of Feminism in the French Enlightenment," in Peter Hughes and David Williams, eds., *The Varied Pattern: Studies in the Eighteenth Century* (Toronto: A. M. Hakkert, Ltd., 1971) asserts that Théroigne was an *enragé*, and actually says she founded the *Club des Citoyennes Républicaines Révolutionnaires* with Olympe de Gouges. See also Léon's dossier, Archives Nationales F[7]4774[9].

13. R. B. Rose, *The Enrages: Socialists of the French Revolution* (Melbourne: 1965), believes the "common assumption" that Lacombe and LeClerc had once been lovers is "gossip" (p. 75). Claire Lacombe's dossier in the Archives (F[7]4756) does contain a statement by two of her former associates in the *Club des Citoyennes Républicaines Révolutionnaires*, Lemoce and Herouart, in which they claim that Lacombe not only lived with Leclerc, but was actually accused by Léon of having slept with Leclerc, and that this confrontation took place "in front of the whole society." At the time this statement was made, however, the society had become divided, with Lemoce and Herouart siding with the Jacobins.

14. Jodin, *Vues législatives*, p. iii.

15. *Lettres d'une citoyenne à son amie sur les avantages que procurerait à la nation le patriotisme des dames* (Grenoble and Paris: Vve Lambert, 1789), p. 2.

16. Jodin, *Vues législatives*, p. 32.

17. *Lettres d'une citoyenne*, p. 3. Most of the abuses to which she referred were, predictably enough, in the area of morality: women should abjure luxury and be obedient wives and good mothers.

18. Etta Palm, "Discours sur l'injustice des lois en faveur des Hommes," in *Appel aux Françaises*, p. 6.

19. Olympe de Gouges, *Lettre au peuple* (Paris: Maradan, 1788), p. 28.

20. Olympe de Gouges, *Dialogue allégorique entre la France et la Vérité. Dédié aux Etats Généraux* (n.p., n.d.), p. 16.

21. Etta Palm, *Réponse à la Municipalité*, p. 15.

22. Olympe de Gouges, *l'Esprit françois, ou Problème à résoudre sur le labyrinthe des divers complots* (Paris: Vve Duchesne, 1972), p. 12.

23. Olympe de Gouges, *Sera-t-il Roi?*, p. 6.

24. Etta Palm d'Aelders, "Lettre d'une amie de la vérité, Etta Palm, née d'Aelders, Hollandoise sur les démarches des ennemis extérieures et intérieurs de la France; suivie d'une adresse à toutes les cityonnes patriotes et d'une motion à leur proposer pour l'assemblée nationale, lue à l'assemblée fédérative des amis de la vérité, le 23 mars 1791," in *Appel aux Françaises*, p. 26.

25. Théroigne de Méricourt, *Discours à la société fraternelle*, 25 March 1792.

26. Ibid.

27. Alexandre Tuetéy, *Répertoire général des sources manuscrites de l'histoire de Paris pendant la révolution française*, 11 vols. (Paris: 1890–1914), Vol. 4, No. 154.

28. Jodin, *Vues législatives*, p. 19.

29. See for instance Thomas, *Essai sur le caractère, les moeurs et l'esprit des femmes*, p. 270.

30. Ibid., p. 269.

31. Saint-Lambert, *l'Analyse de l'homme et de la femme*, pp. 240–241.

32. [Louise Robert], *Mercure national et etrangère*, No. 53, 8 June 1791, p. 840.

33. Olympe de Gouges, *Avis pressant à la convention par une vrai républicaine* (n.p., n.d.), p. 7.

34. Jacques Roux, *Discours prononcé dans l'église des Cordeliers, le 19 avril dernier, par J. Roux, qui vient d'être assassiné par dix-huit aristocrates* (Paris: Vve Petit, 1792), p. 9.

35. See, for example, the anonymous pamphlet, *Les Heroines de Paris, ou L'Entière liberté de la France, par les femmes. Police qu'elles doivent exercer de leur propre autorité. Expulsion des Charlatans, Ec., Ec., le 5 octobre 1789* (n.p., n.d.).

4

The Cult of Republican Motherhood

> If one could hope for a happy revolution in the patrie, it would only
> be one that recalled women to domestic morality. . . .
>
> [Saint-Pierre, *Etudes de la Nature*]

There were few Frenchmen who would deny that the Revolution had
need of a woman's patriotism, yet is is hardly surprising that, according to
the general consensus, a woman's patriotism was a very different thing
from a man's. The Revolutionary concept of a woman's form of patriotism was perfectly in accord with traditional eighteenth-century standards
for feminine conduct. Her place was neither in the tribunes, nor at the
bar of the Assembly, and still less was it in the streets with a pike or
pistol in hand; a good republican woman demonstrated her patriotism by
staying at home.

The more ambitious feminine aspirations of the late eighteenth century
clashed headlong with the objectives of the Revolution itself. The French
Revolutionaries were not only bent on destroying aristocracy and monar-
chical tyranny, they were also out to build a better world, and "better" in
this instance meant "virtuous" and "moral." The society of the *Ancien
Régime* had been neither moral nor virtuous, and the guilty party had
been identified even before the Revolution began: it was, of course,
Woman. It was Woman who had scorned her natural destiny of wife and
mother and who had deserted the sacred retreat of her home to appear
brazenly in public. It was Woman's voracious appetite for luxury that had
ruined the economy, and her insatiable craving for influence and power

that had corrupted and ruined the government. The Revolution had need of a woman's patriotism, it was true, but the patriotic Frenchwoman of the Revolution was none other than the traditional Ideal Virtuous Woman, incarnated as a republican *mère de famille*.

If it was woman who had tempted man out of the paradisaical garden of a pure state of nature and into the corrupting decadence of frivolity and an artificial society, then it must also be woman who could lead him back again into the promised land. Women could save both France and the Revolution by domesticity. According to the Revolutionary creed, a patriotic woman must be modest, simple, and hardworking. She must pass her days in the quiet retreat of her domestic sanctuary, dedicating herself to home, husband, and children (and the more children, the better). If a Frenchwoman truly wished to be patriotic, she must, in a word, become a *mère de famille*.

"The revolution also depends on you," wrote Prudhomme in his journal *Révolutions de Paris*:

It spares you from employment, and reserves you the delicate occupations; without leaving your homes, you can already do much for it. The liberty of a people is based on good morals and education, and you are their guardians and their first dispensors. Coming back to his home, it is from your patriotism, and it is in your arms that the citizen must taste, in the shade of the laws that he decreed at the senate, its chaste pleasures.[1]

The same sentiment was expressed in a 1790 pamphlet entitled *Adresse au beau sexe, rélativement à la révolution présente:* "The most agreeable virtues . . . in a woman and those that win for her moreover the homage and respect of men," asked the author. "Are they not *pudeur*, the care that she gives to nurse and raise her children, to watch over her home and to contribute to the happiness of her husband?"[2]

The Revolutionaries of eighteenth-century France were not creating a brave new world; they were recreating a vision of the glorious past—the past of virile, virtuous, austere, Republican Rome. And in the Rome of the Republic, as Rousseau pointed out in his *Emile*, women shut themselves away in their homes and devoted themselves to house and family. Ever one to take Jean-Jacques as his mentor, Prudhomme wrote:

One of the means by which we can climb to the height of the liberty of Rome in its best days is without a doubt to recall that among the Romans of this epoch, each sex was in its place. Women were not doctors, men were not flatterers. Closer than us to nature, men made the laws, regulated the cult; and women, without allowing themselves to question it, agreed in everything with the wisdom and knowledge of their husbands or their parents. . . .[3]

Frenchwomen were urged to adopt Portia, the daughter of Cato and wife of Brutus, as their model. Portia did not think about religion or politics, but blindly followed her menfolk, who were her gods and heroes—her virtual eyes and ears, even. If the Revolution had not yet produced a Cato or a Brutus, it was obviously the women's fault: they were not acting like Portia.[4] Another favorite role model was, predictably enough, Cornelia. In the *cercle social*, an orator rose one day and proclaimed: "The throne of a woman is in the middle of her family. Her glory is in the glory of her children that she raises for the State. Cornelia was neither general, nor consul, nor senator; she was the mother of the Gracchii."[5]

As often as the men of the Revolution advised their women to emulate the behavior of the ancients, it was seldom that they chose the Amazons as potential role models: references to the Amazons were far more likely to come from women than from men. Likewise, the men of the Revolution were usually quick to turn their women away from the example of the Spartan girls, who were commonly believed to have danced and exercised in the nude (one prerevolutionary writer actually suggested that women not be allowed to read history, lest their delicate imaginations be overset by this discovery). In addition to this rather indecent behavior, the Spartan women also had exercised and trained like men, and such virile virtues were hardly required of the women of the new French Republic.[6]

According to most adherents of the Revolution, patriotic Frenchwomen did not form legions of Amazons; instead, they lived a life as different as possible from the one typically ascribed to women under the *Ancien Régime*. Aristocratic women had destroyed the economy by their addiction to luxury; therefore, as part of her patriotic duty, a virtuous republican woman lived simply and modestly, abjuring luxury and wearing only French-made clothing. One charming project, advocated by Olympe de Gouges and others, was based on the idea that the national economy could be saved if only all the women in the land would donate their jewels to the State treasury. Such a donation was actually made in the Fall of 1789, when a troop of young girls, dressed in virginal white with the *tricolor* at their breast, ceremoniously paraded into the National Assembly, proudly bearing a chest containing the proffered trinkets. Their "decency, grace, and timidity" naturally impressed that august assembly, but the gesture was little imitated.[7]

The truly patriotic woman not only lived simply and modestly, but she also lived "honestly"—in the female sense of the word. If women had been responsible for the decadence of the *Ancien Régime*, then it was now their duty to restore morality to the nation. As a wife, the patriotic Frenchwoman was faithful and fecund; as a girl she was only required to be virginal. If possible, virginity became even more exalted than ever before. Only girls of known purity who lived with their parents were supposedly allowed to participate in public *fêtes*, and of course they always wore white. The conduct of virgins was to be carefully regulated, and the virtuous were to receive recognition and reward. As early as 1789, a number of the *cahiers*, such as that of the united orders of Rozières, had suggested that:

. . . women also receive consideration when, by virtuous conduct, they are an example to their sex, and, having married, contribute by their conduct to the maintenance of the fortune of the citizens to whom they are united, and who give to the State healthy and robust children, well trained in the duties of citizens.[8]

Olympe de Gouges was only one of many who thought that women should be tempted to be good. In 1789 she wrote: "they cause a great deal of harm when vanity does not excite in them the virtues! But what good could they not produce if one piqued that vanity, if one excited it, if one directed it towards honor. . . ."[9] It was all vaguely reminiscent of a scene from Retif de la Bretonne's *Le Gynographe*, and another popular idea of the time could have been lifted straight from the pages of that same work: The Tribunal of Virtuous Women. Suggestions for the creation of a Tribunal of Women can be found in the writings of Etta Palm, Théroigne de Méricourt, Mlle Jodin, and others. To Charles-Louis Rousseau, who denied women any real political existence, it was an alternative way of allowing women to identify with the state and therefore to inspire them with love for the *patrie*. The outlines for all of these projects were basically the same: A set number of virtuous women, always *mères de famille*, would be elected to a Tribunal that was charged with the surveillance of public morality. Sometimes these women would be responsible for education or the assistance of poor women, but they were principally in charge of surveying and correcting female (not male) conduct and morality.[10]

The virtuous republican woman became enshrined in the *mère de famille*—the mother of a family. She was retiring, simple and pure, but above all she was fertile. A song written in honor of the Frenchwomen who had labored so hard to prepare for the *fête civique* of 14 July 1790 included the following stanza:

> To be worthy of the *Patrie*
> More still do you it owe
> Don't border there your duty
> Give us some little heroes.[11]

At the same celebration in 1793, a group of women (dressed in white) carried a banner that proclaimed: *"Citoyennes, give the patrie some children. . . ."*[12]

Motherhood was a woman's duty, her triumph, her glory: "Mother . . . that sacred title, that title, the most beautiful triumph of a woman . . ." wrote the author of *Lettres d'une citoyenne*.[13] "To give to the future generation healthy and robust men; oh! is that not the field of honor where we must gather our laurels?" asked Etta Palm.[14] What more could a woman ask but to be surrounded by the precious fruits of her love? Motherhood gave a woman her place in society; it was the highest rank to which she could aspire. Roussel even wrote:

It seems that a woman only has a right to all the advantages that [society] can give to its members when she has fulfilled all her duties, and she has done only half of her task when she does not nurse the child to which she has given birth. She is only worthy of the rank that she occupies when, after having ornamented it with her charms, she contributes to increasing its force by giving it vigorous and healthy citizens. . . .[15]

It was not enough that a woman merely give birth to her children; she must nurse and educate them herself as well. The aristocratic practice of consigning one's children to the care of an uneducated wetnurse was denounced with horror.[16] "A mother who has not nursed her child has ceased to be a mother in the eyes of the *patrie*," decreed Saint-Just.[17]

The most noble occupation possible for a Republican woman was to raise good little citizens and future husbands. The good, virtuous woman turned her home into a school for patriotism and followed Rousseau's precept that a *mère de famille* should live like a cloistered nun. "When you have the joy to become a mother," wrote the author of *Lettres d'une citoyenne*, "Renounce from then on dissipation and pleasures, so that you can consecrate yourself entirely to the education of your children, no longer live but for them; sacrifice with joy your youth for them, your time, your health even, if it is necessary. . . ."[18]

Nothing was more unfortunate than a naturally sterile woman, and nothing was more vile than one who was sterile by choice. Any attempt even to limit the size of a family was not only criminal, it was unpatriotic. In Charles-Louis Rousseau's vision of the perfect society, "There, one sees . . . virtuous women, tender mothers, and submissive girls. Patriotism is in their hearts, morality is on their lips, and utility in their actions. There women nurse their children, and pride themselves on their number, because it is the prosperity of their home and the trophy of their glory."[19]

It was generally believed that the tender sentiments of a good wife and mother could only be nourished and preserved in the quiet retreat of the home; exposure to society and public life was fatal. Even modesty and decency assigned the female to domestic obscurity. It was J.-J. Rousseau who had written: "There is no such thing as good morality for women outside of a retired and domestic life," and it was also Rousseau who had said: "A woman outside her home loses her greatest luster; and, stripped of her true ornament, shows herself with indecency."[20] Abjuring the world and living unknown, the good republican mother devoted herself to family and house. This was the female vocation, her duty; the home was presented as a *petite république*, where the woman governed supreme while her man busied himself with the affairs of society and state out of doors. This was, of course, the old time-honored diffentiation of sexual destinies and duties, but to revolt against the established order was no longer merely unchristian and unnatural; it had now become unpatriotic.[21]

The idealization of motherhood had not, of course, begun with the Revolution. Its origins lay in the increasing popularity of sentimentalism that characterized the second half of the eighteenth century, and which was reinforced by the writings of Jean-Jacques Rousseau and his disciples. It was a phenomenon that was confined neither to France nor to the Revolution, and one that would not even reach its culmination until the nineteenth century. But as revolution turned to war and republic to empire, the apotheosis of woman as Mother could only intensify. The wealth of a nation was still equated with the size of its population, and only women had the ability to produce new citizens and soldiers. In her role as incubator of the male race, woman was honored and perhaps even appreciated as never before. Yet despite the increase in respect and esteem that it undeniably generated, this virtual cult of republican motherhood was as debilitating to the female sex, in its own way, as the more classical forms of veneration. A woman's worth was still located neither in the depth of her intellect nor in the development of her talents, but in the fertility of her womb. Whether the mother figure is exalted or degraded, as long as the female is exclusively identified with the mother, the effects on the individual woman are much the same. Her entire life must be lived in relation to that one role. As a child, it is the duties of housewife and mother that form the basis of her education; as a young woman, her virginity becomes the guarded promise of undefiled future fecundity, her most sacred treasure and gift; as a wife, her whole existence is centered in the children, which are the greatest, in fact the only, contribution she is allowed to offer to society.

The more important the function of the Mother is perceived to be, the more circumscribed the life of the woman becomes. Neither wealth nor rank can free her from the demands of even the most minute and trivial aspects of housewifery and motherhood. When this attitude is reinforced by the belief that the essential traits of simplicity, innocence, and self-sacrifice, which were believed to characterize the good mother, can only be cultivated in retreat and are irreparably damaged by exposure to the world, then anything that draws a woman beyond the protective confines of the home must be wrong. In the end, the cult of republican motherhood provided the men of the French Revolution with one of the best rationalizations they had to deny women everything from political rights and employment opportunities, to a basic education.

What is most surprising is the extent to which these very same attitudes and beliefs repeatedly appear in the writings and speeches of those revolutionary women who are most famous for their advocacy of women's rights. Much as their own lives might have deviated from the prescribed norms, they were as one in condemning the frivolity and immorality that was believed to have characterized the *Ancien Régime,* and in advocating a return to republican virtue and morality. Olympe de Gouges continually criticized the behavior of her own sex. In *Le Cri du sage*, she wrote: "Oh, Women! What have you done? What have you produced? Could you have thought that by throwing yourselves at men you would conserve your *empire*? It is destroyed, and your natural graces have disappeared with that noble *pudeur*. . . ." In the same work she also accused women of neglecting the duties and responsibilities of motherhood: "You have abandoned the reins of your homes," she wrote. "You have separated your babies from your maternal breasts; left in the arms of corrupted servants, they have learned to hate you, to despire you. . . ."[22] Etta Palm was another who warned her sex that "to be the companions of the regenerated French, of free men, it is necessary [to practice] patriotism, modesty, and the virtues."[23]

These same women even complained about the extent to which so many of their sex were following their own example and becoming involved in the Revolution. Being single women themselves, they felt freed from the restraints imposed on the *mère de famille*, but they still believed that a mother's first duty was to her home. Claire Lacombe said: "And you, *mères de famille*, whom I criticize for leaving your children to follow my duty of fighting the enemies of the *patrie*, fulfill your own by inculcating in your children the sentiments that every Frenchman must have at birth."[24] Olympe de Gouges expressed a similar sentiment: "Women today are mixing in the public assemblies and clubs; they are deserting their homes, it is necessary to lead them back there. . . ."[25] Even Pauline Léon, when she was arrested in April of 1794, after her marriage to the *enragé* Théophile Leclerc, made a statement in which she stressed that, since becoming a wife, she had devoted herself to the care of her household and had "provided an example of marital love and the domestic virtues that are the bases of love for the *patrie*."[26]

While the more active revolutionary women often joined together in societies and clubs in order to better express their patriotism, most of these women's clubs revealed a surprisingly limited concept of what a woman's contribution to the Revolution should be. Although several different men's clubs such as the "Société fraternelle des Halles" or the "Société fraternelle des patriotes de l'un et l'aute sexe" did accept women as members, a number of exclusively feminine associations were formed, not only in Paris, but also in other French cities, such as Bordeaux, Nantes, and Besançon, to name only a few.[27]

These women's clubs were formed to further the cause of the Revolution, not to advocate women's rights. Their members invariably swore an eternal love for liberty, equality, and the *patrie*, combined with a never-ending hatred of despotism, aristocracy, and tyranny. They also promised to live virtuously and modestly in the seclusion of their homes and to teach the Rights of Man and the Constitution (along with the alphabet) to their children. The new members of a women's club in Lyon took the following vow: "I swear to be faithful to the nation, to the law, and to the King; I swear to persuade on all occasions my husband, my brothers, and my children to fulfill their duties towards the *patrie*: I swear to teach my children and all others over whom I might have influence to prefer death to slavery."[28] The women of Lille recited a similar oath. In a solemn ceremony performed at the tribune of the local Jacobin club, they declared: "Dear fellow citizens, despite the weakness [which is the] appanage of our sex, we aspire to defend, to confirm if necessary with our blood, the rights that man holds from nature, the sacred and imprescriptible rights of liberty and equality. . . ." After swearing to hate despotism and aristocracy, they ended: "Such are, dear fellow citizens, the resolution in which we are determined to live; such are the principles from which we will never depart; we will inculcate them early in the minds of our children. . . ."[29]

Many women's groups also vowed careful surveillance and eternal vigilance against the "plots of the forces of counter-revolution." In 1791, the *citoyennes* of the rue de Regard sent to the Cordeliers an address on "the influence of the revolution on women." It is interesting to note the extent to which these women were careful to portray themselves as *mères de famille*. They began by rendering respectful homage to the immortal principles of Jean-Jacques Rousseau, which, they stressed, must always govern the conduct of a good wife and mother. As good *mères de famille*, these women lived, they said, retired in the depths of their homes, where they were tirelessly occupied in helping their children to learn by heart the "sacred principles of the constitution." Yet even in the depths of their domestic retreat, these women asserted, they, too, could learn of "enemy plots," and they, too, were "worthy to fight, to die for the *patrie*." Alarmed by the present state of affairs, the women of the rue de Regard told the Cordeliers: "For a few moments we suspended our domestic labors, we gathered together and spoke about the misfortunes that beset our liberty, and here is what we say to you. . . ." Having deliberated, they now urged the men: Do not sleep; be vigilant; do not just talk, but act. "If you betray our hope," the women warned, ". . . indignation will precipitate us into the public places." But, they promised, if the men faithfully performed their duty, then the women would quit talking and quietly return to their children and their assigned role of domestic obscurity.[30]

In practice, most of these women's clubs assumed the character of service organizations, or "ladies' aid societies." As early as 1789, the "Assembly of mothers, sisters, wives, and sweethearts of the citizens of Angers" announced that, since physical strength had been denied them by nature, in case of trouble they promised to undertake responsibility for provisions, baggage, departure preparations, and "all those cares, consolations and services that depend upon us."[31] The president of the "Société des amies de la liberté et de l'égalité" of Lyon explained in a 1793 letter to the editor of the journal *Révolutions de Paris* that the members of her club met together to study and to instruct themselves and their children in the principles of the Constitution and the decrees of the Assembly, as well as to seek ways to aid the unfortunate. In the same issue, the president of the "Société des amies de la République" wrote from Dijon to say that her society was almost exclusively concerned with collecting patriotic gifts, preparing equipment for the French army, succoring the poor and ill, aiding the authorities in the care of prisoners, and setting up spinning workshops for women without work.[32] Even Etta Palm d'Aelders' "Société patriotique et bienfaissance des amies de la vérité" was primarily devoted to good works, particularly raising poor girls and training them for careers.

As long as the women's clubs confined their activity to patriotic speeches and traditionally feminine tasks, the men of the Revolution were more than willing to accept their aid and contribution. The services that the women rendered were not only useful, they were badly needed in a nation whose government was unable to either finance or organize such undertakings by itself. Moreover, the enthusiasm of these French women for the Revolution was an undeniable boost and encouragement to their men, who might otherwise have faltered in their perserverance.

Yet however grateful the men of the Revolution might have been, even in their praise they made it clear that in a revolution, as in everything else, the duties of the sexes must be carefully deliniated. It was for the women to roll bandages, to reward virtuous citizens with their esteem, and to crown the glory of the male heroes:

The women . . . are showing themselves as moved to maintain the holy flame of liberty in the hearts of our young republicans, as the vestal virgins had care to maintain the sacred fire on the altar of the ancient goddess. While virile hands occupy themselves with robust labors, one sees our interesting *républicaines* using their delicate hands for the tasks that are proper for them. One sees young girls prepare the bandages that must stop a precious blood . . . with as much calm as they would have joy to weave the *couronnes civiques* destined for the beloved conquerors. Oh! but liberty is strong, when it is seconded by the most powerful motivation of the human heart.[33]

This was a sentiment that was repeated so often by so many different orators and writers that it almost became trite. Yet even as a cliché, it remained powerful. As Prudhomme wrote in 1792, it was not at all proper for women to "show men the way," and they would be tolerated only so long as they were content to play a supporting role.[34] When a women's group known as the *Club des citoyennes républicaines révolutionnaries* was formed in 1793, it created a veritable sensation by the aggressively political nature of its activities, and this deviation from the accepted pattern ultimately would bring down the wrath of the Revolution not just onto its own members, but onto every active female revolutionary in France.

NOTES

1. [Prudhomme], *Révolutions de Paris*. "De l'influence de la révolution sur les femmes," Vol. 7, No. 83, 12 February 1791, p. 231.

2. *Adresse au beau sexe, rélativement à la révolution présente, par M.L.C.D.V.* (n.p., 1790), p. 9.

3. [Prudhomme], Révolutions de Paris, Vol. 10, No. 127, 10–17 December 1791, p. 499.

4. Ibid., p. 198.

5. F.-A. Aulard, "Le Féminisme pendant la Révolution française," *Revue bleue*, 19 March 1898, pp. 362–366.

6. [Prudhomme], *Révolutions de Paris*, Vol. 14, No. 170, 7–13 October 1792, p. 105.

7. See ibid., Vol. 1, No. 9, 17 September 1789, p. 20.

8. Hyslop, *French Nationalism*, p. 182; *Archives parlementaires* (AP), Vol. 4, p. 90, Art. 47.

9. Olympe de Gouges, *L'Ordre national, ou le Comte d'Artois inspiré par Mentor, Dédié aux Etats Généraux* (n.p., 1789), p. 10.

10. See Charles-Louis Rousseau, *Essai sur l'éducation et l'existence civile et politique des femmes*, pp. 33–34; Jodin, *Vues législatives pour les femmes*, p. 34; Etta Palm, *Lettre d'un amie*, p. 314; Théroigne de Méricourt, *Aux 48 Sections* (Paris: Imprimerie de F. Dufart, n.d.); and Retif de la Bretonne, *Le Gynographe*, p. 164. Under the old regime, of course, there actually had been "juries" of women, charged with verifying things such as virginity, pregnancy, and male impotence.

11. *Hommage rendu au dames françaises, sur leur patriotisme pour accélérer la fête civique du 14 juillet 1790* (Paris: Imprimerie de Valleyre, n.d.), p. 6.

12. *Cronique de Paris*, 14 July 1793.

13. *Lettres d'une citoyenne*, p. 8.

14. Etta Palm, *Lettre d'une amie*, p. 27.

15. Pierre Roussel, *De la Femme, considérée au physique et au moral*, 2 vols. (Paris: 1788–1789), Vol. 2, pp. 260–261.

16. The use of wet nurses had been condemned long before the Revolution. The practice was probably most widespread among working women of the cities, who had little recourse but to consign their young children to the care of country women in order to continue to earn money to help support their families. See Owen Hufton, "Women and the Family Economy."

17. Louis-Antoine Saint-Just, *Fragments sur les institutions républicaines 1793–1794* (Paris: Techener, 1831), p. 57.

18. *Lettres d'une citoyenne*, p. 10. Despite its title, this pamphlet was probably written by a man.

19. Charles-Louis Rousseau, *Essai*, p. 19.

20. Jean-Jacques Rousseau, *Oeuvres complètes*, "Lettre à d'Alembert sur les spectacles," pp. 115 and 122.

21. Although sixteenth- and seventeenth-century writers had stressed paternal power, the vision of the home as the woman's sphere was still an old one. In his very successful 1513 treatise, *De re uvoria libelli duo*, Barbaro, for example, talks about women running the house and directing the family, although the *ultimate* power, of course, rested with the male. See Ascoli, *Les Idées féministes en France*.

22. Olympe de Gouges, *Le Cri du sage, par une femme* (n.p., n.d.), p. 3.

23. Etta Palm d'Aelders, "Adresse de la Société patriotique et de bienfaisance des Amies de la vérité aux quarante-huit section; rédigée par Etta Palm, née d'Aelders," in *Appel aux françaises*, p. 44.

24. Claire Lacombe, *Discours du 22 juillet 1792*.

25. Olympe de Gouges, *Sera-t-il Roi?* p. 16.

26. Archives Nationales, F⁷4774⁹, dossier Leclerc.

27. A great deal has been written about the provincial women's clubs. See, for example: G. Langeron, *Le Club des femmes de Dijon pendant la Révolution* (Dijon: 1929); H. Perrin, "Le Club des femmes de Besançon", *Annales Révolutionaires*, 9 and 10 (1917–18), pp. 629–653, pp. 37–63, pp. 654–672; Bloch, "Les Femmes d'Orleans pendant la Révolution," *Révolution française*, 43 (1902), 49–62; Marc de Villiers, *Histoire des Clubs de femmes et des légions d'amazones* (Paris: 1910); Claude Brelot, "Besançon révolutionnaire", in *Cahiers de l'Association interuniversitaire de l'Est*, no. 10, *La Révolution à Besançon et dans quelques villes de l'Est de France* (Strasbourg, 1966).

28. Leopole Lacour, *Les Origines du féminisme contemporaire* (Paris: Plon-Nourrit, 1900), p. 339.

29. [Louise Robert], *Mercure nationale et etrangère*, No. 53, 8 June 1791, pp. 840–841.

30. [Prudhomme], *Révolutions de Paris*, Vol. 12, No. 86, 26 February–5 March 1791, p. 383. Prudhomme was not impressed with this address. "Sisters," he told them, "return to the depths of your house." See also the deputation of women to the Assembly described by Prudhomme in Vol. 12, No. 143, 31 March–7 April 1792, p. 20.

31. It is both interesting and important to note that these women identified themselves as the "mothers, sisters, wives, and sweethearts" of the "citizens" of Angers; they did not call themselves *citoyennes*, but identified themselves only by

their relationship to their men. *Réimpression de l'Ancien Moniteur* (Paris: Plon-Frères, 1847), Introduction, p. 544.

32. *Révolutions de Paris*, Vol. 40, No. 189, 16–23 February 1793, pp. 367–371.

33. F.-A. Aulard, *Recueil des Actes du Comité de Salut Public*, 28 vols. (Paris: Imprimerie Nationale, 1893–1964), Vol. 9, pp. 361–362.

34. [Prudhomme], *Révolutions de Paris*, Vol. 12, No. 150, 19–26 May 1792.

5

A Woman's Work

> Men, by the prerogative of their sex and by the force of their temperament, are naturally capable of all sorts of employment and engagements; whereas women, due to the fragility of their sex and their natural delicacy, are excluded from many functions and incapable of certain engagements.
>
> [*Encyclopédie*, Vol. 6, p. 475]

The majority of the journalists, orators, and even some of the best-known of the active women of the French Revolution seemed to agree with the philosophers and moralists of the *Ancien Régime* on at least this one point: a woman's place was in the home, and her only proper occupations were those of wife and mother. This relegation of the female to the domestic sphere was eventually to be used by the Revolutionaries to justify everything from a lack of expanded educational and job opportunities for women to the exclusion of women from politics.

But how well did this Ideal World—as the eighteenth century typically envisaged it—square with reality? The truth was that the period's philosophical and moral portrayals of marriage as a woman's sole destiny and occupation were misleading: only among the upper classes did marriage provide a woman with the relative luxury of having nothing more to do than to survey the management of her home and children, or to abandon herself to her own amusement. In all other orders of society, a married woman was expected not only to keep house and raise her children, but to contribute financially to the maintenance of the family as well. A woman's wage-earning ability formed a vital part of the family economy.[1] Wives worked beside their husbands both on the farm and in the shop, they took work into their homes under the putting-out system, or they ran their own independent businessess. Nor was the married state every woman's ultimate or final destination. Widows, spinsters, and young women still seeking to accumulate the dowry required for marriage, all worked to support themselves. Women were therefore a vital, contributing part of the national economy, and in order to appreciate properly the full ramifications of the period's debate on the question of women and equality, it is necessary to understand just how extensive women's employment beyond the domestic sphere really was, as well as to know which occupations were or were not open to these women.

The industrial revolution, which was to bring with it a diversity of jobs for women in factories, retail outlets, and the rapid expansion of domestic servitude, had barely begun in the France of the late eighteenth century. Agriculture still remained the largest single employer of women, and it has been estimated that 80 to 85 percent of all women in late eighteenth-century France were peasants.[2]

The woman was a vitally important and productive part of the peasant family. In addition to her feminine responsibilities for home and children, the peasant woman was also expected to work in the fields. She did the hoeing and weeding, gathered fodder, and was active in haymaking and gleaning. It was usually the women who carried the produce to market, and they were also largely left in charge of the care and feeding of the family's domestic animals. In fact, the dairy industry was almost entirely in the hands of the female sex; it was the women who milked the cows and turned the yield into butter and cheese. In many areas land holdings were insufficient for the maintenance of a family, causing the males to become seasonal migrant workers; in those circumstances, the women who stayed at home were also forced to take on the traditionally "male" areas of agricultural labor, since their menfolk were away from home most of the time.[3] Furthermore, women themselves also constituted a considerable portion of the migratory workers who moved from the north to the south of France, following the vintage, the olive harvest, and the vagaries of the mulberry and silkworm industries.[4] It was a hard life, and one that left a woman old before her time. On his journey through France in the late eighteenth century, the Englishman Arthur Young made the following entry in his journal on a summer's day in 1789:

Walking up a long hill, to ease my mare, I was joined by a poor woman who complained of the times, and that it was a sad country. . . . This woman, at no great distance, might have been taken for sixty or seventy, her figure was so bent, and her face so furrowed and hardened by labour; but she said she was only twenty-eight.[5]

Like the peasant women on the farms and in the fields, the women of the villages, towns, and cities also worked alone, or alongside their men. On the lowest end of the scale, women performed many of the menial tasks associated with urban life: they emptied privies, served as "*les portefaix*" (carriers of produce, water, wood) and as rag sorters, cinder sifters, and refuse collectors. Wives and daughters were particularly prominent in cookshops and bakeries, restaurants, taverns, and hostelries, and in small industrial enterprises.[6] Nevertheless, it is important to note that even though women were expected to work alongside their husbands and fathers at their trades, they were formally denied actual admittance to most of the male artisan guilds.

The effects of this nonadmittance of women varied. In a number of guilds, a daughter was allowed to pass her father's mastership on to the man she married, but she was ineligible to succeed to it herself. Likewise, the widow of a master often had the right to continue her dead husband's trade, but usually only so long as she did not remarry. Since women were commonly married to men at least ten years their senior and (once the dangerous childbearing years were past) enjoyed greater longevity, the sight of a woman engaged in a "male" occupation was quite common.[7] Even if the husband had been engaged in a trade that was strictly forbidden to women, such as surgery, his widow often possessed the right to "rent out" the privilege of practising that occupation.[8]

Although there did exist some mixed corporations,[9] women usually had the ability to enter them only as successors to their husbands, a right that, again, they frequently lost if they remarried. There were only a few corporations, such as those of the *poissonniers* and *graniers* in Paris, which a woman was able to enter in her own right. And even when women were admitted, their condition was usually inferior (they were often admitted not "*à titre d'ouvrière qualifiée*" but only "*de manoeuvre*"), and their wages were invariably lower. Indeed, in 1776, Turgot gave the unfavorable position of women as one of the reasons for abolishing the corporations.[10]

In addition to the many trades dominated by men, however, there were also a number of trades that were almost exclusively practiced by females, and these women often formed their own corporations. The best-known of these are perhaps those established by the washerwomen and midwives, but there were also the *couturières, filassières, lingères,* and *bouquetières*, among others. These women's corporations often faced open opposition from competing men's corporations. For example, the male *tailleurs d'habits* in many cities for a long time successfully prevented the formation of the female *couturières*. In those areas where the *couturières* did manage to establish themselves, the *tailleurs d'habits* then sought to relegate the *couturières* to making only underclothes, while reserving the more lucrative dressmaking business for themselves.[11]

The *couturières* were only one group of women among the many who worked in the clothing and textile trades, where the traditionally female occupations tended to be clustered. The mid-eighteenth century had witnessed the expansion of the domestic manufacturing system, and tens of thousands of women were hard at work spinning, lace-making, knitting, hemming handkerchiefs, cuffs, and collars, and trimming hats and bodices. Weaving, one of the most lucrative aspects of this trade, was barred to the female sex, but women were employed at most other stages in the production of cloth and clothing: milliners, mantua makers, embroiderers, and seamstresses were all traditionally female. In fact, more than any other occupation, employment in the garment and textile industries was identified as "female" in the popular mind. When charitable organizations, convents, or governments set up schools to teach poor girls a trade, or when prostitutes condemned to the *hopitaux généraux* were set to work to give them a more socially acceptable way to earn a living, it was invariably something such as needlework or lace-making that these young girls and women were taught.[12] Even during the Revolution, calls for improving the economic plight of women continued to focus on training women for these trades, or else on preventing men from competing with women in these industries.[13] And these tendencies persisted despite the fact that it was widely known that it was the chronic instability and inordinately low wages associated with the garment and textile industries that typically had driven women into destitution in the first place.[14] One of the major problems was that, whether it was in the silk or lace-making industries, wives often took such work into their homes on the putting-out system. This created a situation that traditionally tends to characterize "female" occupations: the willingness of women living within the family unit to work for low wages makes survival difficult for the single woman who must use her salary to pay for her own lodging, heating, lighting, and nourishment.[15]

In addition to their activity in the garment and textile industries, women were also highly visible in commerce, particularly at its lower levels. In a 1788 article in the *Tableau de Paris*, Mercier left the following valuable survey of women's participation in this facet of the economy:

. . . the shops of the clockmakers and goldsmiths are attended by women. In fact, they weight out for you anything from a pound of macaroons to a pound of gunpowder.

Women are employed in the smallest aspects of commerce, relating to jewelry, bookselling, and hardware; they buy, transport, exchange, sell, and resell; all foodstuffs pass through their hands, it is they who sell you poultry, fish, butter, cheese, and oysters. . . . Women also manage small offices for the distribution of salt, tobacco, letters, *papier timbre*, and lottery tickets.[16]

Yet, however important they were at these lower levels, women were conspicuously absent from the ranks of the higher merchants and entrepreneurs. In her 1785 *Les Femmes comme il convient de les voir*, for example, Mme de Coicy complained that the *"commerce en grande*, that which calls for any speculation, correspondence, danger, or traveling, is entirely forbidden them by the imperious law of custom."[17] Not only custom, but also the law itself actually excluded women from membership in a number of different merchants' guilds.

The inescapable fact remained that, despite their active and vital role in the economy, the employment opportunities open to women of all classes in eighteenth-century France were rigorously circumscribed by both law and custom. If anything, the position of women in this respect had actually declined in the past several centuries, particularly among the upper classes, for in the chaotic conditions of the Middle Ages some women had managed to obtain a foothold in government, law, and the professions. With the coming of the Renaissance and the reimposition of Roman law, however, the female sex had been gradually but firmly excluded from all of these "virile" occupations. This loss of their former expanded role was not unknown to the women of the time. In her 1789 pamphlet *Demands des femmes aux Etats généraux*, Mme de Coicy drew harshly unfavorable comparisons between the virtual impotence of the eighteenth-century woman as opposed to the relative power of her medieval counterpart.[18]

Although its effects were perhaps more severely felt among the lower classes, the eighteenth-century exclusion of women from power and the professions actually started at the top. France was one of the few European countries in which women were categorically eliminated from succession to the throne. Although women could be appointed to act as Regents, this practice was hotly debated even under the *Ancien Régime*, and the Revolution, bent on reducing the power and influence of the female sex in government, soon deprived women even of that right.

Also under the *Ancien Régime*, a woman was eligible to inherit a fief, but by the eighteenth century her ability to enjoy the feudal privileges associated with it had steadily been eroded. As a result, women found themselves excluded from the various offices and professions emerging from those ancient feudal rights. For example, as feudal overlords, women had once been empowered to act as arbiters and to dispense justice personally within their own territories. But by the eighteenth century, as the *Encyclopédie* noted, "since *seigneurs* are no longer allowed to dispense justice personally, women may no longer be either judges or arbiters."[19]

In the legal arena, by the eighteenth century a woman only had the right to present herself for judgment—prosecutors, lawyers, judges, and juries were all male. In *Les Femmes comme il convient de les voir*, Mme de Coicy complained bitterly against this legal impotence of women: "A woman [who is] injured, insulted, wounded, attacked in her goods or in her honor, has no woman who can plead for her," she wrote; "It is to a tribunal of men, and by men, that her case is prosecuted, defended, and judged."[20] Her exclusion from the legal arena was so complete that a woman could not even be appointed to act as a guardian or a trustee, except in the case of her own children. Nor, incidentally, could she even stand as witness for a will or for any acts taken before a notary.[21] Legally, a woman was regarded and treated virtually as a child, although she most certainly could be (and was) tried and punished as an adult.

The loss of their old feudal rights and privileges also affected women's ability to enter other, newly emerging occupations. Again, as the *Encyclopédie* noted, "[women] formerly could act as peers, and in this capacity sat at the *parlement*. Currently they can still possess a *duché-fémelle* and assume the title, but they can no longer act as peers."[22] By the time of the Revolution, the ability of female fief holders even to vote for representatives to the Estates General had similarly been reduced to the agency of male *procureurs*. And with the destruction of feudal privileges in 1789, even this minor political role, enjoyed by so few women, was lost, and with it any opportunity for pursuing a career in the political sphere.

Women therefore were left with no overt part in either government or public services. That plethora of lucrative public sinecures that provided employment and wealth for a host of Frenchmen—the magistrates, registrars, procurators, commissioners, bailiffs, clerks, public scribes, etc.— were all, by definition, male occupations and therefore completely unavailable to women.[23]

The military was another popular—and potentially lucrative—male occupation that was, theoretically at least, denied to women.[24] Women were also barred from attending the universities and, by extension, from any position, such as the medical profession, that required a higher education.[25]

There was one profession that was, in some ways at least, open to both men and women, and that was the church. But while it offered a comfortable and even opulent living for a considerable number of Frenchmen, the church only provided women with what Mme de Coicy called "the prison of the cloister." By canonical law, only men were eligible to become priests, so that the lucrative possibilities of the entire church hierarchy were effectively closed to women. Even as a child, a male was allowed to assist the priest in the celebration of Mass at the altar, whereas a guarded barrier eternally separated the female sex from the sanctuary.

Desite this exclusion, the church nevertheless offered "employment" of a sort to tens of thousand of women. It has been estimated that there were 56,000 nuns in France in 1789.[26] Although there had been a decline throughout the eighteenth century in male monasticism and in the contemplative female orders, the active teaching and nursing orders of nuns had actually grown. And, unlike the monks, the nuns were not intimidated by the Revolution's attempts to repress them. The convents offered the women who entered them shelter, companionship, and social identity, and as a prioress or an abbess a woman could in fact rise to a position of surprising wealth and power (at least within the confines of her convent); but it all came at a price. A dowry was as necessary for a woman wishing to become a "bride of Christ" as it was for the future wife of any eighteenth-century Frenchman, and the woman who chose that option had to be content to live her life retired from the world and from society.

The existence of convents in France also had a certain effect on the availability of employment opportunities for French laywomen: teaching and nursing, two professions that were offering employment to a growing number of women in England, were in France almost entirely in the hands of the nuns.[27] Until the suppression of the convents during the Revolution, there was virtually no such thing as a lay female teacher in France. In contrast to the English practice of hiring an impoverished but genteel lady to act as governess, French "governesses" were traditionally selected from the lowest classes and could more accurately be likened to nurses or maids. Even the special professors who were engaged to teach dancing, music, drawing, and foreign languages to young ladies, both in the seclusion of the cloister and in the homes of the wealthy, were all men.[28]

Nevertheless, although the masculine establishment successfully managed to bar women from government, the professions, and the universities, there were at least two areas into which it was virtually impossible to prevent them from encroaching: literature and the arts. If a woman could pick up a pen or pencil, then she could, if so inclined, use it to draw; likewise, once a woman was literate, there was little outside her own inhibitions that could stop her from writing. As professional artists and writers, eighteenth-century women could and did earn their own living by becoming painters, journalists, playwrights, and novelists; in fact, it has been estimated that in the second half of the eighteenth century, the majority of all novels published were actually written by women.[29]

The emergence of women as authors and artists aroused both opposition and outrage. To many in the eighteenth century, there was something vaguely indelicate about the thought of a female aspiring to authorship. If a woman wanted to write, then it was generally felt that she might do so for her own pleasure or even for the amusement of a few of her closest acquaintances. And, if her works were truly worthy of merit, then in due time—preferably after the author's death—they might be brought out into the public light through the agency of friends or relatives. But for a woman actually to seek publication personally in her own lifetime was virtually indecent. This was a sentiment shared by men and women alike. As celebrated a personality as Mme Roland once wrote:

I am often angered to see women contend for certain privileges that are inappropriate for them. The very title of author, under whatever reference it might be, seems ridiculous to me for them. However truthfully one might speak of their ability in this respect, it is never for the public that they must have either knowledge or talent.[30]

The problem was, of course, that it was widely perceived that successful authorship could only be harmful to those two praiseworthy and entirely necessary feminine virtues, obscurity and modesty; it therefore could hardly be considered fitting or proper for a woman.

The works of many eighteenth-century feminine authors are full of bitter protests against this rigid notion of propriety, which prevented or at least discouraged a woman from cultivating to the fullest possible extent her intelligence and talents. Mme de Lambert, for example, wrote:

How great is the tyranny of men! They would like us not to make any use of either our mind or our consciousness: isn't it enough for them to regulate all the movements of our heart, without further taking possession of our intelligence? They would like our *pudeur* to be as injured when we employ our intelligence as when we give away our heart: that is to extend their right too far.[31]

Nevertheless, despite this opposition, many women continued to exercise their talents in the face of public disapproval and condemnation. But those who did were subjected to a daunting barrage of hostility. Not only her works, but even a female writer's person were subjected to criticism and harsh attack by the members of both sexes. "I never had the slightest temptation to one day become an author," explained Mme Roland; "I saw at a very early age that any woman who gains that title loses much more than she has acquired."[32] And those women who, like Mme Roland, lacked the courage or else the ability to rival the acknowledged female author or intellectual, could find a variety of ways in which to seek their revenge. "Of what sentiments of jealousy and hate are the great successes of woman not the object!" complained Mme de Staël:

What pains are caused by the means without number that envy takes to persecute her! The majority of women are against her, by rivalry, by foolishness, or by principle. A woman's talents, such as they may be, always upset their sensibility. Those to whom the distractions of the intellect are forever forbidden find a thousand ways to attack them when it is a woman who possesses them. A pretty girl, in eluding these distractions, flatters herself by pointing out her own advantage.

A woman who believes herself remarkable for her prudence and the tone of her mind and who, never having had two ideas in her head, wishes to pass for having rejected all that she never understood; such a woman departs a little from her customary sterility, to find a thousand ridiculous things in her where intelligence animates and varies her conversation; and the mothers of families, thinking, with some truth, that even the successes of true intelligence are not consistent with women's destiny, attack with pleasure those who have obtained some.[33]

Although they had to contend with this hostility from their own sex, the animosity directed towards intellectually active women by the members of the male sex was even more marked. In an article entitled "Femmes-Auteurs," published in the *Tableau de Paris* in 1788, the journalist Mercier presented a penetrating analysis and explanation of the eighteenth-century Frenchman's constitutional dislike of female authors:

Man always dreads any superiority whatsoever in the woman; he would like her to enjoy only half of her being. He cherishes the modesty of a woman—let us say, rather, her humility—as the most glorious of all her traits; and since woman has more natural *esprit* than the man, he dislikes that ability to see, that penetration. He fears that she will perceive in him all his vices and, above all, his faults.[34]

According to Mercier, men valued women far more for their beauty than for their minds. They wanted a woman to have enough intelligence to understand them, he explained, but not so much as to enable her to rival them or even to show herself their equal. "The man demands for himself a daily tribute of admiration," he wrote; "These sentiments, hidden in the heart of all men, are forcefully aroused when they are *en masse*. . . ." According to Mercier, the male sex was virtually united by a common desire and commitment to depress female aspirations and presumptions. Gallic gallantry played no part in their judgment of a woman's productions: "All men have a secret disposition to humble the woman who wishes to raise herself to the level of renown," he explained; "This fancy annoys them, because it is by far enough to be subjected by beauty, without being subjected by talent as well. . . . Women authors pay for their whole sex. A brilliant triumph would be highly alarming to the men's pride. . . ."[35]

Unable to suppress feminine artistic aspirations entirely with accusations of impropriety or unfemininity, those who objected to such female ventures had another formidable weapon: the depressing application of scorn and ridicule. A woman's work was never judged on its own individual merit, as that of a man, but always in relation to the sex of its author, which left it highly vulnerable. The entire sex could be—and frequently was—summarily dismissed as strangers in both essence and taste to the finer arts. For example, in his *l'Analyse de l'homme et de la femme*, the writer Saint-Lambert decreed that *all* women's novels and poems lack the originality, the sublime contrasts, the complicated intrigues, and pro-found ideas found in male works.[36] In the same tradition, another author found all women's novels, paintings, and music to be as weak and spirit-less as their bodies and minds: "All without genius, without vigor, with-out foresight, without any great talent . . .," he wrote in 1786.[37] This expression of masculine contempt was often deliberately patronizing and paternalistic. When the *Comédie Française* rejected a play written by Olympe de Gouges on the plight of the black slaves, its representative sent her a letter saying: "I like pretty women; I like them even more when they are gay; but I only like to see them when they are at home, and not in the theater. I refuse this play.[38]

Nevertheless, as challenging, rewarding, or frustrating as it might be, a career as an author or artist was open only to those women who pos-sessed both the education and the leisure to develop their talents. In general, most women in late eighteenth-century France had neither. The eighteenth-century Frenchwoman was caught in a classic Catch-22 situa-tion: lacking an education, she was found eligible for only the most me-nial employment, while her ineligibility for higher employment was used as an effective argument against female education.

For a middle- or upper-class woman, or even for a woman "of the people" living within the support of the family unit, such an exclusion might have been both irksome and humiliating, but it was hardly life-threatening. But for the woman struggling independently to support her-self and possibly even her children, this disparity between a woman's perceived role in society versus her very real economic contributions and needs could be deadly.

Eighteenth-century France contained a surprisingly high percentage of women who fell into this unenviable category. There were a number of reasons for this phenomenon, among them being a large population of celibate males, unequal inheritance laws, and the hampering effects of a custom that made it virtually impossible for an undowered female to wed, as well as the hardships caused by economic changes and the pressures of an expanding population.[39]

Estimates for the number of women on their own in eighteenth-century France vary. Some put the figure almost as high as one half of the entire female population.[40] According to the demographer Dupaquier, widows accounted for between 12 and 14 percent of the population, while those who never married comprised 8.5 percent of those women born between 1720 and 1724, rising to 14 percent of those born between 1785 and 1789.[41] It is also important to note that, according to demographers, "never marrieds" are identified as women over the age of 50 who die celibate. Therefore, to these figures for widows and aged spinsters must be added a large number of younger women working to accumulate the dowry that would someday enable them to marry. In the years immediately preceding the Revolution, the number of such young women still financially unable to marry was rising, as falling real wages both upped the average age of marriage and increased the number of "never-marrieds."[42]

This increasingly large percentage of women without men faced real hardship, for not only were most occupations barred to a woman outright on the basis of her sex, but wages for "female" work simply were not calculated with an independent existence in mind. As a result, social historians have shown that "criminal records, *maréchausée* reports on prostitution, and the *déclarations de grossesse*. . . all bear witness to the problems of the unmarried woman seeking to maintain herself outside a family setting."[43] It must also be remembered that even a woman who was actually married could suddenly find herself as the family's sole breadwinner, due to the illness, injury, or departure of her husband, or because of his addiction to gambling, alcohol, or other forms of dissipation.

Eventually, many of these women found themselves driven into one of the world's oldest professions: prostitution. According to even the most conservative estimates, the number of prostitutes to be found at any one time in Paris and the larger cities of France was staggering.[44]

Like the practitioners of a number of other professions, not all prostitutes belonged to the same class. Most were a miserable lot, but it was nevertheless true that at the top of this demimonde hierarchy could be found some women who managed to earn a fairly comfortable existence for themselves. These were the courtesans: those women of unusual beauty, talent, and shrewdness who lived a life of rare luxury and leisure by serving as mistresses to a succession of wealthy and generous protectors. These women scandalized more exquisite eighteenth-century sensibilities by appearing brazenly in public, clad in rich but generally indecent raiment and boldly displaying at least a portion of their ill-gotten gain in the form of opulent and obviously very expensive jewelry.

Many of these courtesans had begun their careers as actresses, singers, or dancers, a circumstance that did not rebound to the credit of the practitioners of those professions, who were generally (whether rightly or wrongly) classed with the prostitutes. The acting profession had only recently opened up to women, and it was hardly considered a respectable occupation. The attitude of Jean-Jacques Rousseau was typical. In his *Lettre à d'Alembert*, Rousseau viciously lashed out at actresses, demanding: "How can a profession, of which the unique object is to show oneself in public, and, which is worse, to show oneself for money, be fitting for virtuous women, and be compatible in them with modesty and good morality?"[45] As far as Rousseau and most of his contemporaries were concerned, it obviously could not, and the fact that so many members of the profession refused to conform to eighteenth-century standards for feminine virtue only seemed to prove their point.

Nevertheless, although they formed one of the most visible and highly resented components of their sisterhood, the courtesans, actresses, and dancers actually constituted only a fraction of the women who earned their living by prostituting themselves. Most lived a miserable existence, crowded together in back-street brothels or, lacking even that, plying their trade in darkened doorways and under bridges.

Many women actually engaged in prostitution on only a part-time basis. Because women's wages were inordinately low and women were traditionally paid a substantially lower salary than men doing identical work, many sold their bodies to subsidize the inadequate wage they received at some other labor. Or, since many women's jobs were seasonal and peaked at harvest-time or during the fashionable "season," many women in those trades were forced to turn to prostitution for subsistence in off-periods.

It was not a pleasant alternative. The results were degradation, social ostracism, increasing poverty, and the risk of pregnancy and disease followed by an early death. The treatment prostitutes received was harsh, and their fate uniformly grim. If arrested, a prostitute could expect at the least to have her head shaved and to be sent out to clean the streets; if she were found to be diseased, she was immediately bundled off to a prison-like hospital from which the most likely escape was through death.[46]

Although there would always be stern moralists who could see prostitutes only as debauched women seeking to lure virtuous men into sin, it had long been recognized by a number of clearsighted individuals that most women were reduced to prostitution not from choice but out of economic necessity. In the early part of the century, for example, Benoit Melon had written: "So many girls are wretched only because work is either lacking or insufficient to nourish them. Debauchery offers the money at hand, and it is difficult not to succumb."[47] Likewise, in his 1789 *Mes Cahiers*, the Marquis de Villette insisted that what prostitutes needed most was not prisons, but jobs.[48]

Discussions on what to do about the widespread problem of prostitution were so frequently interwoven in the literature of the period with recognition of the need to do something about the economic situation of women in general that it becomes difficult to separate the two. This is particularly true for the period after 1789.

With the coming of the Revolution, the plight of those women already living on the edge of subsistence became even worse. The flight of the aristocracy precipitated the collapse of the luxury trade, which had traditionally offered employment to a number of women, and this crash soon coupled with the general disruption of society caused by revolution and war to render the situation of women desperate. More and more women lost their jobs or were left alone with a family to support amid the rising costs of food and the collapse of the currency.

As a result, one of the complaints most frequently voiced by French women throughout the Revolution concerned the economic plight of their sex. And these complaints were also, predictably enough, interwoven with concern for a situation that forced woman into prostitution out of economic necessity. Olympe de Gouges, for example, wrote:

A great number of women . . . are lost because men, who have taken all for themselves, have deprived women of the means to rise and to procure for themselves useful and durable resources.[49]

There was not always agreement, however, on how to go about alleviating either the economic plight of women or what many people regarded as a veritable epidemic of prostitution. As often as not, complaints about the present situation of women looked to the past for their salvation. In 1789, for example, the flower merchants of Paris had complained in their *Doléances particulières* that the edicts of 1776 and 1777 had provided too great a liberty of access to their trade; the result was a flooded market, low prices, and a situation in which no one could make a living. "Since their business cannot sustain them," the merchants explained, "they seek the resources that they lack in libertinage or the most shameful debauchery. The cause of the suppliants is also that of morality."[50] What the flower merchants wanted, of course, was a return to stricter access to their trade.

In 1790, there appeared an interesting pamphlet entitled *Motion de la pauvre Javotte*, which also cited female deprivation as a cause of prostitution. The author of this pamphlet (who is obviously not one of the Revolution's most fervent admirers) presents an unflattering description of the economic effects of the Revolution on the female sex.

"*La pauvre Javotte*" begins by talking about the condition of her poor family before the Revolution, and how each member was helped to find a position by a "privileged" aristocrat. Unfortunately, with the coming of the Revolution and the "just" destruction of aristocratic privilege, they all lost their jobs and were once more poor. (At least, she concedes, they are now all equal with the *Grands*, who no longer have anything either.) "*La pauvre Javotte*" then goes on to explain how her father, brothers, and uncles all sought work from the government and, with difficulty, finally received it. But when she, her mother, and her sisters also asked the government for work, she says: "We were told that there was none for women. Are there therefore no poor women in this city, I asked?" According to Mlle Javotte, the truth was that one no longer saw anything but poor women.

As the story continues, Javotte encounters an old crone, with whom she discusses their plight. The old woman listens sympathetically to the younger woman and says: "You have the same needs as [men], but the government does not have the same care for you." Javotte then tells the old woman all the different things that she is capable of doing:

Javotte: My uncle gave me a good education; I have a tolerably fine handwriting, and I have learned all that is required to be employed in a trading house.

Old woman: It is only men who are employed in trading houses.

Javotte: I can copy music very exactly.

Old woman: It is only men who copy music.

Javotte: I am even more skilled at design, also painting.

Old woman: It is only men who know how to draw and paint.

Javotte: I play the harp, the guitar, and I am passable at the harpsichord; I could give lessons to young ladies.

Old woman: It is only men who give lessons to young ladies.[51]

Obviously, the talents and abilities catalogued by "*la Pauvre Javotte*" were not typically those of a "poor woman." Nor is the pamphlet exactly typical of complaints about the economic plight of women that appeared at the time, for there were actually only a few brave souls who ventured to suggest that traditional male careers ought to be made accessible to women, and not very many more who even protested against their inaccessibility.

Mme de Coicy, for example, wrote two notable works, one before and one during the Revolution, in which she raged against the entrenched discrimination shown to women in the area of employment, but the only changes that she suggested were that women should be admitted to orders of chivalry and that they be allowed to share in their husband's honors.[52] Likewise, the author of *Cahier des doléances et réclamations des femmes* wrote in 1789:

Pardon me, oh my sex! If I believed legitimate the yoke beneath which we have lived for so many centuries; I was persuaded of your incapacity and of your weakness; I believed you capable, in the lower or poor class, of only spinning, sewing, and devoting yourself to the economic cares of the household; and in a more distinguished rank, singing, dancing, music, and play seemed to me to be your essential occupations. I had not yet acquired enough experience to discern that all of these excercises are, on the contrary, so many obstacles to the development of genius.

Nevertheless, although she now had been disabused of these notions and had seen that women were capable of working beside men, Mme. B... B... made no real demands for the actual expansion of employment opportunities for women.[53]

Ironically enough, the solution to female unemployment and indigence most commonly suggested was not to expand the number of jobs for which women were considered eligible, but to reserve for them certain specified occupations, usually those that had traditionally been female in the past. The anonymous author of the *Petition des femmes du tiers état au Roi*, for example, demanded that "men may not, under any pretext, exercise the trades that are the appanage of women, such as woman's tailor, embroiderer, fashion retailer, etc., etc.; leave us at least the needle and the spindle, and we will undertake never to wield either the compass or the square."[54] The same idea appeared in, among others, the anonymous *Observations sur la rédaction des cahiers de Paris* and the *Motions adresses à l'assemblée nationale en faveur du sexe*, as well as in the cahiers of Paris and Rouen. Similar proposals also came from a number of known male authors, although these were often fairly patronizing in attitude and almost openly insulting in tone, since the authors make it plain that they believe both that such women's work is degrading to the male sex and, by inference, that the male is a far more noble creature than the female. Thus the abbot Jardineau suggested that "all trades formerly exercised by women and girls, such as fashion, hairstyling, dresses, and clothing, should be forbidden to men forever as a labor that is shameful for them, and under ignominious penalties; by this means, the Sex, finding it easier to live, will give less trouble. . . ."[55] Likewise, the journalist Mercier wrote that he actually "blushed" to see strong and robust men engaged in doing "women's work" and thus debasing and insulting "the name of man."[56]

There were also numerous schemes to improve the economic condition of women by training them in traditional "female" trades. Mme Elbée was only one of many who wanted to build more homes to save girls from prostitution by teaching them needlework and other similar trades, despite the fact that it was the low wages and depression in those areas of the economy that was forcing so many women into prostitution in the first place.[57]

Although there were some rare souls who recognized that what women lacked was not so much job skills as job opportunities, they were in reality very small in number. And the puritanical strain always present in the French Revolution virtually guaranteed that their message would be given little credence. In fact, the Revolutionary emphasis on morality was more likely to produce vicious attacks against the women driven into prostitution than it was to foster a sense of sympathy for those whom the economic realities of the day forced into such a situation.

These attacks against prostitutes often came from unexpected sources. Some of the better-known active women of the Revolution, who might have been supposed to be sympathetic to these women's plight, were instead overtly hostile, perhaps fearing any possible association of their sex as a whole with this one segment, which was so universally despised.

The Society of Revolutionary Republican Women, for example, carried a petition before both the Jacobins and the National Assembly in which they demanded the immediate arrest of all prostitutes.[58] Likewise, Mlle Jodin, the obscure author of a pamphlet extolling women's virtues and insisting upon their right to participate in the Revolution, ended her essay with a strident complaint about the "toleration" of prostitutes and insisted, not that they be helped by expanding the job opportunities available to women, but that they be comprehensively exterminated.[59]

In fact, the Revolutionary period produced very few people who were willing to go as far as had Poullain de la Barre in the seventeenth century, when he had announced that, in his opinion, it was funny to think of women in the professions only because people were not used to seeing such a thing, and that he personally would not be surprised to see women attending universities or acting as doctors, theologians, ministers, and soldiers.[60] It was truly a revolutionary idea, and far before its time. At the end of the eighteenth century, the orthodox although highly unrealistic concept of a sexual division of labor still stood firm.

NOTES

1. The death of the mother could throw a family over the line from poverty to destitution. Olwen Hufton estimates that it usually took the combined wages of both husband and wife to support 2 to 3 children; a widower deprived of his wife's income often had no choice but to abandon his children to local charities. Hufton, "Women and the Family Economy in Eighteenth-Century France," *French Historical Studies*, Vol. 9, 1 (Spring, 1975).

2. For general works on the subject, see especially J. Chauvin, *Des professions accessibles aux femmes en droit romain et en droit français* (Paris: Giard, 1892), Edmond Charles-Roux, *Les Femmes et le travail de moyene age à nos jours* (Paris: Editions de la Courtille, 1975), and Evelyne Sullerot, *Histoire et Sociologie du travail féminine* (Paris: Gonthier, 1968), For the social historians' findings on the "women of the people," see especially Olwen Hufton, *The Poor of Eighteenth-Century France* (London: Oxford University Press, 1974); Hufton, "Women and the Family Economy"; Hufton, "Women in Revolution, 1789–1796," *Past and Present 53* (November, 1971), pp. 90–108, and Angela Grappi, "Le Travail des femmes à Paris à l'époque de la Révolution Française," *Bulletin d'histoire économique et sociale de la Révolution Française* (1979), 27–46.

3. Hufton, "Women and the Family Economy", p. 10, and Elizabeth Fox-Genovese, "Women and Work," in Samia Spencer, ed., *French Women and the Age of Enlightenment* (Indiana University Press: 1984).

4. See Patricia Branca, *Women in Europe Since 1750* (New York: St. Martin's Press, 1978), and Hufton, "Women and the Family Economy."

5. Journal entry for 12 July, 1789, quoted in Arthur M. Wilson, "Treated like Imbecile Children: The Enlightenment and the Status of Women," in Paul Fritz and Richard Morton, eds., *Women in the Eighteenth Century and Other Essays*. (Toronto: Hakket, 1976), p. 91.

6. Olwen Hufton, "Women in Revolution" and "Women Without Men: Wid-

ows and Spinsters in Britain and France in the Eighteenth Century," *Journal of Family History* (Winter, 1984), p. 359.

7. A survey of the eighteenth-century publications listed in the bibliography will show that, in a surprising number of cases, the name of the publisher is preceded by the abbreviation for the word "*veuve*," or widow.

8. See the *Encyclopédie*, "Femme, jurisprudence," Vol. 6, p. 476.

9. Abensour lists those of the *drapiers, tisserands, graniers, passementiers, cabaretiers, tonneliers, tailleurs, boulangers, merciers, imprimeurs, limonadiers, macons, corroyeurs, orfevies, chaudronniers,* and *charcutiers*. He notes, however, that they were often found as "mixed" in only one or two cities. Leon Abensour, *La Femme et le féminisme avant la Révolution* (Paris: E. Leroux, 1923), p. 184.

10. Ibid, pp. 190–196.

11. In some provincial cities, they succeeded. Ibid., p. 184.

12. See, for example, the discussion on this subject in Colin Jones, "Prostitution and the Ruling Class in eighteenth-century Montpellier," *Historical Workshop*, 6 (Autumn, 1978), pp. 7–28.

13. For example, the anonymous pamphlets *Pétition des femmes du tiers état au Roi, Observations sur la rédaction des cahiers de Paris,* and *Motions adressées à l'assemblée nationale en faveur du sexe*; L.-A. Elbée, *Asyle toujours ouvert aux plus infortunées;* l'Abbé Jardineau, *32 articles à Mm les représentants de l'Assemblée électorale et à Mm les deputes aux Etats généraux*; and Mercier, *Tableau de Paris.*

14. Restif de la Bretonne estimated, for example, that food, lodging, and other necessities cost an individual woman about 20 sous a day, but noted that a seamstress made only 10 or 12 sous and an "*ouvière en modes*" commanded about 15 sous. *Le Palais Royal* (Paris: 1790), Vol. 1, p. 65. According to Hufton, in "Women and the Family Economy," p. 2, wages for lace-making were as low as 4 sous a day in the Massif Central (equal to the price of about 2 lb of bread) and rarely rose above 8–10 sous.

15. Hufton, *The Poor of Eighteenth-Century France*, pp. 24–41.

16. Mercier, *Le Tableau de Paris*, Vol. 9, 1788, p. 174.

17. Mme de Coicy, *Les Femmes comme il convient de les voir*, 2 vols. (London and Paris: Bacot, 1785), Vol. 2, p. 62. According to Hufton, however, the women of Le Puy had complete control of the lace-making industry, "from the very merchants who purchased the silk thread from Nimes or the linen thread from Flanders and who bartered the price of the finished object with the lacemaker and then made provision for it in Spain and South America." Hufton, "Women and the Family Economy," p. 15.

18. Mme de Coicy, *Demande des femmes aux Etats généraux, par l'auteur des femmes comme il convient de les voir* (n.p., n.d.).

19. "Femmes, jurisprudence," *Encyclopédie*, Vol. 6, p. 475.

20. Mme de Coicy, *Les Femmes*, Vol. 2, p. 65.

21. Women were allowed to enter testimony in both civil and criminal affairs, although it was commonly said that it took the testimony of two women to equal that of one man: "the evidence of women is in general light and subject to variation," explained the *Encyclopédie*; "that is why one considers it less than the evidence of men. . . ." *Encyclopédie*, "Femmes, jurisprudence," Vol. 6, p. 475.

22. Ibid.

23. See the complaints of Mme de Coicy in *Les Femmes comme il convient de les voir*, Vol. 2, pp. 64–65. It should be noted, however, that since even quasi-official jobs were seen as a kind of property, and because wives frequently assisted their husbands in performing their duties, widows often obtained the right to continue in their husbands' position and functioned in this capacity as jailers, janitors, inspectors, or poor house and hospital officials, even though a woman would never be appointed to such a position, herself, in the first place. See Hufton, "Women Without Men," p. 365.

24. Although some women had always served in the military, it was usually in male disguise. And while in the early days of the Revolution some women did volunteer and were reluctantly admitted to the army, they were categorically excluded in 1793. See, among others, Raoul Brice, *La Femme et les armées de la Révolution et de l'Empire*, 1792–1815 (Paris: n.d.) and Alfred Tranchant and Jules Ladimir, *Les Femmes militaires de la France* (Paris: 1866).

25. Although, in rare cases, some women were allowed to attend lectures. Also, it should be noted that although women were not allowed to be surgeons, the nursing profession was in the hands of the nuns.

26. F. Le Brun, *Histoire des Catholiques en France du XVe siècle à nos jours* (Paris: Privat, 1980), pp. 216–217.

27. This professionalization of nursing in the hands of the nuns apparently worked to the benefit of the French people. In 1789, there were 100,000 in hospitals in France, compared to only 3,000 in England. French nursing nuns who fled to England during the Revolution were appalled at the conditions they found there. See Hufton, "Women Without Men," p. 370.

28. See, for example, the complaints in the anonymous pamphlet, *La pauvre Javotte*, discussed below.

29. Paul Fritz and Richard Morton, eds., *Women in the Eighteenth Century and Other Essays* (Toronto: Hakket, 1976), p. 123.

30. Mme Roland, in L. J. Larcher and P. J. Martin, *Les Femmes peintées par elles-mêmes* (Paris: Edition Hetzel, Librairie Magnin, Blanchard, et Co., 1858), pp. 68–69.

31. Lambert, *Réflexions nouvelles sur les femmes* (London: chez J. P. Coderc, 1730), pp. 11–12.

32. Marie-Jeanne Phlipon Roland, *Mémoires de Mme Roland* (Paris: Baudoin fils, 1820), p. 195.

33. Mme de Staël, cited in Larcher and Martin, *Les Femmes peintes par elles-mêmes*, p. 85. Despite this famous passage, Mme de Staël had considerable difficulty reconciling her need to write with the traditional view of a "woman's role" she inherited from her adored father. She also wrote: "Les femmes sont peu faites pour suivre la même carrière que les hommes! Lutter contre eux, exciter en eux une jalousie si différente de celle que l'amour leur inspire! Une femme ne doit avoir rien à elle et trouves toutes ses jouissances dans ce qu'elle aime." See Gutworth, "Mme de Staël, Rousseau, and the Woman Question," *Publications of the Modern Language Association,* 86 (1971), p. 103.

34. Louis-Sebastian Mercier, "Femmes-Auteurs," *Tableau de Paris*, Vol. 9, 1788, p. 334.

35. Ibid., pp. 335–336.

36. Saint Lambert, *L'Analyse de l'homme et de la femme*, p. 186.

37. d'Artaize, *Réflexions d'une jeunne homme*, p. 73.

38. Olympe de Gouges, *Addresse aux Représentants de la Nation; Mémoire pour Mme de Gouges contre la Comédie Française* (n.p., n.d.).

39. As noted above, a dowry was even necessary in order to become a bride of Christ. It was almost impossible for a portionless girl to become a nun; her only hope was to be accepted as a lay sister.

40. Branca, *Women in Europe*, pp. 25–28.

41. Jean Dupaquier, *La Population française au XVIIe et XVIIIe siècles* (Paris: P.U.F., 1979) pp. 60–61.

42. Conversely, "permanent celibacy recedes in times of rising real wages and the same conditions lower the age at marriage." See Hufton, "Women Without Men," p. 357.

43. Ibid, p. 363. According to Hufton, "periods of price rises dramatically multiplied the number of widows and older single women appearing before the courts" for larceny and prostitution. Hufton also notes that "the widow is the only woman represented in crime statistics in the same proportion as she is represented and appears in the population as a whole" (p. 367).

44. Retif de la Bretonne estimated the number of prostitutes in Paris at 20,000; Mercier put the figure at 30,000, while a document in the archives of the police estimated their number at 25,000; Paris at that time had a population of about 600,000. There is no really satisfactory investigation of seventeenth- and eighteenth-century prostitution. A.-J.-B. Parent-Duchâtelet, *De la Prostitution dans la ville de Paris,* 2 vols. (Brussels: H. Dumont, 1837), is probably still the best, but, like W. W. Sanger, *The History of Prostitution* (New York, 1859), it contains some glaring inaccuracies. Both Fernando Henriques, *Prostitution in Europe and the New World* (London: Macgibbon and Kee, 1963), and Vern L. Bullough, *The History of Prostitution* (New York: University Books, 1964), repeat them.

45. Jean-Jacques Rousseau, *Lettre à d'Alembert*, p. 126.

46. See Parent-Duchâtelet, *De la prostitution.*

47. Benoît Malon, *Essai politique sur le commerce*, quoted in Dessens, *Les Révendications*, p. 42.

48. Charles-Michel Villette, Marquis de, *Mes Cahiers* (Senlis, 1789), p. 20.

49. Olympe de Gouges, *La Bonheur primitif de l'homme ou les Rêveries patriotiques* (Paris: Royer, 1789), p. 72.

50. *Doléances particulières des marchandes bouquetières fleuristes*, in Chassin, *Les Elections et les cahiers de Paris en 1798*, p. 536.

51. *Motion de la pauvre Javotte, députée des pauvres femmes. . . . Les quelles composent le second ordre du Royaume depuis l'abolition de ceux du clergé et la Noblesse* (Paris, 1796), pp. 9, 10, and 11. Although this pamphlet is bitingly satirical, the satire is entirely directed against the Revolution itself, not against women. Its complaints concerning the economic plight of women appear quite genuine, for it has none of the characteristics that distinguish the satires discussed in Chapter 8. On the topic of relief for poor women during the Revolution, see David Cohen, "Women's Work, Women's Welfare: the Ateliers de Filiature in Paris, 1790–92," *Proceedings of the Consortium on Revolutionary Europe, 1983* (1985), 654–680, and Shelby McCloy, "Charity Workshops for Women; Paris, 1790–1795," *Social Service Review*, 11 (1937), 274–284.

52. Mme de Coicy, *Les Femmes comme il convient de les voir* and *Demande des femmes*.

53. *Cahier des doléances et réclamations des femmes, par Mme B... B...* (1789), p. 2.

54. *Pétition des femmes du tiers état au Roi*, 1 January 1789, p. 6.

55. l'Abbé Jardineau, *32 articles à Mm les représentants de l'Assemblée électorale et à Mm les députés aux Etats généraux*, in Chassin, *Les Elections et les cahiers de Paris en 1789*, p. 386.

56. Mercier, *Tableau de Paris*, Vol. 9, 1788, p. 177.

57. L.-A. Elbée, *Asyle toujours ouvert aux plus infortunées et aux plus à plaindre des jeunes filles qui veulent toujours être honnêtes et vertueuses* (Paris: Imprimerie de L. Jarry, 1789).

58. *Monituer*, XVII–699, 21 September 1793; Aulard, "La Société des Jacobins," *Recueil de Documents*, 6 vols. (Paris: Quantin, 1889–1897), Vol. 5, p. 402.

59. Jodin, *Vues législatives pour les femmes*.

60. François Poullain de la Barre, *De l'Egalité des deux sexes; discours physique et moral où on voit l'importance de se défaire des préjugés* (Paris: chez Jean du Pais, 1673), pp. 12, 162–163, 168–169, and 175.

6

Marriage,
Adultery, and Divorce

> Marriage, by forming a society between the husband and the wife, of
> which the husband is the master, gives to the husband in his capacity
> as head of this society a right of power over the person of his wife,
> which extends also over her property.
>
> [Pothier, *Traité de la Communauté*]

The French laws dealing with marriage, especially those concerning adultery and divorce, were the object of intense criticism and debate throughout the Revolution. No other topic relative to equality between the sexes, not even education, received quite so much attention. In any society in which the female's existence is defined first and foremost by her marital status, the nature of the laws that govern the institution of marriage understandably assumes a position of paramount importance in the life of a woman. Furthermore, even the man who might view with indifference or vague detachment a discussion of the laws on the education or employment of women is likely to become intensely interested by any proposed modification in the laws that regulate his relationship with his wife.

To understand the nature of this debate on the legal framework of the institution of marriage, it is important to realize that in France in 1789 the authority of a husband over the person and property of his wife was, under law, virtually absolute. When a woman married, her name, her identity, and even her nationality were all submerged beneath those of her husband. According to Robert Pothier, one of the most respected eighteenth-century authorities on marital law, this custom was founded on the idea that, once married, a woman "is from then on considered to form with her husband only one single person, of whom he is the head."[1] As a result, if a woman married a man from a different province or country, she was considered to have forsaken her own original domicile and to have acquired that of her husband. A woman likewise assumed her husband's name, and his rank. For this reason a nonnoble woman wed to a noble man was herself ennobled, just as a noble woman who married beneath her class was considered to have forfeited her nobility as long as the marriage endured.[2]

Although a husband's rights and powers were very carefully supported by law, his obligations were few: he was required to receive his wife, to furnish her with the necessities of life by working at an occupation appropriate for him, to love her, to bear with her faults, and to fulfill his "marital duties" when requested to do so, while forsaking carnal commerce with all others.

The obligations that a woman owed her husband were more extensive and binding. According to Pothier, "She must love him, be submissive to him, obey him in all things that are not contrary to the law of God, and support his faults." She was also expected to work for the common good of the household and to fulfill her "marital duties" when asked to do so, forsaking carnal commerce with all others.[3]

The husband was considered the "*chef*" of a marriage, and he ruled his wife by right of what was known as the "*puissance maritale*," or the power of a husband. This *puissance maritale* was divided into two types, that which the husband exercised over the person of his wife, and that which he enjoyed over her property.

As a result of his *puissance maritale* over his wife's person, a husband had the right to require her to follow him wherever he chose to go, and to live wherever he chose to live (as long as he did not propose to take her out of the country, the reason for this exception being that a woman was considered to belong to the country even more than she belonged to her husband). If a wife left her husband, she could by law be forced to return to him. She could not say that the place where her husband had chosen to live was dangerous, or unhealthy, or disease-ridden; nor could she offer as an excuse her husband's ill treatment of her (if she had not requested a "*separation d'habitation*" for this reason). Unless she had been granted a legal separation, the husband of an errant wife was fully empowered to drag her back home again, as well as to take legal action against the people to whose home she had fled, even if they were her parents or relatives. Conversely, if a husband kicked his wife out of his house, she might have him ordered to take her back again, but the man always retained the right to refuse, in which case he could only be required to grant his wife a pension considered in keeping with his resources.[4]

The law required a wife to render full obedience to her husband. "The power of the husband over the person of his wife," wrote Pothier, "Consists, by natural right, of the right that the husband has to require from her all the duties of submission that are due to a superior." Every man was considered to be the sovereign lord and master of his own home. It was quite commonly said that a woman owed to her husband the same respect and obedience that he owed to his God, or that the position in which a man stood to his wife could be likened to the relationship between Christ and his church.[5]

The male was repeatedly warned to be jealous of this vulnerable position as God and King to his wifely subject and worshiper. "Conserve your authority early," Jean-Baptiste Blanchard advised young husbands; "It is one of the most beautiful rights that you have received from nature, and one despises those imbecile men who let themselves be stripped of it by their wives." In the *Ecole des moeurs*, Blanchard presented a veritable manual on the proper training of a good and submissive wife. He cautioned young husbands not to be *too* anxious always to show their wives who was master: "It almost always suffices that a wife knows that the man can be it, and that he sometimes makes her remember it, if she comes to forget it." But it was very important, he stressed, that a wife never be allowed to forget who really was the ruler, lest she try to usurp the man's command: "The wife who makes herself mistress, takes pleasure in being contrary to her husband in everything," wrote Blanchard, warning of dire consequences:

She cannot have dominance over him without changing it into a tyranny, nor see him her subject, that she does not make him her slave: usurpations are only maintained by violence. The wife that one fears, is truly to be feared. As soon as one trembles before her, she is terrible; and the more a husband is quick to obey her and to please her, the more she is insupportable and cruel.[6]

The idea of a marriage between equals was completely foreign to the times. In the society formed between a man and a wife, just as in any other society, someone had to be the leader, and it was thought to be against the laws of nature, God, and reason that it should be the woman. Nature had shown its preference for the male by making him the stronger, God had seconded this choice in Genesis and the writings of St. Paul, while the laws of society had reasonably added their confirmation by investing power in the spouse described by the *Encyclopédie* as the one who "is gifted with a greater strength of mind and body, and [who] contributes more to the common good, in matters both sacred and profane."[7]

The only legally recognized way in which a wife was allowed to "participate" in her husband's authority was through meekness and complaisance. Women were repeatedly assured that if they would only just do everything that their husbands told them to do and if they would only just agree with them in everything their husbands said, then their husbands would be so struck by their wives' nobility and generosity that they would be rendered incapable of doing anything to displease them. According to Blanchard's version of this theory:

There only remains one legitimate means for wives to share authority with their husbands, even to possess it almost entirely, and that is [by] submission, complaisance, and meekness. A wife who tries to take pleasure only in what her husband wishes and commands will soon put him in the position to dare and to be able to command only what pleases his wife.[9]

Since a wife was expected to submit to her husband in every way, if a marriage was troubled, the wife was commonly held to be at fault. It was a woman's attempts to argue with her husband or to dispute his authority over her that were assumed to upset the familial harmony and cause bad marriages. "The majority of the dissensions that arise between husband and wife," wrote Blanchard, "Come from the latter's wish to leave the state of dependence where nature has placed her."[9]

According to Pothier, a wise woman would tell you that the secret of her happy marriage lay "in doing all that pleases [my husband], and in patiently suffering all that which he does, even when it does not please me."[10] A good wife was expected to agree with her husband in all matters of religion, politics, taste—everything. She should also dress to please him. If he should happen to be the jealous type, she was told to hide herself away and not to speak to a soul; if, on the other hand, he wanted her to take her place in society, then she must do so. If a wife balked at even one little thing her husband wanted, then it was considered obvious that she did not truly love him. "That is the way men think of it," wrote Retif de la Bretonne; "We do not recognize as wife an infidel who, of set purpose, goes against our known intentions and opposes herself to the execution of our will." The bridal vow that he so fondly envisaged in the *Gynographe* admirably reveals the degree of total wifely self-abnegation idealized by his society:

I swear complete submission and obedience to my husband; promising to do in all things that which will please him. . . . I promise and bind myself to use all the qualities that I may have received from heaven and all my acquired talents, only to please my husband. . . . I will place my happiness in making that of my husband. . . . I will try to form myself to my husband's character, to bend mine to it, to the effect that his wishes will be my wishes, his desires my desires . . . convinced that the first virtue of a Woman is to be identified with her leader.[11]

In eighteenth-century France, a husband not only possessed the right to demand full and complete obedience from his wife; he also had the right to exact it. As part of his *puissance maritale*, a husband had the legal right to beat his wife. The full enjoyment of this privilege had recently been slightly impaired by the requirement that a man's use of physical correction not be so excessive as to actually endanger his wife's life, but beyond that minor consideration he was free to act as he saw fit. In contrast, unless she could prove herself to be in mortal danger, a wife was required to bear the faults and vagaries of her husband in silence. Her only legal weapons of self-defense were those same two female virtues, meekness and complaisance, which were so often expected of her sex. "She may oppose only patience to her husband's bad manner, and even to his bad treatment," wrote Pothier; "She must regard them as arriving by the order of God and as a cross that he has sent her to expiate her sins. They must not prevent her from in all cases going beyond all that she can do to please her husband, and she must not leave him, unless things are carried to the greatest extremities."[12]

The *puissance maritale* exercised by a husband over the person of his wife was so extensive that she was considered virtually powerless to act without his consent. "Our laws have placed the woman in such dependence on her husband," wrote Pothier, "That she can do nothing that is valid or has any civil effect, unless she has been enabled and authorized by him to do it." In this respect a wife's legal position was identical to that of a minor, although there was no real attempt made to attribute the cause of her civil impotence to the existence of some inherent weakness in the female intellect. Such a contention could have been too quickly countered by the simple argument that the mere act of marriage could hardly be considered to have rendered a wife any less intelligent than an unmarried woman or a widow, neither of whom required such authorization. In fact, Pothier deliberately emphasized the difference in the intent of the law that required a minor to obtain the consent of his guardian, versus that of the law that required a husband's authorization for his wife. The purpose of the first was to protect the best interests of the minor, whereas the intent of the second was not to protect the best interests of the wife, but those of her husband, by preserving her state of dependence and his power over her.[13]

As a result of this state of civil nonexistence, a wife could neither buy nor sell anything of value without the expressed authorization of her husband. Nor could she receive payment due her, or pay any sum of money or goods that she might owe. Likewise, a wife required her husband's authorization to either accept or repudiate an inheritance. All contracts made by a wife without the consent of her husband were considered null and void. Nor could a wife either institute civil proceedings against someone without her husband's authorization, or testify in court (unless she was so ordered). About the only thing she could do without his authorization was to sign a contract freeing her husband from prison, although authorities argued over whether or not she had the right to do the same to get *herself* out of prison. In some provinces, such as Normandy and Burgundy, a wife even needed her husband's authorization on her last will and testament, although the laws of other areas considered such authorization unnecessary, regarding the will as coming into being only after the wife's death, at which time the power of the husband over her person might be supposed to have ceased.[14]

It was possible for a husband to grant his wife general authorization to administer her own property, but anything outside day-to-day administration always required special consent. Any attempt made by a man to give his wife complete general authority was illegal. The reason, according to Pothier, was that any such general authorization would "tend to place women outside the dependence in which the laws wish that women should be in relation to their husbands."[15] Only if a woman was constituted a "*marchande publique*," a public merchant with a business of her own in which her husband had no part or interest, was she granted the power to sign all contracts relating to her business without the need to obtain her husband's authorization.[16]

As long as he retained his own civil existence, a husband never forfeited his rights over the person of his wife. A husband who was himself still in his minority nevertheless possessed the right to exercise his full marital powers over his wife's person, be she a minor or not. Even a husband gone insane retained his powers; his wife might be given general authorization to administer her property, but for anything else she was required to receive specific authorization from a judge. A woman whose husband was absent or missing was also required to obtain authorization to act or obligate herself from a judge. Only when a husband lost his civil existence through condemnation to a capital penalty was a wife considered free to act as she saw fit, the same as if she were unmarried or widowed.[17]

In addition to his power over his wife's person, a husband also had control over her property. Under Roman law, a married woman had two kinds of property: *les biens dotaux*, or those goods that comprised her dowry, and *les biens paraphernaux*, her paraphernal or "personal" property. This distinction continued to exist in France in those provinces governed by the *droit écrit*. At marriage, the ownership of a woman's dowry was transferred to her husband, with the stipulation that it must be returned to her at the end of the marriage. For the duration of the marriage, the husband was considered the veritable owner of these goods, although he was not allowed to alienate any of the actual property of which the dowry was comprised without his wife's consent. Any portion of a wife's property that did not form part of her dowry was considered her "paraphernal property," and over this a woman was allowed to retain nominal ownership, although her husband enjoyed its revenues, and his *"puissance maritale"* over her person required her to obtain his consent and authorization in all matters relating to it.[18]

The distinction between *biens dotaux* and *biens paraphernaux* did not exist in those areas of France not governed by the *droit écrit.* According to the customary law of Paris, which was similar to that of most of the provinces governed by customary law, all of a wife's property was considered her dowry. Under customary law, another type of distinction was made, between what were known as *biens de communauté* and *biens propres.*

A woman's *biens de communauté* joined with those of her husband to form the couple's community property. The husband was considered the "absolute master" of the community property. According to Pothier:

The power that a husband has over the person and property of his wife makes him the head of this community and gives him in this quality the right to dispose at his pleasure in whatever style seems good to him, even by *donation entrevifs,* all those things that compose it . . . without the consent of his wife, who on her side, does not have the right to dispose of anything; it is for this reason that the husband is considered, while the community endures, as being in some fashion the only lord and absolute master of the goods of which it is comprised, and that the right which a wife has here is only regarded, as long as the community endures, as an unformed right, which is reduced to the right to some day share in the goods that are found to compose it when it is dissolved.[19]

Any of a woman's possessions that did not become part of the *communauté* were known as her *biens propres,* or "personal property." This property was itself of two distinct types, depending upon whether it was real estate or movable goods. The movable property of the *biens propres* differed from the community property only in the fact that the woman or her heirs had a right, at the end of the marriage, to recover an amount equal to the worth of this property (or to try to, at any rate). The husband had no less right to dispose of this property, at his own will and without his wife's consent, than in the case of the *communauté*. The wife did, however, retain nominal ownership over any real estate that was excluded from the community property and classified as her "personal property" (although even here the husband maintained the right to administer it and to enjoy its revenues).[20] Anything that a wife might earn as the result of her labor during the course of the marriage was considered to belong not to her, but to her husband.[21]

The legal regulations governing the classification of property in a marriage were obviously complicated and involved, and it is easy to see that the drawing-up of a marriage contract was a serious and arduous affair. It is also important to note that even though a woman could not be deprived of either her dowry or her "personal property" (depending upon the part of France in which she lived) by the deliberate action of her husband, she could nevertheless lose it through his negligence.

The only way in which a husband could be deprived of his control over his wife's property was through a "separation of goods." A separation of goods could come about in one of two ways: either as a clause inserted in the marriage contract or as an act of separation instituted in the course of the marriage itself. A woman could ask for a separation of goods for much the same reasons for which she could demand the restitution of her dowry under Roman law: when the poor state of her husband's affairs was endangering her future ability to retrieve her dowry or (even if she did not have a dowry but had worked since her marriage) if her husband was wasting her money. Whether it was enacted before or during the marriage, the results of a separation of goods were the same: the husband lost both the right to enjoy the revenues of his wife's property and his rights to administer it. Even in the case of a separation of goods, however, the husband still retained his authority over his wife's real estate, which could neither be sold nor rented without his consent.[22]

In addition to a separation of goods, a wife might also seek a "separation of habitation." According to Pothier, a wife could demand a separation of habitation for five reasons: if her husband had an "aversion to her," to the extent that she suffered profoundly and grievously; if he beat her badly, and often, and when she had neither deserved nor provoked it, and if he did so to the extent that her life was in danger; if he was depriving her of the necessities of life; if he was accused of a capital crime; if he was a heretic. A wife could *not* ask for a separation of habitation on the grounds that her husband had venereal disease, or any other disease. Nor were epilepsy, deformity, insanity, or the husband's adultery considered just causes.[23]

A separation of habitation usually carried with it a separation of goods. A husband nevertheless retained his marital powers to the extent that his wife still needed his consent to alienate any of her real estate or for any other act that did not concern the simple administration of her property. The separation did not break the marriage tie. Its major effect was that the wife was freed from her obligations to live with her husband and to render him her "marital duties" in the conjugal bed.[24] For whatever reason (except perhaps the last two) that she was granted a separation of habitation, a wife could usually expect to lose her children, who were considered as belonging to the father. He could, if he so chose, prevent their mother from ever seeing them again.

Although a woman was unable to demand a separation of habitation on the grounds of adultery, her husband could. There were any number of explanations and rationalizations that were frequently presented in justification of this acknowledgedly blatant inequality. To begin with, a husband's honor was held to have been besmirched by his wife's infidelity, in some mysterious fashion that apparently did not similarly affect the wife of an unfaithful husband. Secondly, the commission of adultery by a woman required such a violation of *pudeur*, modesty, and decency, that such a woman must be supposed to have renounced all pretense of virtue. Furthermore, as Montesquieu pointed out in *De l'Esprit des lois*, by violating the laws of marriage, a woman was effectively escaping from that state of dependence that was her natural and rightful condition.[25] But even more important than all the rest was the inescapable possibility that an adulterous wife could, without him even knowing it, present her husband with an heir who was not of his own begetting. In contrast, a husband's commission of adultery was considered to have affected his wife in no way whatsoever, the possibility of emotional upset, exposure to venereal disease, and the diminution of the familial fortunes by the diversion of a substantial portion of them in the direction of mistresses and any number of broods of illegitimate children evidently not being thought worthy of serious consideration. Said Pothier:

The adultery that a woman commits is infinitely more contrary to the good order of civil society, because it tends to despoil families, and cause their goods to pass to children who are strangers there; whereas the adultery that a husband commits, however criminal in itself, is in this respect without consequence. Add to which it is not for the woman, who is an inferior, to have the right to inspect the conduct of her husband, who is her superior. She must presume that he is faithful, and jealousy must not lead her to make investigations into his conduct.[26]

Whatever other reasons might be given in defense of the penalties incurred by a woman's infidelity, here, at the end, is the reason why a man could never be held similarly culpable.

A man who committed adultery was guilty both of a crime in the eyes of the law and a sin in the eyes of the church. But although the church might exact a penitence, the law did not. A man's adultery was a crime that carried no penalty, so that he could commit it with impunity. He might set up a mistress in the grandest manner, frequent a hundred harlots, or, in the extremities of libertinage, he might even introduce his partners in debauchery into his wife's own home and force them all to live together in some sort of bizarre *menage à trois*, or *à quatre*, or even *à cinq*. His wife could only endure.

Yet however dissolute and abandoned the husband might be, he could, in all legality, exact the most unflinching fidelity from his wife. If she strayed even once, she was at his mercy. Only a husband could enter an accusation of adultery against his wife, and her fate was in his hands. The old practice of having an adulterous wife stripped and whipped through the streets had been largely abandoned by the late eighteenth century. Instead, the unfaithful woman was locked away in a convent (or, depending upon her station in life, in a house of correction) for two years. During that time, the husband could, if he so desired, go to visit her, and at the end of that period he might even release her and take her back home as his wife. If, however, his desire for vengeance was unsatisfied, then her head was shaved and she was shut away for life.

As one of the most flagrantly unjust examples of the inequality of the sexes in marriage under the law, the French adultery laws of the eighteenth century drew harsh criticism. Long before the Revolution began, Voltaire, Condorcet, and others had used both logic and biting satire to criticize their country's unequal adultery laws. In her *Lettres d'une Péruvienne*, Mme de Grafigny angrily spoke out against what she called "the revolting injustice of the laws":

A husband, without fearing any punishment, can have for his wife the most disgusting manners, he can dissipate in prodigalities, as criminal as they are excessive, not only his own goods, and those of his children, but even those of his victim, whom he makes live practically in indigence, by an avarice for honest expenses that so often accompanies prodigality. He is authorized to punish rigorously the appearance of the lightest infidelity, while delivering himself without shame to all those which libertinage suggests to him. Indeed . . . it seems that in France the bonds of marriage are only reciprocal at the moment of the celebration, and that afterwards only the woman must be subjected to them.[27]

With the coming of the Revolution, public objection to the unequal adultery laws intensified, often coming even from those who were otherwise opposed to any movement towards equality between the sexes. "The laws are visibly unjust," wrote citizen Bouchotte, "When they are not equal. Our laws against adulterers have a double vice," he explained; "They punish, in an atrocious manner, women who have been either unhappy or imprudent. These women alone are punished, even though they may well be less culpable than the lovers who seduce them, and above all less culpable than the husbands who abandon them to be corrupted by others." Bouchotte described the makers of such laws as "as jealous" as "savages": "A false point of honor made them adopt with enthusiasm this refinement of cruelty," he wrote, "Which condemns to a long and sorrowful torment a sensitive woman, whose crime was perhaps the result of those of the husband to whom her parents delivered her."[28]

The traditional justifications for the inequality in the punishment of adultery were all called into question, including the age-old contention that an adulterous wife dishonored her husband: "But your husband's honor has suffered a real outrage. What a ludicrous notion is this!" said one of the characters in the Marquis de Sade's *Philosophy in the Bedroom*; "My libertinage in no wise affects my husband; mine are personal faults. . . . My husband is no more sullied by my debauches than I might be by his."[29]

Even the relative importance assigned to the more physical results of each sex's adultery was challenged. The Montagnard Saint-Just wrote:

I would like just once for someone to explain to me why the husband who puts adulterous children in the house of another, or of many others, is less criminal than the woman who can only put one in her own. There exists a contract between the spouses. . . . The contract is null if any one dishonors it; to say that an unfaithful husband is not culpable, is to say that he reserves for himself, by the contract, the privilege to be bad.[30]

As the Marquis de Sade dryly pointed out, when it comes to the question of the paternity of his children:

Any man who vexes himself with suspicions upon this head seeks vexation; even were his wife a vestal he would plague himself with worries, for it is impossible to be sure of a woman, and she who has behaved well for years may someday interrupt her good behavior. Hence, if this husband is suspicious, he will be so in any case; never, then, will he be convinced that the child he embraces is really his own.[31]

Instead of disowning them, de Sade suggested that a husband should regard his wife's adulterous children rather as he would any children she might have had by an earlier marriage. Olympe de Gouges even proposed a new marriage vow, in which husband and wife would promise to live together for the duration of their "mutual penchants" and to recognize each other's children, "out of whatever bed they come."[32] But de Sade and de Gouges were two free-thinkers regarded by the majority of their contemporaries as something vaguely approaching lunatics.

Most of the Revolutionaries who protested the current adultery laws only went so far as to suggest that the punishment for the crime of adultery should be equal for both man and wife. Charles-Louis Rousseau wrote: "Nothing can justify in my eyes these laws, which, at the same time, strike the weakest and spare the strongest. Is adultery therefore only a crime for the women? I cannot convince myself of it."[33] There were any number of complaints against both the harshness of the penalties imposed on an adulterous woman, and the simultaneous absence of any punishment at all for the adulterous man. The pamphlet *Les Griefs et plaintes des femmes mal mariées* roundly condemned the retribution exacted from an adulterous wife, while, at the same time, protesting the impunity with which a husband could "deliver himself to libertinage, to debauchery even in his home under the very eyes of his wife, if he wishes it," complained the pamphlet; "He keeps his mistress there, living in a public and scandalous adultery, the wife does not even have the right to complain, the law does not allow her to enter an acusation of adultery. She may only be the accused, never the accuser."[34]

More than one writer was aware that such unequal laws could be (and were) used as tools for personal interests or revenge. "One knows too well the abuse of the *lettres de cachet*," reminded one author, "and experience teaches that that which should only punish culpable women, is often the fate of the innocent."[35]

Despite the widespread criticism of the old adultery laws, however, when the new police code was drawn up in the spring of 1791, it once again denied women the ability to complain of their husbands' adultery, while reserving for the men the right to imprison an adulterous wife for two years. Under the new law, as under the old, a woman so convicted also forfeited both her dowry and her dower portion. This infamous "Article XIII" was subjected to indignant attack from, among others, Etta Palm d'Aelders.

Leading a delegation to the National Assembly, Etta Palm informed those august representatives that this new law of theirs surpassed the worst injustices of the centuries of barbarism: "It is a refinement of despotism that [will] render the constitution odious to the Sex," she warned them; "And by the degradation of our existence, in flattering your own vanity, it will rock you to sleep in the arms of a slave and thus deaden your energy, to better rivet your chains." Will you make slaves of those who contributed to your libery? she demanded. "The powers of the husband and wife must be equal," she insisted; ". . . the laws cannot establish any difference between the two authorities. . . ." She begged the French not to "soil" their "immortal" work: "You need a moral code, without a doubt," she agreed; "But morality is the product of the times and of education; it cannot be ordered; [today's] license is the natural result of the oppressive regime of the indissolubility of marriage. . . ."[36]

In this case, as in many others, criticism of the existing adultery laws was often joined to support for the institution of divorce. Before the Revolution, only Voltaire and a very few others had had the courage to speak out in favor of divorce. With the calling for an Estates General in 1788, however, the demands for the legalization of divorce became legion. Even before the Estates met, hundreds of essays, articles, and pamphlets were issued in favor of the institution. Many of the *cahiers* that the representatives from all over the country carried with them to Versailles contained within them requests for the legalization of divorce (or, in a number of cases, arguments against it).

Divorce was by no means a singularly feminine issue. France contained any number of men who would have been only too happy to be released from their marriage vows, however lightly these may have pressed them. Nevertheless, there were few who would have denied that the plight of the unhappily married woman was usually the most desperate. "It is on the weaker sex that the misfortune (of a bad marriage) falls, and more often with the most force," contended the author of one typical pamphlet on divorce. Comprehensively surveying the woman's plight, he wrote:

A young girl almost always marries at her parents' pleasure: she only dares to
influence their choice, and sometimes she dares it in vain; shy, without experience, without will, she walks to the altar, and there beholds herself united to a
man of whom it was impossible or useless to see the faults. And if a woman has
few means to avoid a bad choice, she has still less to correct its effects: the husband is the master.[37]

After marriage, continued the author, the husband's rights of *puissance
maritale* over her person and property could make the life of an unhappily married woman wretched indeed.

An unexpected champion of both equal adultery laws and legalized
divorce was, surprisingly enough, the journalist Prudhomme. In an article
entitled "Du divorce," written in 1791, Prudhomme charged that the laws
on separation were written completely to the advantage of the legislating
sex:

Judge and party in his own cause, he was able thereby to preserve, all at the same
time, his vanity, his jealousy, his tranquility, and his liberty at the expense of the
second sex: his vanity, by making obvious the superiority of his forces; his jealousy, by condemning to celibacy she with whom he no longer desires to share his
bed; his tranquility, by separating from him, in the person of his wife, an important witness of his infidelity towards her; his liberty, because a separation allows a
husband to reenter into the vague circle of pleasures of a dissipated and unbridled
youth. Whereas his companion only changes her prison. . . .[38]

Unlike the "*separation d'habitation*" permitted by present laws, Prudhomme noted, legalized divorce would restore to both parties complete
and equal freedom. Not only would such a law save the unhappy captives
of those marriages that could no longer be salvaged, he said, but it would
also have a beneficial effect on all other marriages, as well. According to
Prudhomme, if it were known "that the doors of the temple of justice
would open at the first reclamation of one or the other . . . that divorce,
far different from a simple separation, would restore to one as to the
other partner all their rights . . .," then, he said, one would see both
wives *and* husbands trying harder to please their spouses, and the result
would be happier homes. The legalization of divorce, predicted Prudhomme, would soon teach men not to talk so much about their rights,
and to be a little more attentive to their wives. Without divorce, he contended, "the temple of Hymen . . . is for women a prison, of which their
husbands are the gaolers."[39]

If there were a number of Frenchmen who spoke out in favor of
divorce, however, there were also a number of Frenchwomen who argued
against it. Some women feared that legalized divorce would allow men to
abandon their ill, sterile, or aging wives in favor of younger and pretty
brides; others were alarmed and frightened by the degree of unknown
liberty and independence that the freedom of divorce threatened. One of

the most persuasive and popular essays written against divorce at the time of the Revolution actually came from the pen of a woman: Suzanne Necker.

According to Mme Necker, divorce was dangerous for the moral fiber of the female sex. In her estimation, the Sex's true virtue was "dependence," its proper sentiment was the "abandonment of willpower," its taste the "desire to please," and its pleasures came from "identification with the happiness of others." For Mme Necker, this was a woman's natural character, and it fitted her, since women were destined never to live in isolation but only as the complement of others. With the usual insight and perspicacity that characterized her, Mme Necker foresaw that the institution of divorce would somehow change all that: "If divorce were permitted," she wrote, "the opinion of the duties of women would perhaps change, and marriage having almost the appearance of a simple love affair, meekness, indulgence, submission even, and all the qualities of sacrifice that maintain domestic peace, would be less esteemed. . . ." This was a prospect that Mme Necker could only find disturbing. If women were allowed the right to divorce, she asked, how could they retain that "taste for retreat" so necessary for the exercise of the duties of wife and mother? With their futures never permanently decided, worried Mme Necker, women would form some sort of "species of amphibians, neither girls, nor mothers, nor wives"; their position in society would never be defined.[40]

Mme Necker's sense of morality was deeply shocked by the thought of divorce. In the eighteenth century, as in ages past, a wife was expected to bring with her to her marriage bed the "talisman" of her virginity, which she presented to her husband as a wedding gift. Mme Necker's bourgeois imagination found the thought of any kind of voluntary change of partners utterly revolting and indecent. In her mind, there would soon be little left to distinguish married women from the actresses and *filles* of the Palais Royal.

She was also haunted by the vision of a society in which women felt free to judge their husbands and to compare them with others. In words startling coming from one of her renowned intelligence, she wrote:

The women who are the most lovable in the eyes of their husbands are certainly those whose virtues are natural and whose innocence has never been altered or fortified by reflexion; they neither judge nor compare [their husbands]; there exists only one man for them.[41]

Fully cognizant yet peculiarly frightened of the inevitable changes that it would bring, Mme Necker warned that the legalization of divorce would lead to the veritable overthrow of what she saw as the natural order of things. "The purpose of [women's] creation will be missing," she wrote;

"They will leave their place in the chain of being, and they will suspend the decree of the system that they did not wish to follow. . . ." She admitted that it would indeed be nice if there were some way in which a woman who was truly made miserable by the wickedness and cruelty of her husband could escape from his tyranny, but such a thing could never be. The unhappy victim had to be sacrificed for the greater good of the rest of society.[42]

Yet perhaps because it was desired as ardently by men as by women, a divorce law was in fact passed in September of 1792. What is startling is its almost unprecedented degree of liberality. Both sexes were given the equal right to file for divorce on the grounds of mutual consent, incompatibility, insanity, desertion, criminality, or immorality. If there were children from the marriage, all girls and any boys under the age of seven were confided to the custody of their mother; boys seven years of age and older went with their father, although the parents had a right to agree to any other arrangement they might prefer.[43]

Those who had predicted that women would be the greatest beneficiaries of legalized divorce were soon proven correct. Of the 5,994 divorces granted in Paris from 1 January 1793 to 29 prairial in the year III, 3,870 were demanded by women and only 2,124 by men. When one considers that 548 of the 559 divorces granted on the grounds of mutual consent were attributed to the husband, it becomes even more obvious that the overwhelming majority of those who took advantage of the new law to seek release from unhappy marriages were women.[44]

Although it was destined not to endure, for a while, at least, women had obtained both the right to divorce and more equitable adultery laws. Of all the issues concerning the institution of marriage that attracted attention during the Revolution, it was in these two areas that women had received the greatest support from the masculine sector of the population, and it was for this reason that their demands became law. In contrast, women's requests for a reduction of the *puissance maritale* over a wife's person and property were met with little but hostility.

It was a rare soul who proposed a complete and untrammeled equality between the sexes, in marriage as in anything else. Condorcet, with the unflinching consistency that characterized his thought, was one of the few who categorically denounced the *puissance maritale* as a tyranny: "The law cannot sanction any authority in husbands," he wrote, "which deprives wives of any of the rights of natural liberty."[45] Olympe de Gouges, with perhaps less consistency but more emotion, shared the same conviction. In 1788 she wrote: "I think that two independent beings . . . whom marriage has united, must be equal masters of their destinies and their actions."[46] One woman even went so far as to petition for the right to continue to bear her own name along with that of her husband. The request was rejected.[47] Only a few acute individuals seemed to be aware that although the Revolution might claim to protect a Frenchman's rights to life, liberty, and property, it did not seem to extend any similar protection to married Frenchwomen. "Hey!" cried Etta Palm d'Aelders in her *Discours sur l'injustice des Lois en faveur des Hommes*; "Our life, our liberty, our fortune are hardly our own."[48]

After the questions of adultery and divorce, a married woman's lack of control over her own property generated the greatest controversy. Women like Olympe de Gouges and Etta Palm d'Aelders, as well as anonymous authors of pamphlets such as *Du sort actuel des femmes* or *Mémoire sur le divorce*, all campaigned for a woman's property rights after marriage. Some argued from a philosophy of sexual equality and the guarantees of the Declaration of Rights, while others, such as the pamphlet *Les Griefs et plaintes des femmes mal mariées*, sought to appeal to their readers' sense of justice.

The author of *Les Griefs et plaintes des femmes mal mariées* was one of several to contradict the popular belief that French community property laws (which, it is noted, did not even apply to all of France) allowed women to share in the fruits of her husband's labor. When, asks the pamphlet, does a wife enjoy these so-called rights? "After the death of her husband," says the author; "And if she dies the first, what has she enjoyed? Nothing. If the husband leaves nothing, then what will she enjoy after his death? Nothing." The pamphlet also attacked the popular idea that a woman is supported by her husband and gives little in return:

The arrears of her dowry, her care of the house, the economy and intelligence with which she aids her husband, in commerce for example, the discomforts of pregnancy, the pains of childbirth, the nurture and education of the children, are they of no consideration? And if she receives some fruits from the community property, are they not legitimately acquired? But how will she enjoy them? At the good pleasure of the lord and master of the community property.[49]

Nevertheless, as interesting as these protests and others like them appear in retrospect, they were actually few in number. The sovereign control of a man over his own and his wife's property continued.

The atmosphere of freedom that characterized the beginning of the French Revolution stimulated criticism not only of the various laws governing the relationship between man and wife, but also of that venerable French institution, the *mariage de convenance*. At all levels of French society, marriages were traditionally arranged. In the upper classes, girls were commony married as soon as they emerged from the convent, somewhere between the ages of sixteen and eighteen. The engagement was usually contracted while the girl was still in the cloister, and many a bride who went to the altar met a groom she had barely seen before.

It was a system that revolted the sensibilities of the adherents of the cult of sentimentalism, and, even before the Revolution, it was regarded with disfavor by many. In his *Système social*, the *philosophe* Holbach roundly condemned what he called the French practice of sacrificing their daughters to the ambition and avarice of their parents. In a style typical of these denunciations, he wrote:

[A girl] is led to the altar like a victim and forced to swear an inviolable love to a man for whom she feels nothing, whom she has never seen, or even detests. She is placed in the power of a master who, content to possess her person for an instant and to enjoy her dowry, disappoints her, neglects her, makes himself odious by his bad manners and lack of regard and who very often, by his example and harshness, pushes her to wrong, as a means to revenge herself on the despot become the arbiter of her destiny.[50]

In 1789 one author called forced marriages "a form of rape, conducted on the altar of Hymen."[51]

Writers often cited arranged marriages as one of the most common causes of the alarming incidence of adultery, and it was also one of the most cogent arguments in favor of divorce. In his 1789 pamphlet, *Observations sur le divorce*, the Comte d'Antraigues contended that as long as people were forced to marry, they should be granted the alternative of divorce. The Comte was wise enough to realize that the French custom of arranged marriages was not likely to be destroyed by the Revolution: "In the National Assembly," he so astutely observed, "the majority of the Deputies are fathers, and however virtuous a father might be, it is rare that while wanting to destroy political despotism, he does not wish to conserve domestic despotism."[52]

The fact was that the practice of arranging marriages continued to maintain a hefty block of adherents. If left to themselves, these partisans contended, girls always make bad marriages. "In general," wrote Ferrières, "You see women prefer a fool to an honest man, a libertine to a lover who has morals."[53] The allegation that women always prefer the most despicable sort of fellows was repeated *ad nauseum*, particularly by men who were themselves rejected lovers. That self-styled *"ami des femmes,"* Boudier de Villement, warned: "A girl will be, from the moment of her entrance into the world, the dupe of a lively and brilliant exterior, and will give her hand to the man the most unworthy to possess it, if the experience that she lacks is not supplied by that of her parents."[54]

The frailty of the female intelligence and powers of judgment was not the only factor that was believed to necessitate parental guidance and control in this area; the degree of independence and self-assertion entailed in the selection of one's own marriage partner was seen by many as simply not compatible with the female condition. Montesquieu was only one of many whose sensibilities were revolted by what was perceived as a shocking eruption of female impertinence and contrariness across the channel, and which was thought to exist as a result of the dangerous English practice of allowing their daughters what struck Frenchmen as an irresponsible degree of influence in the selection of their husbands. Montesquieu, however, decided that such license had to be tolerated in a country like England, since Protestant girls who rejected their parents' choice were denied the alternative course of taking the veil and retiring to a cloister.[55]

In August of 1792, a law was finally passed freeing all children over the age of 21 from the dictates of parental authority, and in some ways this law brought a measure of relief in this respect. But its beneficial effects were felt far more by sons than by daughters, for most girls of the upper and middle classes, at least, had been resolutely led to the altar long before their 21st birthdays were reached.[56]

Intimately connected with the practice of arranging marriages was the French dowry system, for in a society where marriage is above all else an economic contract, the relative wealth of a prospective bride is of paramount importance. Sentimentalists and moralists alike had long denounced this custom as a barbaric ritual, in which young girls of marriageable age were brought to market and auctioned off without regard to their intrinsic personal merit or virtue. The egalitarian spirit of the Revolution only increased the criticism of the dowry system, although the protests were quite as likely to be motivated by disgruntled allegations that a girl's dowry depleted her brothers' potential inheritance, as by sympathy for the fate of the dowerless daughter. Nevertheless, the French custom of dowering their daughters and demanding dowries from their wives continued.[57]

In fact, with the exception of the new laws on divorce and adultery, the institution of marriage remained virtually the same in 1792 as it had been in 1789. The laws on marriage had been written long ago in favor of the male sex, and, as the Comte d'Antraigues pointed out, it is rare that even those who are dedicated to the destruction of political despotism are not equally dedicated to the preservation of their own domestic despotism. In reality, there was actually comparatively little demand for more sweeping changes. Many of the polemics written in favor of equal adultery and divorce laws are couched in terms that could very easily be interpreted as support for a broader equalization of the powers in marriage, but such usually was, in fact, far from their intent.

A classic example of this may be found in Prudhomme's article "*Du divorce.*" The essay begins with sweeping and dramatic periods: "For a long time," says Prudhomme, "[society] has sanctioned the tyranny of one sex over the other; for a long time marriage has only been a sales contract; for a long time man has taken woman like an American planter buys a slave; like the *code noir*, the *code matrimonial* is almost entirely in favor of the master." He continues in much the same vein:

Because the woman leaves her own name to take that of her husband, one demands that she also deprive herself of her individual will; one demands from her a complete abnegation; she must only receive existence from her husband; all for him, she is no longer anything by herself!

Yet despite these unguarded histrionics, Prudhomme was in reality one of the Revolution's most vocal opponents of sexual equality, and he ended his article on divorce by saying:

Let us hasten to restore to women all the plentitude of their most dear and precious rights, that they may dispose of themselves in all liberty, that they may be the absolute mistresses of their choice, and free again to retract it when they judge it proper. A law in favor of divorce will acquit us towards them of all that we owe them and probably shut the mouths of the most exacting.[58]

Likewise, when a man by the name of Sédillez proclaimed, near the beginning of his pamphlet *Du divorce*, that "Liberty and equality do not yet exist in France for women!" he would have been startled indeed at the idea that the situation could only be alleviated by something far more revolutionary than a divorce law that would give women an "equal" opportunity to "free" themselves from an unhappy marriage.[59]

One of the best examples of this reluctance (displayed by some of even the more fervent supporters of women's rights in marriage) to commit oneself to a comprehensive demand for female emancipation can be found in the pamphlet entitled *Les Griefs et plaintes des femmes mal mariées*. This pamphlet begins with a typical appeal to the National Assembly, in which the author seeks to identify and associate the needs and wants of the female sex with those of the downtrodden French masses:

In this confusion of voices which rises and implores the august assembly that represents the nation, will it close its ears to the plaints of that amiable half of the human species. . . ? Will its rights continue to be misunderstood and despised?

As in so many other works of the period, the condition of women is likened to that of slaves: "Like slaves, [women's] persons and goods are, by law, a property of the husband." In fact, the pamphlet proclaims, the condition of wives is actually *worse* than that of slaves, since the dowry requirement in France forces women to pay for the privilege of serving their masters. Surveying the position of women in marriage, the author observes: "In this society, the one is all, the other nothing!" He (or she) also exclaims: "The one oppresses, the other is oppressed, and can never cease to be so."

But the author of *Les Griefs et plaintes de femmes mal mariées* is not as revolutionary as might first appear. When protesting the traditional idea that a wife must meet the mistreatment of her husband with nothing more than modesty and meekness, he or she does say: "The brutal and ferocious man will hardly cease to be so: meekness must not be the sole resource against brutality." Yet the author does not propose that husbands should be denied the right to beat their wives; he or she only wants a law that would "punish the excesses." In another passage, the author actually agrees that the female sex, as the weaker, must be submissive to the stronger (although to be "protected," not oppressed). The pamphlet continues:

One does not hide the fact that the man must be the head of the community, because his faculties, his education, and his intelligence render him more fitting than the woman for administration. He should be the *chef*, but not the master.

At another point the author writes: "One will say [that] women must only be second in rank in the order of society. I agree, but they must never be assimilated with slaves. . . ."[60] The fact is, this author has no desire to end the subordination of women, but only some of the hardships that resulted from it.

Alongside those who, with varying degrees of thoroughness, sought the amelioration of the condition of women under eighteenth-century marriage laws, there were others who were equally committed to an effort to fortify and even extend the powers and privileges enjoyed by the French husband. Many, such as the journalist Mercier, actually believed that the laws of Paris, among others, had given women *too much* power and authority: "As a result of the law," he wrote, "Women have become virtually the mistresses."[61] One man demanded some sort of law that would protect men from the fruits of their wives' adultery, which, under the law of "*pater quem nuptiae demonstrant*," they were forced to acknowledge. "What will be the encouragement of morality and the bonds of marriage in society," he asked, "If the man is entirely subordinate to the vices of a sinful woman. . .? The one on whom rests the extent of political rights," he complained, "will then be only her slave. . . ."[62] In a similar spirit, another man wrote:

After having rendered man free and happy in public life, it remains for you to assure his liberty and his happiness in private life. . . . It is proper, therefore, after the declaration of the rights of man and the citizen, to make, so to speak, the declaration of the rights of husbands, fathers, and sons. . . .[63]

This last suggestion shows, as clearly as anything else, that as far as most Frenchmen were concerned, the Declaration of the Rights of Man and of the Citizen was written as exclusively for the male sex as it was written by it.

NOTES

1. Robert Pothier, *Traité du contract de mariage*, 2 vols. (Paris: Letellier, 1813), Vol. 1, p. 325. On this general subject, see also the secondary works of P. Granotier, *L'Autorité du mari sur la personne de la femme et la doctorine féministe* (Paris: Giard et Briere, 1909); G. Krug, *Le Féminisme et le droit civil français* (Nancy: Imprimerie Nanceienne, 1849); Louis Trenard, "La Famille et la femme dans l'Ancien France," *Information historique*, 43 (no. 5, 1981), 234–240; Francois Lebrun, *La Vie conjugale sous l'ancien régime* (Paris: Armand Colin, 1975); James F. Traer, *Marriage and the Family in Eighteenth-Century France* (Ithaca, NY: Cornell University Press, 1980); Martine Segalen, *Mari et femme dans la société paysanne* (Paris: Flammarion, 1980); Martin Olivier, *La Crise du mariage pendant la Révolution* (Paris: A. Rousseau, 1901).

2. F.-A. Aulard, *Recueil des Actes du Comité de Salut Public*, Vol. 12, p. 720, séance du 2 floréal an II. Children of such unequal marriages always followed the rank of the father. Thus, whether a woman was noble or not, her children would be considered noble only if their father was.

3. Pothier, *Traité du contract de mariage*, Vol. 1, p. 312.

4. Robert Pothier, *Traité de la communauté, auquel on a joint un Traité de la puissance du mari sur la personne et les biens de la femme* (Paris: DeBure, 1770), p. 2.

5. See, for instance, Dinouart, *Le Triomphe du sexe*; Saint-Pierre, *Discours sur cette question*; and Retif de la Bretonne, *Le Gynographe*.

6. Blanchard, *l'Ecole des moeurs*, pp. 180–181.

7. *Encyclopédie*, "Femme, droit naturel," Vol. 6, p. 471. The Chevalier de Jaucourt, author of this article, goes on to remark, however, that it is difficult to show that the husband's power comes from nature, both because such a principle would be contrary to the natural equality of men and because the *ability* to command does not necessarily entail the *right* to do so; he also notes that the male does not always have more strength, wisdom, or intelligence than the female. As a result, Jaucourt concludes that the subordination of the wife in marriage is the result only of civil law and could therefore be changed. In this conclusion he was at variance with most other contributors to the *Encyclopédie*. See, for instance, the article "Mari," Vol. 10, p. 101, which makes heavy use of biblical quotations to support the existence of husbandly supremacy: "The man did not come from the woman, but the woman from the man, and he was not created for woman, but rather woman for the man . . .," etc.

8. Blanchard, *l'Ecole des moeurs*, p. 184.

9. Ibid., p. 182.

10. Pothier, *Traité de la communauté*, p. 185.

11. Retif de la Bretonne, *Le Gynographe*, pp. 101, 102, and 485.

12. Pothier, *Traité du contract de mariage*, Vol. 1, p. 66.

13. Pothier, *Traité de la communauté*, pp. 3 and 5.

14. Ibid., pp. 33–55.

15. Ibid., p. 66.

16. In her position as public merchant, such a woman was considered to have obligated not only herself by these contracts, but her husband as well. Ibid., p. 21.

17. Ibid., pp. 22–27.
18. Ibid., pp. 80–82.
19. Ibid., pp. 2–3.
20. Ibid., pp. 81–93.
21. *Encyclopédie*, "Mari," Vol. 10, p. 102.
22. Pothier, *Traité de la communauté*, pp. 54, 93–94.
23. Pothier, *Traité du contract de mariage*, Vol. 1, p. 67.
24. Ibid., pp. 91–92.
25. Montesquieu, *De l'Esprit des lois*, Book 26, Chap. 8, p. 134. See also the *Encyclopédie*, "Infidélité," Vol. 8, p. 701, and Blanchard, *l'Ecole des moeurs*, pp. 163–164.
26. Pothier, *Traité du contract de mariage*, Vol. 1, p. 81.
27. Mme de Grafigny, *Lettres Péruviennes* (Paris: 1749), pp. 68–70.
28. M. Bouchotte, *Dernières Observations sur l'accord de la Raison, et de la Religion, pour le rétablissement du divorce, l'anéantissement des Séparations entre époux, et la réformation des loix relatives à l'Adultère* (Paris: Imprimerie Nationale, 1790), p. 47.
29. Marquis de Sade, *Philosophy in the Bedroom*, p. 224.
30. Louis-Antoine Saint-Just, *Esprit de la Révolution et de la constitution française* (n.p., 1791), p. 68.
31. Marquis de Sade, *Philosophy in the Bedroom*, p. 223.
32. Olympe de Gouges, *Les Droits de la femme*, pp. 17–18.
33. Charles-Louis Rousseau, *Essai sur l'éducation*, pp. 29–30.
34. *Les Griefs et plaintes des femmes mal mariées*, pp. 17–18.
35. [Hennet], *Du divorce* (Paris: Desenne, 1789), p. 74.
36. Etta Palm d'Aelders, "Adresse des citoyennes française à l'Assemblée Nationale," in *Appel aux Françoises*, pp. 38–39.
37. [Hennet], *Du divorce*, pp. 70–71.
38. [Prudhomme], "Du divorce," *Révolutions de Paris*, Vol. 7, No. 85, 19–21 February 1791, p. 331.
39. Ibid., pp. 335 and 337.
40. Mme Necker, *Réflexions sur le divorce* (Lausanne: Durand Ravanel, 1794), pp. 29, 78, and 86.
41. Ibid., pp. 67–68.
42. Ibid., pp. 63 and 79.
43. *Loi du divorce*, 20 September 1792, Archives Nationales, AD IIᵉ 33.
44. Oliver Martin, *La Crise du Mariage pendant la Révolution dans la législation intermédiaire, 1789–1804* (Paris: A. Rousseau, 1901), p. 164.
45. Jean-Antoine-Nicolas Condorcet, *Déclaration des Droits*, in *Oeuvres,* Vol. 12, p. 265.
46. Olympe de Gouges, *Philosophe corriegé* (1788).
47. *Moniteur*, 3 July, 1790, Vol. 35, p. 34.
48. Etta Palm d'Aelders, "Discours sur l'injustice des lois en faveur des Hommes," in *Appel aux Françoises*, p. 4.
49. *Les Griefs et plaintes des femmes mal mariées*, pp. 18 and 23.
50. Holbach, *Système social*, pp. 350–351.
51. "Duc d'Orleans," *Traité philosophique, théologique et politique de la loi du divorce* (n.p., June 1789), p. 210. If the union was one of love, however, the

author contended that the "woman is justly beneath the yoke, and, remarkably enough, she likes it there."

52. Emmanuel-Louis Antraigues, *Observations sur le divorce* (Paris: Imprimerie Nationale, 1789), p. 17. Sons as well as daughters could be forced into unwanted marriages. One such well-known victim was the Marquis de Sade.

53. [Ferrières], *La Femme et les voeux*, p. 52.

54. Pierre-Joseph Boudier de Villement, *L'Ami des femmes ou Morale du sexe* (Paris: Royez, 1788), p. 172.

55. Montesquieu, *l'Esprit de lois*, Vol. 2, pp. 80–81.

56. As stated above, most girls of the upper and middle classes were married at the age of 16, as soon as they emerged from the convent. The women "of the people" tended to marry later, usually in their mid-20s. This delay was caused by the fact that many had to work to acquire their own dowry, which, presumably, also gave them relatively greater freedom of choice in the selection of their husbands. On this subject, see Hufton, "Women without Men."

57. On this topic see the anonymous pamphlet, *Avis interéssant concernant les jolies filles à marier ou De l'abus des dots dans le mariage* (Paris: Imprimerie de Momoro, 1789); also *Motions adressés à l'Assemblée Nationale en faveur du sexe.*

58. [Prudhomme], *Révolutions de Paris*, Vol. 7, No. 85, 19–21 February 1791, pp. 331 and 339.

59. M. L. E. Sédillez, *Du divorce et la répudiation, Opinion et projet de Décret, Archives Nationales*, AD XVIIIe 192.

60. *Les Griefs et plaintes des femmes mal mariées*, pp. 19–20.

61. See John Lough, "Women in Mercier's *Tableau de Paris*," p. 114, in Eva Jacobs, ed., *Women in Society in Eighteenth-Century France.*

62. *Petition sur les effets des moeurs des épouses dissolues* (Paris: Imprimerie du Lycee des Arts, n.d.), p. 3.

63. Gossin, *Motion sur l'article XII du titre 9 du nouveau project sur l'ordre judiciare,* Archives Nationales, AD XVIIIe 162.

7

The Rights of Women

Learn that one only leaves slavery by a great revolution. Is this revolution possible? It is for you alone to say, because it likely depends on
your courage.

[Choderlos de Laclos, *De l'Éducation des femmes*]

The French Revolution had proclaimed the dawning of a new era, characterized by the reign of liberty and equality for all. In the 1789 Declaration
of the Rights of Man and of the Citizen, and again in the 1793 Declaration presented by Robespierre, the fundamental principles of this new
order were enumerated. The equality of rights was established by nature,
and liberty was defined by Robespierre as "the power that belongs to
man to exercise, at his pleasure, all his faculties." These rights belonged
equally to all men, "whatever might be the difference in their physical or
moral forces." They included the right of every individual to the possession of his own property and to be admitted to all public functions. The
nation was declared sovereign, and it was stipulated that no portion of
the people could be allowed to exercise the power of the population as a
whole.

However defective the Revolution may have been in the application of
these principles to the male population, there was hardly even any
attempt to apply them to the female sector of the nation. The discrepancy
between the wording of the Declaration and its actual practice in relation
to the two sexes is so glaringly maladroit that, in all probability, the
authors who drew up the Declaration of the Rights of Man did not even

110

pause to consider what would have been the incontestable fact that women constituted fully one half of the "people" of France. When they said "man," the authors thought of man the male, not man the human being, simply because the females of their society were always submerged, in both thought and reality, beneath the men in their lives. Yet there were those who read the Declaration of Rights who interpreted it in terms of all of humanity. In a society where both sexes enjoy few stipulated rights, the preference of one sex over the other is far less noticeable than in a situation where the rights of one are very carefully enumerated, to the obvious exclusion of the other. The contradiction in this respect between the principles and the practice of the Revolution, as perceived by a small minority of men and women, motivated some of the most far-reaching and unabashed declarations of sexual equality yet seen in the history of mankind. Under the influence of the Revolution, these men and women were prompted to expand beyond the age-old arguments of relative ability and capacity and into the increasingly relevant and ultimately productive territory of "natural" and legal rights.

By far the most important and influential eighteenth-century advocate of women's rights was the *philosophe* Condorcet. Condorcet had first broached the subject in 1787, in his *Lettres d'un Bourgeois de New Haven à un citoyen de Virginie*. In the guise of a stolid and commonsense-type American republican, Condorcet advocated the implementation of a written constitution. This new constitution was to be founded on what the Enlightenment was so fond of referring to as the "natural rights of man." In Condorcet's conception, these rights were derived from man's existence as a sensible being, capable of reason and accessible to the acquisition of moral ideas. One of the most essential of these natural rights was, of course, the freedom of every individual to vote on all matters relative to the common interest, either personally, or through the agency of an elected representative.

However alarming such ideas might have been to an eighteenth-century monarchist, in its basic conception this theory contained nothing that would have surprised either Condorcet's similarly inclined fellow *philosophes* or the more pedestrian minds that were to become the apostles of the Revolution. But Condorcet carried his philosophy one vital step farther. Fully cognizant of the fact that summarily to exclude some one-half of the human race from any such pretensions to rights and liberty could only serve to undermine irretrievably the credibility of the principal assumptions supporting his entire system, Condorcet unhesitantly extended to women every right that he granted to men. In so doing, he placed himself apart from all other great thinkers of his time, for he was virtually the only one who both perceived the inherent contradiction involved in the exclusion of women and, having once recognized it, made no attempt to shoo it away with sophisms and ingenious excuses.

In *Lettres d'un Bourgeois de New Haven*, Condorcet startled his contemporaries by proclaiming that no true republic had ever existed, because women had never yet been allowed to exercise the rights of citizenship. On what grounds, he asked, do men claim the rights of citizenship? "Is it not in the quality of sensible beings, capable of reason and possessing moral ideas, that men have these rights? Then women must have absolutely the same ones . . .," he said.[1]

It was popularly believed that the participation of women in government was both unnecessary and redundant. Women were assumed to have the same interests and opinions as the men who ruled their lives, and the female sex was repeatedly assured that their husbands, sons, and fathers would always have their best interests at heart. Condorcet flatly denied this comfortable assumption: "The facts have proven that men have, or believe themselves to have, very different interests than those of women, because everywhere they have passed laws that oppress them, or at least establish a great inequality between the sexes."[2] The fact that current civil laws had created a situation in which it could be assumed that women had no will of their own he described as simply "one more injustice." Women must, he insisted, be allowed to vote for themselves. Taking advantage of the American cry of "No taxation without Representation," Condorcet continued: "You admit without a doubt the English principle that one is only legitimately subjected to the taxes that one has voted, at least by one's representatives; it follows from this principle that every woman has the right to refuse to pay taxes. . . ."[3]

Having thus masterfully dismissed all justifications for the denial of women's *droit de cité*, Condorcet then turned to an examination of the eligibility of women for public office. The exclusion of women from any public office, he argued, entails not one but two injustices: first, to the person who is denied a right enjoyed by others, and, second, to the electors, who are denied the right to vote for such a person. Therefore, Condorcet concluded, the law cannot justly exclude women from any public office or position.

The political system envisaged by Condorcet presupposed similar changes in two other areas: first, in civil law, which would have a decided effect on the character of women, and, second, in the laws on education, which would allow women to improve their minds. With these alterations, said Condorcet, "Objections that today seem plausible would cease to be so. . . ." Condorcet did admit that women's physical constitution made them less capable than men of marching off to war; he also agreed that the exigencies of childbearing would, for a portion of their lives, require some women to restrict their activities. But, in all other respects, Condorcet could discern no differences between the sexes that he believed could not be ascribed to their education.[4]

Where men like Voltaire and Diderot had restricted themselves to expressions of condolence on the pitiful lot of women, Condorcet suggested concrete changes. "It is a question," he wrote, "Of the rights of half of the human species, rights forgotten by all legislators." But Condorcet had few illusions about the world in which he lived. He was fully aware that his proposals would probably meet with almost as much opposition from the one sex as from the other: "I am afraid that I will be in trouble with [the women] if ever they read this article," he wrote:

I speak of their rights to equality, not of their *empire*; one could suspect me of a secret desire to diminish it, and since Rousseau earned their approbation by saying that they were made only to care for us and are fit only to torment us, I must not hope that they will declare in my favor. But it is good to tell the truth, even if one must expose oneself to ridicule.[5]

Condorcet's ideas were met by both opposition and ridicule, but he persevered. His support of women's rights to equality was not mere idle philosophy. As a sincere and dedicated humanist, he was profoundly troubled by what he perceived to be one of the most deeply entrenched and least understood prejudices of his day, and he referred to this injustice again and again in his works. When France began to prepare for the convening of the Estates General, Condorcet once more brought up the subject of women's rights.

In his *Essai sur la constitution et les fonctions des Assemblées provinciales*, Condorcet returned to the question of women and the *droit de cité*. No longer speculating on some desirable yet unforeseeable future, but instead discussing a set of elections that were already imminent, in this work Condorcet insisted that women must be allowed not only to vote for the representatives to the Estates General, but to compete for that position themselves, as well. "By this means," he wrote, "women will not be deprived of the *droit de cité*, a deprivation contrary to justice, however authorized by an almost general practice." Condorcet would acknowledge no legitimate reasons for depriving women of this right, a right that, he said, men exercised, not by virtue of their sex, but "in their quality of reasonable and sensible beings, which they have in common with women."[6]

Although he made few converts, Condorcet's works did attract attention. His opponents took to prefacing their reaffirmations of women's traditional position in society with remarks such as "Despite the contentions of *some philosophers* . . ." or "Contrary to the dangerous maxims suggested by *some writers*. . . ." Condorcet had founded his belief in women's rights on their quality as reasoning and moral beings; his opponents countered by saying that women were no such beings. In defense of what was rapidly becoming a campaign with him, Condorcet again took to his pen. The result was the article *"Sur l'admission des femmes au droit de cité,"* printed in July 1790 in the *Journal de la Société de 1789.*

Condorcet begins the article with the observation that both convention and prejudice have habituated not only the vulgar, but even philosophers and legislators, to accept without question a world in which all members of the female sex have been deprived of their natural rights:

Have they not all violated the principle of the equality of rights, by tranquilly depriving half of the human species of [the right] to participate in the formation of the laws, by excluding women from the *droit de cité?* Is there a stronger proof of the power of habit even over enlightened men, than to see the principle of the equality of rights invoked in favor of three or four hundred men whom an absurd prejudice had deprived of them, and to forget in this respect twelve million women?[7]

In order to avoid a charge of tyranny, Condorcet warns that the men of the Revolution would have to prove either that the rights of women were in no way similar to those of men, or, if they were, that women were incapable of exercising them.

Condorcet returns once more to his principle that it is the existence of women as moral and reasoning beings that entitles them to the same rights as men. "Either no individual of the human species has any true rights, or they all have the same ones," he reasons; "He who votes against the right of another, whatever be his religion, color, or sex, from then on abjures his own."[8]

Condorcet then proceeds to enumerate and demolish the age-old rationalizations for the disenfranchisement of women. He makes short shrift of those who would eliminate women on the grounds of their alleged physical infirmities by asking: "Why should beings exposed to pregnancies and passing indispositions be unable to exercise the rights that one has never dreamed of depriving men who suffer from gout every winter, or catch cold easily?"[9] The charge of mental inferiority was less easily dismissed.

Declining an argument on the relative mental abilities of the sexes, Condorcet contends that even if men are capable of greater genius than women (a point that he in no way concedes) that is still not an excuse for denying women the right to participate in government. So what if no woman ever made an important discovery in the sciences, he argues, or showed great genius in the arts? "Without a doubt," he says mockingly, "One does not claim to grant the *droit de cité* only to geniuses." Furthermore, he notes:

Except for a small class of very brilliant men, there is a complete equality between women and the rest of the men; setting aside this small class, [mental] inferiority and superiority is equally divided between the two sexes. Now, because it would be completely absurd to restrict the *droit de cité* . . . to this superior class, why should one exclude women, rather than those men who are inferior to a great number of women?[10]

Condorcet also confronts the popular allegation that no woman, however wise or intelligent, is ever guided by reason:

This observation is false: it is true that they are not guided by the reason of men, but they are by their own. By the fault of the law, their interests are not the same, and the same things do not have the same importance for them as for us; they can, without lacking reason, be determined by other principles and tend towards a different end. It is as reasonable for a woman to take care of the charms of her face as for Demosthenes to take great pains with his voice and his gestures.[11]

Condorcet does admit that most women are more influenced by their feelings than by their consciences, but blames this not on their nature, but on the education they receive and the life they are forced to live. "It is unjust," he writes, "To continue to refuse women the exercise of their natural rights on the basis of causes that only have some sort of reality because they do not enjoy their rights." It would be possible, he points out, to use the same argument to deny the rights of that segment of the population that is forced to work and is unable to pursue an education. "If one admits such principles," he warns, "It is necessary by an unavoidable consequence to renounce any free constitution. The sundry aristocracies have only been founded and perpetuated by similar pretexts." Condorcet likewise rejects the idea that the existence of the *puissance maritale* is an excuse for denying women political rights. This "tyranny" should also be destroyed, he says, and "one unjustice can never be a legitimate reason to perpetuate another."[12]

There remained only those objections based on the theory of utility, and once again Condorcet reminds his readers that such pretexts have long been the excuse of tyrants. To those who contended that women already have too much influence over men as it is, he replies that such influence is far more redoubtable in private than in public:

Since up until now women have never in any country been admitted to an absolute equality, and since their *empire* has nevertheless existed everywhere, and since the more women have been degraded by the law the more dangerous it has been, it appears that one must not have much confidence in this remedy.[13]

If women were allowed to act openly in public, Condorcet contends, they would not be forced to seek such devious means in private. The allegation that women cannot be admitted to politics because no gentleman would argue with a lady in public he dismisses as absurd.

The most formidable of all the objections based on utility was the contention that the participation of women in public life would distract them from the duties of wife and mother. It is this argument that Condorcet finds most difficult to answer. He does so not by denying that women are destined for a domestic existence, but by repudiating the belief that the acquisition of equal rights would lead all women to automatically abandon home, husband, and child. In the actual nature of things, he points out, only a very small percentage of citizens are ever actively engaged in government: "One would no more tear women away from their homes than one would tear the farmers from their plows or the artisans from their ateliers." A woman's domestic responsibilities might be a reason not to prefer her in an election, but, he maintains, "It can never be the foundation for a legal exclusion."[14]

Condorcet returned to the question of women's rights once more before his death, in his *Esquisse d'un tableau historique des progrès de l'esprit humain*. Proscribed along with Girondins and hounded by the Jacobins, Condorcet maintained to the end his unswerving belief in progress and the perfectability of the human condition.

In his last work, Condorcet identified the age-old inequality in the rights of the sexes as one of the greatest impediments to the progress of the human spirit. As a "fecund source of injustice, cruelty, and crime," he wrote, sexual inequality reduces the relationship between the sexes to one founded on the privileges and hypocrisy of pride and maintained by a fear of shame and retribution. "The pride of the strong," he said, "easily leads him to believe that the weak was created for him, but that is neither the philosophy of reason, nor that of justice." Reiterating his belief in the absolute equality of rights between the sexes, Condorcet insisted that not only justice but the "common good" requires that this equality be respected in the laws, institutions, and, in fact, all parts of the social system.[15]

Although Condorcet was the only intellectual of any stature to champion the cause of sexual equality, his thoughts echo through the works of a scattering of less-known or even anonymous authors. There survives only a handful of pamphlets that appeared at the beginning of the Revolution and that go beyond the type of immediate demands in the areas of employment, education, and marriage that characterized works such as *Les Griefs et plaintes des femmes mal mariées* or the *Petition des femmes du tiers-état au Roi*, to develop an actual philosophy of equality between the sexes.

Condorcet's influence is probably most easily discernible in the 1792 pamphlet, *Du sort actuel des femmes*. "Half of the human race," writes the anonymous author, "is deprived of its natural rights." It is a situation, we are told, to which both men and women have become so accustomed as to accept it as natural. The result has been the corruption and debasement of both sexes. But our author is indebted not only to Condorcet, but to the Enlightenment Conspiracy Theory as well. We are told that the denaturing of the sexes was some sort of masterful plot concocted by priests and the political tyrants of old:

They inspired a taste for the extreme virtues and created false ones, for fear that the native virtues would upset their designs. They persuaded women, by an excess of sensibility, to seek their merit and happiness in servile dependence. Following the same views, they excited men to callousness and pride, by according them excessive power, by permitting them disorder in morality and dominion. To create submissive victims, and arrogant victims, ready to serve and to fight for them, behold what the artificial usurpers who have too long burdened the nations did and still do.[16]

The author explains that women have been misled by "false homages," which only "seem" to restore to them what they have lost, and, thus betrayed, they have abandoned themselves to frivolity and idleness. The only way to restore morality, says our author (who is almost certainly female) is to give women their rights. Again echoing Condorcet, she says:

If one wants health, strength, justice, and virtue, one wants morality; if one wants morality, women must acquire honor; if one wants women to acquire honor, it is necessary to give them their rights, and their property, all as holy, all as sacred, as are the rights and property of men.[17]

Yet, instead of being given their rights, asks the author, how have women been compensated for what she calls "that most sacred duty" of bearing and raising children? Is it with honors? No, she answers. Is it with education? No. Is it with wealth? No; even their own goods are forfeited the instant they agree to fulfill this function, she replies. In reality, women are, she writes, "without rights, without property, without position, without power."[18]

Now that France has declared the Rights of Man, the author contends, the situation has become even worse, for instead of including women in its application, "One hears . . . with ostentation," she says, "that the rights of women were not included there; that women are nothing and cannot be anything else. . . ." This author does not want women to be pitied; she simply wants them to be given their rights. Yet, instead of giving them rights, she protests, the Revolution does not even seem to consider women citizens. Descending from the general to the particular, she quotes Article 29 of the penal code, which condemns "women, girls, and foreigners" to the stocks in cases where French men are punished by civil degradation. "Yes, sirs," she accuses; "No doubt without wanting to, you have assimilated French women and girls with men who are strangers to the *patrie*." What! she asks, "Are women not citizens?"[19]

An even earlier Revolutionary pamphlet to approach a philosophy of sexual equality was the *Cahier des doléances et réclamations des femmes, par Mme B... B...* (which also appeared as the *"Cahier des doléances et réclamations des femmes du departement de Charente,"* reprinted by Mme Vuignerias). Writing in 1789, this author is full of enthusiasm and optimism for the Revolution. Dwelling less on the causes of inequality than on its effects, she is confident that although the "centuries of ignorance" had deprived women of their inheritances, left them uneducated, and denied them participation in government, with the coming of this glorious Revolution women will no longer be told that it is their duty to "work, obey, and keep quiet."

Unlike Condorcet, Mme B... B... does not proclaim the right of women to participate at all levels of government. She does, however, insist that women must be allowed to vote and to represent themselves in assemblies. The idea that women can be represented by male *procureurs* she utterly rejects, saying:

It has been rightfully demonstrated that a noble cannot represent a commoner, or the latter a noble; for the same reason a man cannot, with more equity, represent a woman, because the representatives must have absolutely the same interests as those they represent. Women can therefore only be represented by women.[20]

The inequality in the moral firmity expected of each sex also comes under her fire as another result of prejudice and an example of inequality:

Perverse and unjust men! Why do you require from us more firmness than you have yourself? Why impose dishonor on us when, by your maneuvers, you have been able to make us susceptible and thus obtained your end? What right have you to claim that we must resist your importunate entreaties, when you lack the courage to control the irregularity of your passions?[21]

In education, inheritance and even morality, the law, she says, must be uniform for both sexes.

Although not solely devoted to the question, another Revolutionary pamphlet that protests the eighteenth-century inequality of the sexes is the anonymous *Offre généreuse des dames françaises du Tiers Etat, ou Moyen de rétablir les finances en 24 heures*, also published in 1789. In all ages, writes the author, men not only have forbidden women to act in both public and private affairs, but they have even denied them the right to think or reason about such matters. "If a woman should venture to talk to her husband about public affairs, the operation of finance, . . . administration, etc.," complains the author of the pamphlet, "he tells her:

'Take care of your house; that is your sphere; only masculine heads are organized for science and affairs.'[22] Taking offense at the constant Revolutionary tendency to refer to women as wives, sisters, and daughters, the author reminds her readers that men are also husbands, brothers, and fathers—yet that does not prevent them from being recognized as citizens, or being considered worthy to work for the public good. Since women have proven their ability in philosophy, letters, government, and business, it is wrong, she says, to claim that they lack aptitude. Declaring man and woman to be "two beings of the same species," she says: "It is time, at last, that things change, and that we regain our rights. . . ."[23]

An even more militant espousal of the cause of women's rights can be found in the anonymous *Remontrances, plaintes et doléances des Dames Françaises, à l'occasion de l'assemblée des Etats-généraux.* Writing in 1789, the author begins by denying the pretensions of the Estates General to the claim that it represents all of France:

One would wish to persuade us that this respectable assembly . . . as it is presented to us, can truly represent the entire nation, while half and more of the nation, does not sit there, is exluded from it. . . .[24]

She also denies that women can trust to their fathers, husbands, sons, and lovers to protect their interests: what she calls "the pride of their sex, and their attachment to the ancient prejudice of their claimed superiority" would, she contends, soon tempt them away from any such self-sacrifice. Is it not possible, she asks, for women to form their *own* assembly? Do not women have their own religious communities, nobility, and third estate? Women cannot, insists the author, justly be denied all knowledge and influence in government, and she warns all members of the male sex:

Know you well . . . you would have much to fear from a decree of the council of State of French Women and the whole feminine species, which would shatter and annul all your fine operations; you are ignorant of to what point the resentment of women can go.[25]

The author also accuses men of having deliberately denied women an education and kept them ignorant in order to ensure their continued submission. And when is this done, she asks, but in an age that calls itself "enlightened"? She ends with the expressed hope that one day, perhaps, women will have their rights restored to them with interest. This pamphlet is so belligerent, in fact, that it might actually have been intended as a satire.

In addition to the works of these anonymous authors, all of the more famous female Revolutionaries, such as Claire Lacombe, Théroigne de Méricourt, Pauline Léon, and others, left interpretations of the revolutionary rhetoric of equal rights and freedom that included women. Some of the best presentations of these beliefs came from Etta Palm d'Aelders and Olympe de Gouges.

Etta Palm presented most of her ideas in the form of speeches, which, after she was accused of counterrevolutionary activities and conspiracy, she eventually collected together and published under the title *Appel aux Françoises, sur la régéneration des moeurs et nécessité de l'influence des femmes dans un gouvernement libre*. One of her first speeches was a "Discourse on the injustice of the laws in favor of Men, at the expense of Women," which she read at the Federal Assembly of the Friends of Truth in December of 1790.

She began her speech by congratulating Frenchmen for having allowed women to join their clubs and help to fight for the Revolution, two improvements that she called "the first shock" to the prejudices and despotism that oppressed women. But this was not enough for Etta Palm. "Justice must be the prime virtue of free men," she said, "and justice requires that the laws be common for all beings. . . ." Instead of justice, however, she found that "everywhere the laws are in favor of men, at the expense of women, because everywhere the power is in your hands." Women were left uneducated and given only a "secondary existence" in society, with the result, she protested, that they were forced to the humiliating necessity of earning by ruse and seduction what they should have exercised as a right. Do you think, she challenged, that we value success and fame any less than you? She also reminded the men of France that women had helped to make the Revolution as much as they had. She then asked them if they would have said to the women at the Bastille: "Abandon your just reclamations. You are only born for slavery; nothing can free you from the need to eternally obey an arbitrary will." Etta Palm could not seem to believe that the "glorious Revolution" could continue the abuses of the centuries of ignorance. She pleaded with the men: "Oh! Sirs, if you want us to be zealous for the happy constitution that gives men their rights, then begin by being just towards us."[26]

In her *"Adresse de la Société patriotique et de bienfaisance des Amis de la Vérité aux quarante-huit sections,"* Etta Palm turned her criticism to the custom that restricted women to domestic chores and eternal dependence:

Deprived of a civil existence, submitted to the arbitrary wills of their nearest, even in the secret penchants of the heart; slaves at all times and at all ages: girls, to the will of their parents; wives, to the caprices of a husband, of a master; and when chance seems to have freed them from every despotism, that of the servile prejudices with which their sex has been surrounded, still keeps them bowed before its laws; thus, from the cradle to the grave, women vegetate in the form of slavery.[27]

But she once more reiterated her assurance that in the "new order of things" the situation of women was certain to improve.

In speech after speech, Etta Palm again and again referred with undeterred optimism to the "glory" that she was so sure France would acquire by being the first to establish sexual equality. In a letter read to the Friends of Truth in March 1791 she exclaimed: "Glory, immortal glory to the legislators of France, to have given [women] their rights. . . ."[28] She optimistically heralded the first steps they had already taken in this direction by freeing women from convents (which she called "those odious caverns where you were forced to smother the gentlest sentiments of the heart") and by ensuring them equal inheritance. In her *"Adresse des citoyennes françoises à l'Assemblée nationale"* (precipitated by the infamous Article XIII of the police code), she said confidently: "You have restored man to the dignity of his being by acknowledging his rights; you will no longer leave women beneath an arbitrary authority—that would be to reverse the fundamental principles on which rests the majestic edifice that you have raised." Philosophy, she announced, had delivered truth from the shadows: "The hour sounds: justice, sister of liberty, calls all individuals to the equality of rights, without difference of sex." At least until 1793, Etta Palm remained sure that Frenchmen would not make "slaves" of those who had contributed to their liberty.[29] Then, threatened with arrest, she found it prudent to retire to her native Holland.

The most thorough and pointed application of the principles of the Declaration of the Rights of Man to the condition of women was undoubtedly made by Olympe de Gouges, who wrote a Declaration of the Rights of Woman. It appears unlikely that Olympe ever read any of the works of Condorcet on this subject: she never mentions him as a champion of equal rights for women, and none of his more recognizable arguments appears in any of her writings (she was never one to hesitate to borrow the ideas and even the words of others).[30] Her devotion to the cause of sexual equality was derived from her belief in the capacities of her sex, and her dedication to the principles of the Revolution. The Declaration of the Rights of Woman was born from her perception of the contradiction that existed between the essence of these principles as formulated by the organs of the Revolution and the blatant way in which the female sex was so obviously excluded in their application.

Les Droits de la femme is patterned after the more famous original, and its form gives order and direction to Olympe's usually flamboyant and wandering style. It is a declaration of what she calls the "natural, inalienable, and sacred rights of women." Borrowing even the wording of her model, Olympe subtly alters and enlarges it, at every step demonstrating and underscoring the extent to which the mandate of the Revolution had ignored and betrayed one half of the population of France. The first three articles are especially effective:

ARTICLE PREMIER
Woman is born and remains free and equal with man in rights. . . .

II
The end of every political institution is the preservation of the natural and imprescriptible rights of Man and Woman: these rights are liberty, property, security, and above all resistance to oppression.

III
The principle of every sovereignty essentially resides in the nation, which is only the union of Woman and Man; no corps, no individual may exercise authority which does not expressly emanate from it. . . .

She continues in the same vein: the law is "the expression of the general will," and all citizens and "*citoyennes*" must have the right to contribute to its formation; the law must be the "same for all," with "all equal" before it; men and women must be equally eligible for all honors, offices, and public employments (Article VI). Article X contains probably her most famous line (not an original one, however):

Woman has the right to mount to the scaffold; she must equally have the right to mount to the Tribune.[31]

Olympe contends that if the Revolution is to remain true to its principles, then women must enter into the plentitude of their rights. If all men (interpreted in the sense of species, and not gender) are born free and equal, then that must mean that women are equal to men, and being equal they must have the same rights. Therefore, she concludes, any law or custom that deprives a woman of her property, denies her rights to an equal education or equal employment opportunities, prevents her ability to exercise her free will or her right to resist, is counterrevolutionary. A full and unhesitating application of the Rights of Man as amplified by Olympe de Gouges would have revolutionized French society in a way its authors never imagined and certainly never intended. But if the rights of women were not respected, Olympe warned, then the Revolution would not succeed.

The *Droits de la Femme* is followed by a lengthy "post-amble," in which Olympe de Gouges calls her sex to action: "Women, wake up!" she cries; "The tocsin of reason is making itself heard." Accusing men of having used women's help to free only themselves, she now charges them with injustice:

Oh Women! Women, when will you cease to be blind? What advantages have you received in the revolution? A more marked contempt, a more pointed disdain. . . . If they persist in their weakness, to [deny you rights] in contradiction with their principles, courageously oppose the force of reason to the vain pretensions of superiority; unite beneath the standards of philosophy; deploy all the energy of your character, and you will soon see these arrogant men, not servile adorers rampant at your feet, but proud to share with you the treasures of the Supreme Being. Whatever might be the barriers with which they oppose you, it is in your power to free them; you have only to wish it.[32]

The one advocate of women's rights who was second only to Condorcet in scholarship and originality was not a Frenchwoman at all, but the Englishwoman Mary Wollstonecraft. The child of a genteel but profligate father, Wollstonecraft had been forced at an early age to earn her own living in a society that was not at all hospitable to penniless young ladies. An enthusiastic partisan of the French Revolution, she wrote a reply to Burke, and eventually moved to Paris to enjoy the whole experience first-hand. Her *A Vindication of the Rights of Women* was written in hopes of inspiring her adopted nation to extend the application of its principles to include the female sex; translated into French, it was published in 1792, running to several editions.

Unlike Condorcet, who founded his philosophy of equal rights on the principles of justice and natural rights, Mary Wollstonecraft meets the enemy in their own territory and bases her arguments on utility. It is her contenton that if woman "is not prepared by education to become the companion of man, she will stop the progress of knowledge and virtue. . . ."[33]

Although   developing   her   thesis   with   arguments   of   utility, Wollstonecraft does not hesitate to have recourse to those of justice, as well. Addressing herself to Talleyrand (to whom she dedicated a later edition, in response to his *Rapport sur l'instruction publique*) she says:

Consider . . . whether, when men contend for their freedom, and to be allowed to judge for themselves respecting their own happiness, it be not inconsistent and unjust to subjugate women, even though you firmly believe that you are acting in a manner best calculated to promote their happiness? . . . In this style, argue tyrants of every denomination. . . .[34]

She calls the exclusion of women from participation in the "natural rights of mankind" a "flaw" in the new French constitution and warns that women will never be forcefully confined to domestic concerns but must always, however dangerously ignorant they are kept, manage to interfere in the affairs that one seeks to forbid them.

The bulk of Mary Wollstonecraft's work is a biting, satirical attack on her age's perception of and attitude towards women. What emerges is, for its day, a masterful sociological and psychological study of the causes of the subjugation of women and its effect on the characters of both sexes. She accuses her society of "considering females rather as women than human creatures," as though they were not quite part of the human species, but something strangely alien and different. It is the state of ignorance in which women are kept ("under the specious name of innocence") that Wollstonecraft blames for much of the folly and weakness for which men satirize and condemn them. Woman is treated, writes Wollstonecraft, as if "she was created to be the toy of man, his rattle, and it must jingle in his ears whenever, dismissing reason, he chooses to be amused."[35] Wollstonecraft complains that women are not only denied the opportunity to cultivate their reason, but they are also repeatedly told that it is not in their best interest to do so. "Confined . . . in cages," she says, "like the feathered race, they have nothing to do but to plume themselves, and stalk with mock majesty from perch to perch. It is true that they are provided with food and raiment . . . but health, liberty, and virtue are given in exchange."[36] To liberate them, Mary Wollstonecraft would not only grant women full and equal educational opportunities, but she would also open access to numerous new areas of employment. As it is, she says, virtually the only means of subsistence open to women is prostitution, either of the common or "legal" variety (by the latter she means marriage). The degree to which women are forced to depend on men, insists Wollstonecraft, humiliates and degrades them. Women will never be truly virtuous, she argues, until they can exist independently of men and acquire self-respect.

Mary Wollstonecraft also rejects the eighteenth-century notion that the virtues of women are distinct and different from those of men. The virtues of the sexes must be the same, she reasons, otherwise virtue is a relative idea, and she harshly castigates Rousseau, who would have women revel in their weakness and cunning. Wollstonecraft agrees, however, that it may take a long time to convince women that it is really not in their best interest to be weak, and that "the illegitimate power, which they obtain by degrading themselves, is a curse, and that they must return to nature and equality. . . ."[37]

Returning again and again to the need to educate women, Wollstonecraft argues that it is the gift of improvable reason that distinguishes man from the animal and that, as human beings, women must be allowed to cultivate their minds ("for a gift is a mockery if it is unfit for use"). She sardonically concedes that the education of women will end their blind obedience to their husbands ("The *divine right* of husbands, like the divine right of kings, may it is to be hoped in this enlightened age, be contested without danger. . . .") as well as their meek submission to the unjust laws of society, but she insists that there can be no such thing as virtue without knowledge. And to be truly virtuous, she argues, women must also share equal rights with men:

Let women share the rights, and she will emulate the virtues of man; for she must grow more perfect when emancipated, or justify the authority that chains such a weak being to her duty—if the latter, it will be expedient to open a fresh trade with Russia for whips: a present which a father should always make to his son-in-law on his wedding day, that a husband may keep his whole family in order by the same means; and without any violation reign, wielding this sceptre, sole master of his house, because he is the only being in it who has reason:—the divine, indefeasible earthly sovereignty breathed into man by the Master of the Universe. Allowing this position, women have not any inherent rights to claim; and, by the same rule, their duties vanish, for rights and duties are inseparable.[38]

Although Condorcet had predicted in 1787 that his support of equal rights would find little favor with the female sex, those few writers who joined him in the advocacy of sexual equality were far more likely to be women than men. One of the few males to join the cause was Pierre-Mark-Augustin Guyomar, author of *La Partisan de l'égalité politique*.

Guyomar began his treatise on sexual equality by asking the question: "Is the Declaration of the Rights of Man common to women?" His answer was "yes." Then what, he asked, is the "prodigious difference" between the Sexes? Guyomar could find none in their characteristic traits, and he could not conceive how a mere sexual difference could create a corresponding difference in rights: "What! Would that be the line of demarcation traced by nature between the sovereign and the subject parts of the human species?" he asked; "In that case women are born and remain slaves . . .," which, he said, was an obvious contradiction of Article II of the Declaration. It was common in literature of this type to compare the subjugation of women to the enslavement of the Negroes (who had been declared free and equal by the Revolution), and Guyomar reasoned that a condemnation to slavery based on the differences between the sexes was no better founded than one based on color:

A white skin, a black skin, no more characterizes exclusion from the sovereignty of the human species than a male sex, a female sex. . . . All or nothing, behold the alternative that the partisans of equality and liberty can and must propose. In this great cause, half-means are as illusory as they are derisory.[39]

Inexorably running through the various articles of the Declaration of Rights, Guyomar insisted that women had an equal right to their personal safety and property, as guaranteed by Article II. He also drew attention to Article III, which stated that no one corps could represent the entire nation:

Either one of two things, either the nation is composed of men and women, or it is only composed of men. In the first case, the men form a corps, against the spirit of the article; in the second case, women are the helots of the Republic.

If women were not considered to form a part of the "general will," then, Guyomar contended, they were under no obligation to obey any of the laws to which they had neither directly nor indirectly concurred. "I maintain," he wrote, "that half of the individuals of a society do not have the right to deprive the other half of the imprescriptible right to express its will." By what right, Guyomar demanded, were women excluded? By the law of the strongest? If that was the basis of its new government, he warned, then France had no need of either legislators or a constitution.[40]

Calling the subjugation of women "a crime of *lèse-humanité*, which fouls even the land of liberty and equality," Guyomar urged his fellow countrymen to destroy what he termed "this barbarous and feudal prejudice." Reiterating the "feudal" nature of this custom of sexual inequality, Guyomar accused the male sex of being even more unjust than the *seigneurs* of old. "Blush," he told them, "for your ridiculous feudal error":

This liberty, this equality belongs equally to man and to woman, or truly the immortal declaration of rights contains a mortal exclusion. Then I see [the existence of] a privileged caste, an aristocracy formed of men. . . .[41]

In support of his declaration of sexual equality, Guyomar concluded his essay with a defense of the capacities and abilities of the female sex. He accused men of judging women "by the companions of your debauches, or by badly raised dolls." He turned their attention instead towards the women of the lower classes, who, he pointed out, worked both long and hard at a variety of jobs, or to the successes of those women who had been allowed to dedicate themselves to literature and education. He even pointed to the reigns of the Queens of England and Russia, who, he noted, had shown themselves as capable of making themselves loved or hated as men. How, he asked, could the "free French" refuse to allow women to be magistrates, when even the enslaved Russians allowed them to become Queens? Returning again to the Declaration of Rights, Guyomar directed his countrymen's attention to Article VI, saying:

The French who have abolished privilege, and proclaimed the aptitude of every individual, according to his talents, to all places, can they without the most monstrous inconsistency establish an exclusion injurious to women?

If women were denied the rights of citizenship, Guyomar contended, then "the name of *citoyenne* is only a ridicule, and must be struck from our language." He also denounced the idea that a husband could and did vote for his wife: a man is no more capable of voting for his wife, said Guyomar, than he is capable of eating or drinking for her. Noting that women were treated as equal to men when punished for a criminal act, he denied that a distinction based on sex could justifiably be applicable in one case but not in the other. Such injustices might have been tolerated in the past, but the nation proposing to establish "the new order" could not, Guyomar said, continue to leave women languishing in the old; "Defenders of liberty," he urged his countrymen, "let us proclaim that of women."[42]

There were only a few other men who spoke out in favor of political equality for women, and most of these hesitated to commit themselves to the same extent or with the same intensity as Condorcet and Guyomar. Charles-Michel Villette would have admitted women to political assemblies, but only if they were over 25, and unmarried or widowed.[43] David Williams, an Englishman whose enthusiasm for the Revolution had carried him to Paris to participate in it, believed that women should be allowed to vote, although he, too, restricted this right to unmarried women or widows. Williams also believed that women should be allowed to sit on juries, but only in cases involving a member of the female sex.[44] In his *Projet d'acte constitutif des Français*, Francois Chabot took a somewhat opposing view, restricting the female right to vote to those women who were *"mères de famille."* In Chabot's plan, such women would also be eligible for magistratures, but only those of security and education, and once again their participation on juries would be restricted to cases involving their own sex.[45] The citizen Lanjuinais was another who proposed extensive rights for women, but only at some unspecified future date. He found the moral tone of the women of his day quite shocking, and was utterly appalled at the excesses being committed by the fair sex in the course of the Revolution. He did not seem to find similar male excesses sufficient cause to deny the natural rights of men, nor did he seem to find it unjust to deny women rights on the basis of what Condorcet called "causes that only have some sort of reality because they do not enjoy their rights."[46]

The more the Revolution talked about the Rights of Man, the more women became aware of their own subordinate position in society, which, it was becoming more and more obvious, the Revolutionaries had little or no intention of improving. "We are all equal, you say," wrote one woman to Prudhomme in 1790; "Why then such a cruel difference? Because I am a girl, I have no pretensions towards my parents' property, and I must live in misery, while my brother peacefully enjoys a property that by natural right I should share with him."[47] In a speech before the National Assembly, another woman laid claim to equal consideration for her sex, saying: "If you propose to break the bonds of servitude, you cannot leave these captives . . . equally born for liberty."[48] Women's enthusiasm for the Revolution, so marked in 1789, began to wane to the extent that it actually occasioned comment. In 1791, *Le Courrier de l'hymen*, a woman's journal, wrote:

Several days ago a man expressed surprise that so many women are opposed to this revolution. One could respond to him: but what has this revolution done for them?[49]

The man in question was probably Prudhomme, who had written an article in response to the number of women who had complained to him about the Revolution. He said they had written him "many letters," saying

that for two years it seems as if there is no longer but one sex in France. In the primary Assemblies, in the sections, in the clubs, etc., it is no more a question of women, than if they did not exist.[50]

It was a sentiment echoed by many women, in speeches, pamphlets, and letters to newspapers. "Oh, my poor sex," wrote Olympe de Gouges, "Oh women, who have acquired nothing in this revolution. . . ."[51] A short-run journal, *L'Observateur féminin* (later "*l'Etoile du matin, ou les Petits Mots de Madame de Verte-Allure, ex-Réligieuse*"), proclaimed in 1790: "The word liberty has finely resounded in all mouths . . . our sex alone has not felt its effects." In another issue, the editor protested: "Sex, jealous of your rights; men, aristocrats who have always made us bend beneath a scepter of iron; we also wish to be free, and to escape your despotic yoke. . . ."[52]

As the sole acknowledged privileged caste left in France, the male sex easily left itself vulnerable to charges of "aristocracy." In her letter to Prudhomme, Blaudin Dumoulin urged him to retract his repressive plans for the female sex, which she called "as despotic towards women as that of the aristocracy towards the people. It is time," she said, "to reestablish [women] in their natural dignity. Eh! what virtue can you expect from a slave!"[53] In her pamphlet on female unemployment, Mlle Javotte wrote:

It will be easy for me to make you understand that the Revolution has done nothing for the poor women, that the inequality of advantages perpetuates at their expense the masculine aristocracy; and that, forced to see in you the privileged sex, they consider themselves as the second order in the Kingdom, since the abolition of those of the clergy and the nobility.[54]

An article in the *Courrier de l'hymen* remarked on the number of women who had complained that they were not even allowed on juries, saying: "That is one of the greatest proofs that our legislators are aristocrats because they reserve for one single part of the human species, the power to judge both. By what right . . . are men exclusively the arbiters of our destinies?" As Olympe de Gouges and others had done, the article reminded French men that women had helped to make the Revolution:

Do we deserve to be treated with this injustice, in a Revolution in which we have had such a part? Do not the men remember having seen us at the attack on the Bastille, on the road to Versailles, and on the field of the Federation? Let them take care to arouse our courage! We have made them free, we can put them back in chains.[55]

NOTES

1. Jean-Antoine Condorcet, *Lettres d'un Bourgeois de New Haven à un citoyen de Virginie* in *Oeuvres*, Vol. 12, p. 20.

2. Ibid., pp. 20–21.

3. Ibid., p. 21.

4. Ibid., p. 24.

5. Ibid., p. 27.

6. Ibid., p. 36.

7. Condorcet, *Sur l'Admission des femmes*, p. 1.

8. Ibid., p. 2.

9. Ibid., p. 3.

10. Ibid., pp. 3–4.

11. Ibid., p. 6.

12. Ibid., pp. 7–8.

13. Ibid., p. 9.

14. Ibid., pp. 10–11.

15. Condorcet, *Esquisse des progrès de l'esprit humain* in *Oeuvres*, Vol. 8, pp. 45, 359–568.

16. *Du Sort actuel des femmes* (Paris: Imprimerie du cercle social, 1792), p. 6.

17. Ibid., p. 8.

18. Ibid., pp. 8–9.

19. Ibid., pp. 11–13.

20. *Cahier des doléances et réclamations des femmes, par Mme B... B...*, p. 5; it would appear, however, that she is only supporting the right of unmarried women and widows to vote.

21. Ibid., pp. 6–7.

22. *Offre généreuse des dames françaises du Tiers Etat, ou Moyen de rétablir les finances en 24 heures* (August, 1789), p. 7.

23. Ibid., pp. 2–3.

24. *Remontrances, plaintes, et doléances des dames françaises, à l'occasion de l'assemblée des Etats-généraux, par M.L.P.P.D. St. L., 25 mars 1789* (n.p., n.d.), p. 2.

25. Ibid., p. 4.

26. Etta Palm d'Aelders, "Discours sur l'injustice des lois en faveur des Hommes, au dépense des Femmes, lu à l'Assemblée Fédérative des Amis de la Vérité, le 30 décembre 1790," *Appel aux Françoises*, pp. 2–3, 5, and 6.

27. Etta Palm d'Aelders, "Adresse de la Société patriotique," *Appel aux Françoises*, pp. 41–42.

28. Etta Palm d'Aelders, "Lettre d'une amie de la vérité sur les demarches des ennemis extérieures et intérieurs de la France; suivie d'une adresse à toutes les citoyennes patriotes, et d'une motion à leur proposer pour l'assemblée nationale, lue à l'assemblée fédérative des amis de la vérité, le 23 mars 1791," *Appel aux Françoises*, p. 29.

29. Etta Palm, "Adresse des citoyennes françoises à l'Assemblée Nationale," *Appel aux Françoises*, pp. 37 and 38.

30. Although in her *Pronostic sur Maximilien Robespierre*, she does accuse Robespierre of wanting to "assassinate Condorcet."

31. Olympe de Gouges, *Les Droits de la femme*.

32. Ibid., pp. 12–13.

33. Mary Wollstonecraft, *A Vindication of the Rights of Women* (London: Johnson, 1796), p. vi. The text cited here is from an English edition.

34. Ibid., p. ix.

35. Ibid., pp. 3 and 66.

36. Ibid., p. 118.

37. Ibid., p. 38.

38. Ibid., p. 451.

39. Pierre-Mark Guyomar, *Le Partisan de l'égalité politique entre les individus ou Probleme très important de l'égalité en droits et de l'inégalité en fait* (Paris: Imprimerie Nationale, n.d.), pp. 2–4.

40. Ibid., pp. 4–6.

41. Ibid., pp. 5 and 10.

42. Ibid., pp. 11 and 20.

43. Villette, *Mes Cahiers*, p. 40.

44. David Williams, *Observations sur la dernière constitution de la France avec des vues pour la formation de la nouvelle constitution* (Paris: Imprimerie du Cercle Social, 1793), pp. 16–17.

45. Francois Chabot, *Projet d'Acte Constitutif des Français* (Paris: Imprimerie Nationale, n.d.), pp. 10, 12, 14, 16, 22, 25.

46. M. F. Alengry, *Condorcet, Guide de la Révolution française, théoricien du droit constitutionnel et précurseur de la science sociale* (Paris: V. Giard and E. Brière, 1904), p. 215. Allengry credits Condorcet with thoughts similar to Lanjuinais, in contradiction to Condorcet's own works on the subject.

47. [Prudhomme], *Révolutions de Paris*, Vol. 2, No. 26, 2–9 January 1790, p. 31.

48. *Motions adressées à l'Assemblée Nationale en faveur du sexe* (Paris: Imprimerie de la Vᵛᵉ Delaquette, 1789), p. 10.

49. *Le Courrier de l'hymen*, No. 7, 13 March 1791, p. 28.

50. [Prudhomme], *Révolutions de Paris*, Vol. 17, No. 83, 5–12 February 1791, p. 226.

51. Olympe de Gouges, *l'Esprit françois*, p. 12.

52. *L'Observateur féminin*, No. 1, 15 March 1790, p. 1; No. 2, 18 March 1790, p. 1; despite its title, this journal has been attributed to a man.

53. [Prudhomme], *Révolutions de Paris*, Vol. 15, No. 189, 16–23 February 1793, p. 367.

54. Mlle Javotte, *La pauvre Javotte*, p. 6.

55. *Le Courrier de l'hymen*, No. 1, 20 February 1791, pp. 2–3.

8

The Beginnings of Reaction

There are some slow people who do not march with their century, but
one must agree, Madames, that you are advancing ahead of yours.
[Anonymous, *Avis aux Dames*]

The advocates of equal rights for women formed a small but deter-
minedly vocal minority in the French Revolution. Nevertheless, it
became more and more apparent as time passed that, however
unknowingly, these proponents of sexual equality had set themselves in
opposition to the mainstream of Revolutionary thought. Refusing to
agree with them, and unable to ignore them, the Revolution could only
react to them. This reaction initially took the form of informal satires, but
it gradually expanded with a growing disapproval of the political activity
of Revolutionary women until it reached its culmination in a direct
refutation of the entire philosophy of sexual equality.

The satires appeared as early as the first days of the Revolution. Issued
in pamphlet form, they can be classified, for the purposes of study, into
four major varieties or categories, although some pamphlets could and
did incorporate elements of up to three of the categories.

The first and most easily defined category of satires consists of those
pamphlets that were highly erotic in content, often to the point of being
pornographic. In the atmosphere of the virtual collapse of censorship that
accompanied the Revolution, sexual as well as political license flourished
in print. Many of these erotic pamphlets purport to originate from the
Palais Royal (well known as the haunt of Parisian "*filles publiques*"), and

they make extensive use of a number of *doubles entendres* of doubtful taste. The second variety of satires is sometimes less easily recognizable and includes those works that make veiled attacks on the Revolution by writing in the guise of foolishly naive and enthusiastic female supporters. These are closely related to those of the third category, which are pro-Revolutionary pamphlets, written in the guise of avaricious and selfish female opponents to the Revolution who supposedly despair at the loss of their *empire* occasioned by the advent of stern revolutionary morality. The fourth group consists of pamphlets that are not overtly erotic and more directly satirize the demands being made by some women for sexual equality, mainly by carrying those demands to extremes that seemed, in that age at least, utterly ridiculous. It is this fourth type of satire that has misled the most historians, and it is not unusual to find them being discussed as serious examples of eighteenth-century "feminism."

Of the erotic satires, some of the most successful were those in a series that followed from a pamphlet that appeared even before the convening of the Estates General, entitled *Procès verbal et protestations de l'assemblée de l'ordre le plus nombreux du royaume, les C....* In this pamphlet, the cuckolds of France, as the most numerous order of society, announce that they have gotten together and issued their demands and suggestions for the improvement of the nation. Although ostensibly intended as a joke, some of the articles included address themselves to issues that were taken very seriously at the time. For example, in order to make women "less capricious, vaporous, crotchety, lazy, expensive, proud, and imperious," and in order to encourage girls to be chaste and desirous of pleasing, the pamphlet suggests that the institution of the dowry should be abolished. All women should also be forced to do their own housework and to raise their own children, rather than going out to risk their honor at the gaming table and the opera. Furthermore, women who have another source of income should be forbidden to compete with the prostitutes, who must be left some means of making a living. Any woman who flatters herself as a *"bel esprit"* or an author should be condemned to return to her needle, since, explains the pamphlet, "experience has proven that what they acquire on the side of knowledge, they lose on the side of chastity, and, believing themselves above prejudices, they brave scandal by principle." The "cuckolds" then end by demanding that all bachelors should be forced to marry, since "it is particularly to them that the order of the C... owes its existence. . . ." There follows a long list of only half-disguised "signatures," including, among others, that of Retif de la Bretonne.[1]

This satire spawned a long line of successors, such as the *Second procès-verbal de l'assemblée de l'ordre le plus nombreux du royaume*, an *Assemblée de tous les bâtards du royaume,* and a *Réponse des femmes de Paris au cahier de l'ordre le plus nombreux du royaume.* The latter complains that the cuckolds have no proof to substantiate their accusations; the response to this assertion was the *Nouvelle Assemblée des notables cocus de Royaume, en présence des Favoris de leurs épouses, appellés pour certifier du cocuage de chacun des membres composant ladite assemblée*. This pamphlet contains an undisguised list of cuckolded husbands, complete with the names of the men who have certified them, which runs to 40 pages and includes such well-known names as Calonne, the duc d'Orleans, La Fayette, and de Staël.[2]

Another addition to this running "joke" is the *Délibérations et protestations de l'Assemblée des honnêtes citoyennes compromises dans le procès-verbal de celle de l'ordre le plus nombreux du Royaume*. This Assembly originally meets divided in orders, in mock imitation of the Estates General, but the women soon decide to join forces ("since the two classes are already intermingled in bed"). The entire pamphlet is couched in terms strongly reminiscent of the rhetoric used by authors advocating greater equality between the sexes, derisively incorporating both their phraseology and style. One woman complains of the treatment she has received at the hands of her husband after his name appeared on "the list":

In this day, when one pleads with such force the cause of liberty, shall we not make an effort to recover our own, shall we be the only slaves who foul the soil of France? Why should this half of the nation wear irons, while the other half only wears horns? If Frenchmen run after the rights of a free people so much today, then Frenchwomen, for their part, [should be able] to obtain these two objects . . .: *divorce and liberty*.

To bring about this new order, the Assembly sets to work writing its own *cahier*, calling for a "revolution" that would improve the condition of women ("always oppressed") by employing in their favor all the ideas of "reason, nature, and liberty" that are illuminating the century. The women faithfully trust that the male sex will agree to renounce its "physical advantages" in order to "submit voluntarily to the law of reason" and "enter without opposition" into the new reign of "equality prescribed by nature." Article One of this "cahier" would free women from "the yoke of servitude beneath which they have languished for so many centuries." The "cahier" also calls for the destruction of the "gothic prejudice" requiring wives to be faithful and demands the institution of divorce and an end to the penalties imposed on bastards. It also suggests that any lover who seduces another man's wife and talks about it should have his tongue cut out. The "Assemblée des honnêtes citoyennes" is then joined by a deputation of prostitutes, who add their names to the inevitable signatures.[3]

Another group of erotic satires, which are far more pornographically inclined than those purportedly published by the cuckolds and their kin, is the large number of pamphlets ostensibly attributed to the prostitutes of Paris. Some, such as the *Requête des filles de Paris à l'Assemblée Nationale* or the *Grande et Horrible Conspiration des demoiselles du Palais-Royal contre les Droits de l'Homme*, are almost purely pornographic. Others, like the pamphlet entitled *Les Demoiselles du Palais Royal aux Etats Généraux*, are similar in intent, but much of their wording is deliberately and provocatively reminiscent of more serious contemporary feminine literature. This particular pamphlet begins with a familiar contention: "All the citizens are allowed to inform you of their complaints and their projects," the "demoiselles" complain; "You have all the grievances of the masculine element of France on your desk. . . . Shall we then be the only ones, sirs, who have nothing to say to you?" After this, however, the tone of the pamphlet rapidly deteriorates.[4]

The *Déclaration des droits des citoyennes du Palais Royal* is another erotic satire that also manages to mock more serious demands for sexual equality. The very first article of this "Declaration of Rights" is oddly reminiscent of Olympe de Gouges' *Rights of Women*, which, however, it predates: "Women are born equal to men and, like them, free," it says; "If they are born free, they must remain free until their last sigh." Since liberty includes the right of property over one's person, says Article II, then women should be free to do with their persons as they see fit. This philosophy is expanded in Article III, which contends that "if men are free to go to women, then women must be free to receive them." The "*citoyennes*" also want to be "free" to practice their trade whenever and where ever they please, without being constrained to pay their customary recompense to the police.[5]

Most of these erotic satires were written in a spirit of fun, oddly rare in this age, which took itself so seriously and generally lacked a healthy sense of the ridiculous. Their satire is directed more toward the Revolutionary assemblies and the various griefs, complaints, and ingenious systems they produced than against the female sex itself. But whatever the intent, its effect was unfortunate. However much of a coincidence it might have been, the similarity in wording between these mock prostitutes' plaints and the very real grievances of the female sex as a whole could only serve to discredit the latter. Women have always been peculiarly vulnerable to association with that class of females which is forced to pander to all male whims merely to stay alive, and ridicule can be a deadly weapon indeed.

Other satires of this period were conceived with a more serious intent. Some were anti-revolutionary and sought to discredit the movement by associating its supporters with naive and very silly females. A good example of this type of satire is the *Lettres de la Comtesse de... au Chevalier de....* This pamphlet purports to be a collection of highly ridiculous letters written in favor of the Revolution by a very foolish

Comtesse. She is finally brought to the sense of her folly by her father, who tells her, among other things:

Women must not mix in the great concerns that one discusses today. Neither their nature nor their education have prepared them for it. They generally have a lot of kindness and no sense of justice, excessive sagacity and no reflection. They feel more than they think. They see nothing in affairs but the individuals and are governed by their affections . . . they even only do good by intrigue. Therefore their qualities are injurious to public affairs, their faults disastrous, and their influence dangerous.[6]

Conversely, there were other satires that sought to support the Revolution by associating its *opponents* with the female sex, portrayed this time not as weak and foolish, but as grasping and power-mad. These satires were some of the first to portray women as the inherent enemies of the Revolution, and they drew on the long tradition that held women responsible for the corruption of society and government under the *Ancien Régime*. In the new era of stern Republican morality, it was popularly believed that women would be deprived of any further opportunity to exercise their famed talents for intrigue, and these satires helped to promulgate the idea that female vanity was piqued by this loss of former influence and illegitimate power.

The *Très Humbles Remontrances des femmes françaises* is typical of this type of satire. By deliberately echoing the phraseology of the pamphlets that were seriously protesting the female sex's lack of political rights, the satire manages to associate women's demands for political power in the new government with their disgruntlement over the loss of the influence that they supposedly exercised in the old. In this pamphlet, the "women" begin by insisting that they, too, have the right to voice their "grievances," along with everyone else. But it soon turns out that their main grievance is the loss of their former ability to scheme and intrigue. They complain bitterly against the "injustice" of men, who secretly confide everything to women but publicly ignore them ("by a base jealousy"). While begging the French to abandon their plans to establish such a "cold" and "austere" system of administration as a Republic, the "women" simultaneously demand to be admitted to governmental office. This satire also uses another popular ploy, that of portraying women who are interested in politics and equal rights as scornful of the more traditional members of their sex and contemptuous of the sacred role of wife and mother. The women of this satire assure their readers that they will not allow such banal considerations as home and children to deter them or to interfere with their ambitions:

One must not judge Women by a few such as which one rarely encounters. This simplicity of morals is the resource of weak minds; this respect for domestic duties is the veil with which one envelops her incapacity; for them, the nation is reduced to their family; the Kingdom is concentrated in their house; and these minds, of such a low level, are well confined to household affairs. But those are not the women we propose to call on. . . . We have no children, or if we do have some, we will arrange things so that we are not inconvenienced by them. . . .[7]

These same tactics form part of the arsenal of the fourth main category of satires: those pamphlets whose primary intent was to ridicule contemporary revindications of women's rights. Laughter was a typical response to the idea of sexual equality, particularly in the years from 1788 through 1790, when most of these satires were published. But in these pamphlets the laughter is forced, and it portrays an underlying sentiment of anger and fear, which would eventually come to be expressed openly in outright denial of what was at first treated only as an object for ridicule.

These satires sought to discredit women's complaints and demands by either exaggerating them or trivializing them. Some such works are so similar to the serious demands for sexual equality appearing at the same time that historians disagree markedly over which pamphlets should or should not be classified as satires. It is generally safe to assume, however, that any author who pretends to regret the passing of women's former influence and intrigue, makes erotic innuendos, disparages the sacred name of motherhood, claims that women cannot "keep silent" at this moment (in obvious reference to their reputation for talking too much), says that the nation has need of their "wise counsels," and demands that the masculine gender be abolished or that women be allowed to wear pants, is writing a satire.

Some satires used sexual innuendos to discredit women's demands for equality. A good example is the *Requête des femmes, pour leur admission aux Etats généraux, à Messieurs composant l'Assemblée des Notables*. This pamphlet begins with the familiar feminine complaint against women's "outrageous" exclusion from the Estates General (despite the sex's well-known interest in government, of course), but these "women" are confident that "French gallantry" will correct this abuse. In faithful imitation of the models it mocks, the pamphlet proclaims:

Women have suffered long enough: the end of our slavery has arrived, and it will no longer be said that of the twenty-four million people who inhabit France, more than half do not have the right to be represented at the Estates General.

If admitted to equal rights, the "women" are confident that they could do much to improve the nation. To begin with, they have some very good ideas on how to increase the French birthrate. They also think that they would do quite well leading the armies—no need to fear that they would turn their backs when meeting the enemy. Women would also make very good ambassadors and spies (for obvious reasons), and so on. In fact, the pamphlet proclaims, women already do much to help the nation—their luxury and changing fashions stimulate trade, and their charms are used to soften men's fiercer passions—yet all they get in return is "black ingratitude." With words deceptively similar to those of serious works of the time, the pamphlet complains:

> Man is born egotistical. . . . It was not enough to deprive us of the sceptre and to close to us the access to all places, he also gave us a futile education, he presumptuously assumed for himself an insolent superiority and, by a ridiculous contradiction, left us in the particular an ascendency of which he deprives us in public. All our study, according to him, must be to please him, and we are perfect when we have attained this marvelous end. In vain did nature give us the spirit for intrigue, and all the seduction necessary to succeed; he aspires to reduce us to the management of his house. . . .

The pamphlet then demands that equal numbers of men and women should be named as representatives to the Assembly. Any girl or woman over 15 years of age who has "known" (in the Biblical sense, of course) a citizen of France is eligible to vote. From that point on the pamphlet rapidly degenerates to the level of pure pornography.[8]

One comparatively innocuous satire of this variety is the *Cahier des représentations et doléances du Beau Sexe, au moment de la tenue des Etats généraux*. This "assembly of women" begins by denying that they talk too much and lays claim to being the "friendliest" part of the nation, besides being capable of enlightening it if people would only just listen to them. "The *Beau Sexe*" then presents a long and curious list of laws that it would like to see promulgated, including one that would permit women to obtain a separation from their adulterous husbands, and another that would allow women to avoid paying their dressmakers' bills. They also would like to see any noble woman who acts and dresses like a whore degraded, while any prostitute who gives herself the airs of a lady should be locked up, and so on.[9]

Other satires of this type were more openly vicious. Both the *Protestations des Dames françaises, contre la tenue des Etats généraux* and the *Lettre de ces dames à M Necker, suivie de Doléances très graves* juxtapose women's demands for political rights with lamentations over the loss of their former "corrupting influence."

The *Lettre de ces dames à M Necker, suivie de Doléances très graves* begins innocently enough, with the protest that some twelve million women also live in France, and should be represented:

> . . . your assembly, the so-called Estates General, where men of all ranks and states have the right to sit, and where it appears that you do everything exclusively for their happiness, has none of us the right to be consulted on what should be done for ours?

Not only have they been denied representation in this assembly, complain the "women," but even their salons have been deserted. "Before," it was the women who set the tone of society, but now men forget them and bore on forever about useless things like the Third Estate. In fact, say the "women," it is enough to give them the vapors, the way their sex seems to be forgotten, as if they "were created only to contribute to the pleasures and amusements of these sirs." The "women" also bemoan the loss of their former influence at court:

Will we be allowed to hope to see again those precious times when . . . without regard for merit or real services . . . our sex distributed in handfuls gratuities, pensions, and employments, to proteges, favorites, and intimates of all kinds, in proportion to the services they rendered us, the pleasures they procured us, the presents they made us. . .?

Indeed, say "the women," their "grievances" against the male sex are infinite. "What will become of our sex's *empire*?" they ask, "Of the power of our charms?" Then (overcoming their natural tendency to talk for a long time) the "women" present their demands. They want, first of all, to establish an Academy of Fashion, to forbid any kind of tax on luxury goods, and to be relieved of the necessity of wearing black when in mourning. They also want to be allowed to wear pants (to show off their figures) and to drive through the streets of Paris as fast as they care to without the need to worry about the life or limb of pedestrians. Furthermore, the Salic law should be abolished ("as injurious to our sex"), and any woman who degrades herself by doing housework and taking care of her children should be relegated to the level of the Bourgeoise and not be admitted to the Academy of Fashion.[10]

The *Protestations des Dames françoises, contre la tenue des Etats prétendus généraux* is similar in tone and content. These "women" announce that they have overcome their natural reticence in order to speak up for the good of the nation, despite the contempt that seems to have left them forgotten at this decisive moment. Proclaiming that "Might does not make right," they demand that the injustice that has excluded women from the Estates General be corrected (so that they may take their place in government and subject all its decisions to their "superior judgment").

Dwelling wistfully on their former influence, the "women" complain that "times have changed." Frenchmen have now become serious instead of frivolous, they despise luxury, and they "intolerably refuse" to recognize "the Sex's right to lead and enlighten men in governmental affairs." The "women" then list all the "evils" that have resulted from their loss of former power and, in response, they issue the following protests:

1 Against the false and outrageous title . . . taken by the assembly of the Estates General; 2 Against the insult that refuses to recognize the rights of the Sex. . . .[11]

Another satire that is so similar to sincere contemporary pleas for sexual equality that it has deceived more than one historian is the *Requête des dames à l'Assemblée Nationale*. This author achieves his semblance of reality by simply lifting entire passages almost verbatim from the works he is satirizing. Thus we are told (as by Mme B... B...) that a golden age is dawning: the black slaves are to be freed, and kings will walk with commoners: "Oh! Sirs," cries the pamphlet, "Will we then be the only ones for whom the age of iron will always exist. . . ? Will we be the only ones not to participate in this brilliant regeneration that is going to renew the face of France . . .?" Having proclaimed the end of despotism and liberty for all, says the author, you have left women in chains; having declared equal rights for all, you have unjustly deprived half the population of theirs. Having granted everyone the right to speak, accuses the pamphlet, you have forced women to remain still; having decreed that dignities and honors are open to all, you have continued to exclude the female sex. Yet this apparent sincerity is belied when the author says, in true satirical fashion:

Is it not [women] who, sacrificing without pain their most precious interests, abandoning the shameful work of the distaff and the trivial and irksome care of the home to vulgar hands, come every day and, with indefatigable constance, ennoble and decorate the tribunes of the French Senate with their presence, direct its work, excite its courage, prevent its errors, applaud its success?

The satirical nature of this pamphlet is also clearly revealed in the inevitable "plan for decree" that is appended to it. The author calls upon France to correct the "ancient" and "unjust" abuses that have excluded women from the dignities and honors of government (for "six million years") by passing "her" recommended decree. According to the decree, all privileges of the masculine sex are to be abolished, and women are to have the same liberty, advantages, rights, and honors as men; the French language is to be altered accordingly; wives are to have equal power and authority with their husbands; women will be allowed to wear pants; cowards will no longer be made to wear women's clothes as a sign of their disgrace, but instead be declared neuter. Women should also be admitted to the assemblies (where they "will take great care to speak one at a time, so that people can more easily understand the fine things that depart from their mouths"), and they should be made magistrates so that they can use their beauty on the bench. Women likewise should be admitted to the army (so that France will be "veritably invincible"), and, so that justice will truly be done, the marshal's baton should be alternately shared by the sexes.[12]

With its faithful imitation of the phraseology and tone of the models it mocks, this satire is by far the most deadly. By subtle alteration, it manages to attribute feminine protests to vanity and pique, while by juxtaposing their very serious demands with the trivial (such as the punishment of military cowards) or with the ridiculous (such as the demand that the marshal's baton be arbitrarily shared), it manages to discredit them all.

Like the more forthright denunciations that followed them, the satires are good indicators of more than one aspect of the reception given to Revolutionary demands for sexual equality. For a number of people, the idea of women sitting in assemblies or enjoying equal authority with their husbands was so highly hilarious that it was treated as a good joke. And in this respect, the satires not only revealed the nature of the eighteenth-century reaction, they also helped to form it. For instead of being taken seriously, those women who did dare to advocate change were laughed at and made the objects of crude sexual suggestions and insinuations.

Yet there is also a darker side to the satires. Many of them, especially those specifically directed against women's claims for equality and recognition, betray a deep-seated, age-old male fear and hatred of the female sex. Women are portrayed as vain and foolish, yet somehow also simultaneously cunning and dangerous. What emerges most clearly is a continuing inability on the part of at least a segment of the male sex to accept women as people like unto themselves; they figure instead as alien beings and as such are treated with hostility and suspicion. The popular myth that women both conquered and corrupted the *Ancien Régime* figures largely in the satires, as does the corresponding idea that women must therefore be intrinsically hostile to the Revolution and all that it stands for. In this respect, the satires contributed to and fostered the growing belief that women (along with priests) were the enemies of the Revolution.

The satires also discredited the movement for women's rights by associating the female sex's very real grievances with the trivial, foolish, or even deliberately provoking ideas presented in the satires. Thus, demands for equal rights for women came to be associated in the popular mind with sexual promiscuity, the disparagement of the feminine roles of wife and mother, and a movement to force all women to wear pants.[13]

The majority of the pamphlets satirizing women's various protests and demands appeared from the years 1788 through 1790. After that time the hostility, which had always been there, came more and more often to be expressed openly, either in the form of criticism of politically active women or by direct denial and repudiation of their demands for sexual equality.

In the early days of the Revolution, most men had been both encouraged and gratified to see women taking such an active interest in the Revolution. The myth of the female sex as the enemy of the Revolution had not yet taken hold, and no one could have denied that women played a vital part in the various *journées* that periodically rocked Paris and kept the momentum of the Revolution going. Yet the seeds of reaction were already there. In 1788, an anonymous author published a pamphlet entitled *Avis aux dames*, in which he complains of the participation of the female sex in the public protests that greeted the suppression of the *parlements*. Women are told that such activity is against their nature: the resistance they make to love is "charming," says the author, but female resistance to authority "disfigures you, it disjoints your traits, it causes the somber and disastrous fire of conspiracies to spread in your eyes, where only decency and gaiety must shine." Women may have always thought that they had the right to decide the fate of books or plays (lightly passing judgment on them "without thought or principles"), but now, accuses the author, they seem to think they have a right to do the same with government edicts, and they are using the same methods. Nevertheless, he tells them, they are advancing ahead of their time: "We are not yet at that transmission of faculties, which confounds the species and puts women in the place of men. . . ." He then, with surprising foresight, warns them against the future they seem to be so eagerly seeking: "The Graces, transformed bourgeois-fashion into *mères de famille*, will become pure repopulation machines: take care, the republican government is cold and severe."[14]

As an obvious monarchist, such an author might perhaps be expected to criticize the political activity of women headed straight for revolution, but he was only the first of many who would lament the political activity that was "denaturing" women. In 1790, Louise-Felicite Robert complained that instead of being "weak and timid," women were abandoning their "essential" qualities of "fear and pity" and boldly assembling in public places to incite men to mayhem and murder. Chaste and moral females are, she says, timid; only "fallen women" are so "hardy, audacious, and cruel."[15]

Even women who were initially praised and congratulated for their patriotic zeal gradually became the objects of criticism and abuse. Etta Palm, who had once had her speeches applauded and who had at one time been ceremoniously awarded the cockade, was accused of trying to stir up trouble.[16] When she led a deputation of women to the legislature in April of 1792, the journalist Prudhomme responded with a long article of condemnation and rebuttal. "In the style of the Lacedaemonians" (who were persona non grata to most Revolutionaries), says Prudhomme, these women dared to take up the legislators' time with promises to teach the Declaration of Rights to their children, to revive the spirit of domestic morality, and to guard against the plots of counterrevolutionaries (a typical revolutionary melange). But this was not all, says Prudhomme, with which these women "distracted" the legislators, who were occupied with "far more important things." First, they demanded the institution of divorce. To this Prudhomme replies:

Nothing is more just, more urgent even, than a law on divorce, but it is not for the women to elicit such a decree; the reserve of their sex forbids them any step in this respect; an unhappy wife should die at her post, rather than leave it for an instant to complain about it. . . .

In response to the women's request for better education for their sex, Prudhomme decides that the petitioners must have spoken without reflection. He agrees that men, who are destined for public employment, need to be educated at school; but the housework and domestic details that are a women's destiny are best learned at home. As for the women's desire that their age of majority be reduced to eighteen, Prudhomme also finds that ridiculous: since they pass from the power of their parents to that of their husband, he says, women have no need for any age of majority. But it is for Etta Palm's demand for equal rights that Prudhomme reserves his greatest scorn. A proper wife, he says, would never want to leave her home to take a seat in the legislature, and a good mother would never abandon her son's cradle to go make a motion in favor of divorce or women's education. These petitioners, he decides, cannot be on a mission that has the approval of the majority of their sex.[17]

Olympe de Gouges also came in for more than her fair share of ridicule and assault. Her plans for the funeral of the Maire d'Etampes were met with the response that "the honor of women consists in cultivating in silence all the virtues of their sex, beneath the veil of modesty and in the shadow of retreat. It is not for women to show men the way."[18] In December 1792, Prudhomme called her a "*mouche du coche*," a busybody. He found her "amusing" and "ridiculous" and reported that, not content to shrug their shoulders at her posters, the people tear them down and say: "Why does she meddle? She would do better to knit some pants for our brave *sans-culottes*!" Prudhomme then adds, rather maliciously, that this was not the opinion of the legislator Condorcet, who thinks that both sexes should be admitted to all assemblies and state offices. Says Prudhomme:

Imagine two hundred women like Olympe de Gouges seated at the Convention beside Bishop Fauchet, the author de Faubles, de Chabot, d'Egalité, Condorcet even. . . . We leave to our readers the pleasure of calculating the results.[19]

Prudhomme obviously finds the whole idea a very good joke.

Thérogine de Méricourt, once so honored for her mission to the Lowlands and her part in the assault on the Tuilerius, also became the object of attack. In 1791 she was satirized in an erotic pamphlet entitled *Julie, the philosopher, or the good patriot, a very nearly true history of an active citoyenne, who was by turns agent and victim in the last revolutions of Holland, Brabant, and France*. In April 1792, she was denounced at a session of the Jacobins, and when she tried to defend herself, she was dragged away.[20]

Even the idea of women joining together in their own clubs and societies began to seem contrary to the best interests of the Revolution. Prudhomme, for one, was revolted by the idea of women holding meetings according to rules, electing presidents, and recording their minutes. Such women were told to go home and take care of their families, "in the name of the *patrie* . . . in the name of nature . . . and in the name of good domestic morality of which the women's clubs are the scourges. . . ." Prudhomme also asks these women to reflect for a moment on what would happen to the republic if all Frenchwomen followed their example: "There would be clubs everywhere and no well-kept houses," he says.[21] Nor was Prudhomme the least bit abashed when a number of women's clubs wrote in to inform him of all the good works that they performed. He answers that the Roman women did not elect presidents or secretaries, and that Frenchwomen should not try to be better than the Romans. Upholding Rousseau as his source, Prudhomme also tells the women that Julie would never have taken her children to their clubs, and Emile would certainly never have let Sophy go to one. "Madame president," he claims Rousseau would have told them; "Concern yourself with the government of your house, and let us take care of the Republic; leave the Revolution to men . . . why are you meddling?"[22]

When Théroigne de Méricourt tried to organize a club among the women of the faubourg Saint-Antoine in 1792, she created a veritable uproar among the men of that district. The tide of masculine outrage carried a delegation before the Jacobins, where the ill-used husbands denounced Théroigne as "the general of the *'incullottées.'*" Highly indignant, they complained that:

This She-devil in ruffles . . . has decided to form a club, to which she attracts all our wives three times a week, engages them in civic feasting that deranges their brains and puts them in full insurrection; since then they have the devil in them, all our households are disrupted, and there is much there that does not please us: we want neither the Théroigne, nor her dog of a club.[23]

From the first days of the Revolution, women had enjoyed the right both to petition the Assembly and to appear personally at the bar, but eventually even these privileges came to be threatened. Delegations of women to the Assembly began to be greeted with amused condescension or stern rebuffs. When a group of women from St. Suplice appeared before the legislature in November of 1791 to denounce the clandestine religious services being held in their district, they were curtly told to leave such matters to their husbands and the magistrates.

Motivated by this incident, Prudhomme published his article "*Des femmes pétitionnaires*," in which he would deny women the right not only to vote and participate in government, but even to have a single independent political thought in their heads. The man who once described in glowing terms the ceremonial gift of jewels made by the women of France to the National Assembly now says that those very women would have done better to have stayed at home and made their gesture through the intermediation of their husbands and fathers. Women are compared to hothouse plants, too delicate to be exposed to the "storms of publicity." The proper place for them is in the home, not at the bar of the Assembly. As Prudhomme explains it,

... each sex has its duties well specified, and morality always suffers when one of the two sexes trespasses on those of the other: to each its functions, its habits, its way of life. The laws of modesty consign women to the home. . . .[24]

Prudhomme would have his readers believe that there is no need for women to appear in public, since a good woman adopts the very same religion and political opinions as her family, reposing complete, blind confidence in the wisdom of her men. When some readers wrote in to complain that a vigorous enforcement of his principles would reduce women to "purely passive beings, veritable automats," Prudhomme not only refused to retreat from his position, he actually expanded it: "What would become of society itself," he asks, "if the women . . . abandoned their homes to go argue with our theologians, or to deliberate with our legislators?" Women lack the depth of understanding necessary to comprehend such matters, he says: "Good God! Where would we be, if women did not adopt with confidence the doctrine of their father or husband!" Prudhomme also vigorously denies that such a system would reduce women to a passive role; it would simply relieve their frail minds of the heavy burden of contemplating such "dry, arid topics" (which are "too abstract and complicated" for them to understand anyway), he says, and allow them instead to concentrate on properly fulfilling their assigned duties:

A woman capable of experiencing pleasure anywhere but beside her child is an indifferent mother, ready to become cruel. A wife who haunts the popular assemblies, who also wants to say her word and make her motion in a public place or club, is rarely of the disposition to abandon these attentions . . . to show that deference . . . which makes the peace of a home and the happiness of a wise and sensible husband.[25]

The message is clear: good wives and mothers stay at home.

The reaction against the idea of politically active women was accompanied by a corresponding repudiation of the philosophy of equal rights for women, which so many of them advocated. It is important to realize that the French Revolutionaries did not fail to grant women equal rights merely because it never occurred to them to do so. They were perfectly aware of the female sex's claims to equality, and they did not simply ignore those claims: they categorically rejected them.

That a number of women were unhappy with their position in society was well known, as was the fact that many of them had expected the Revolution to do something about it. In 1791, one man observed that:

Some [women] . . . are happy with the lot left to them . . . but the greatest number believe themselves injured, and do not cease to cry against the injustice, the tyranny of the strongest, and await the moment of a revolution to complain.

The moment has come, but not to contradict the wise plans of good nature, by yielding in a cowardly manner to the wounded vanity of women without principles. . . .[26]

His attitude was typical.

The men of the Revolution had no need to discover new rationalizations to explain their rejection of women's right to equality; they simply repeated and adapted every reason that had ever been given in the past to explain the age-old subordination of women in society. In his *Essai sur l'éducation et l'existence civile et politique des femmes, dans la constitution française*, Charles-Louis Rousseau broaches the popular question of women in politics, and notes that throughout history women have been denied public office. He then asks, why is this so? His answer: "Women, by being born with supple organs, a delicate mind, an excessive tenderness, and peaceful tastes, appear made for the domestic joy of society and not for the movement of camps or the discussions of counsels." Furthermore, he says, their pregnancies and feminine maladies eliminate women from both the active life and the in-depth study such roles require. So what is a woman's true destiny according to Charles-Louis Rousseau? "To give the *patrie* children, form them by a good education and good example, make a husband happy and maintain . . . the charm of society."[27]

The same arguments of mental and physical incapacity appear in an article written by Prudhomme in support of the movement to exclude women from the Regency. Prudhomme also asks on what principle women have been traditionally excluded from political functions. He finds his answer in the will of nature, which, he says, did not create women to fulfill these functions. Such tasks require a "force of intelligence and a reasoning ability" which, according to Prudhomme, women lack. Their constitution is "feeble and delicate," and their delicate mental organs "produce only a succession of subtle and glib ideas, but none of the strong and sustained conceptions" so necessary for political life. Nature has assigned to each sex its own proper role, says Prudhomme:

Women are born for domestic virtues and cares. Their task does not extend beyond that, and when they wish to escape from that circle, they only present a phenomenon that is often bizarre and rarely authorized by nature.

Despite the widespread use of the word "*citoyenne*," Prudhomme observes that, under the French constitution, women are not really citizens. "They have no political character," he continues. So how, he asks, can women of royal blood be any more capable than the others of being magistrates? The answer is that they obviously cannot be, and Prudhomme insists that there is no middle ground: either women should not be allowed to become Regents, or Frenchmen must be willing to let their mothers, daughters, wives, and sisters come to sit beside them and vote in their assemblies. Having delivered this home-truth, Prudhomme evidently felt that he had clinched his argument.[28]

The Revolutionaries also used the argument that women's participation in politics was unnecessary. In his *Projet de Constitution*, Lanjuinais says: ". . . it is difficult to believe that women must be called to the exercise of political rights . . . everything considered, men and women would gain nothing good by it."[29] Although Condorcet and others had denied it, the idea persisted that women were already represented in government in the person of their men. In response to those readers who claimed the need for women to appear in public to represent the special needs of their sex, the *Révolutions de Paris* answered:

Citoyennes! What! Are we not then your natural representatives, legitimately charged with your affairs. Can we have interests separate from yours? Are you not a part of us? Did we not swear the civil oath in your name at the same time as in ours? Many of you wanted to say it themselves; they were wrong, because this step seems to set a distinction between your rights and ours. Stay in your place, do not leave your homes, and be persuaded that your presence can add nothing. . . .[30]

In apparent contradiction to the vehemence with which it found it necessary to try to convince women to stay out of politics, the journal also argued that women really have no interest in public affairs:

Women have never shown that sustained and strongly pronounced taste, that ardour for civil and political independence, to which everything cedes, which inspires men to such great deeds, and such heroic actions: it is because civil and political liberty are, so to speak, useless for women and, consequently, must be foreign to them.[31]

Others believed that female participation in politics was not only unnecessary, it was actually dangerous. This was a combination of the growing myth that women had ruled and ruined the *Ancien Régime*, and the already age-old belief that men's inability to resist women's beauty and seductiveness already gave the female sex far too much power. In the *Actes des Apôtres*, the journalist Beuvin wrote: "What a wise policy, sirs, that excludes women from the legislative assemblies in France! Otherwise, the decrees would no longer be the results of opinions, but of love. . . ."[32]

A lengthy portion of Prudhomme's 1791 article "On the Influence of the revolution on women," is devoted to an attempted refutation of Condorcet's essay on the admission of women to the *droit de cité*. Prudhomme's arguments are basically those of utility and the natural division of labor, but he also betrays a widespread, growing fear that the Revolution and the ideas it disseminated were irreparably damaging the female character he knew and loved so well. He pleads with women not to envy men their "painful" public duties or the "perilous" honors that are their recompense. "*Citoyennes!*" he cries; "Whatever happens, cultivate in peace and silence your virtues . . . they are no less precious for being obscure." Like so many others, Prudhomme is both haunted and threatened by the idea of women emerging from their homes to compete with men and rival them in their own territory:

Woe unto you, woe unto us all, if by a disastrous rivalry between the sexes, you come to take your duties in distaste! . . . Leave us the anxieties and fatigues of the outdoors . . . do not rival us; do not let a misplaced jealousy alienate you from us . . . these rare and violent crises will cost us too dearly if they make you neglect your duties and take your virtues in disgust. . . .[33]

When arguments, commands, and entreaties failed, the men of the Revolution still had recourse to ridicule. Although the heyday of the satirical pamphlet had passed by 1790, ridicule continued to be used to depress women's pretensions. When Théroigne de Méricourt asked to be admitted to the District des Cordeliers with a consultative voice, she was told that "since a canon of the council of Mâcon had formally recognized that women possess a soul and reason like men, one cannot forbid them to use it . . .," but, said the men, a woman still could not be admitted to discussions of questions of State.[34]

A latter-day satire appeared in August of 1791 in the form of an article entitled "les droits de la femme, pour faire le pendant à ceux des droits de l'homme," in the *Journal des Droits de l'Homme*. In a style reminiscent of earlier pamphlet satires, the author of this article chides his fellow men for their lack of gallantry and gratitude:

The finest work to have come from the head of legislators is the Declaration of the Rights of Man. But they should have created the counterpart; they should have, I say, decreed the Rights of Woman.

Extolling women's charms, their delicacy, humanity, and sensibility, he decides that (with their delicate organs, which receive impressions so vividly) women are just the thing needed to quicken the pace of the assembly. The author then suggests a decree: any woman who has more intelligence and knowledge than her husband is hereby freed to devote herself to public affairs, while her husband must stay home and take care of the children. Only, in its very next issue, the journal announces that since so many men have threatened to quit reading their paper if they persisted in their support of the women's cause, they are obliged to renege on their proposal. Since it is the men who figure in the Revolution, says the journal, it is only fair not to use them to wash their children's diapers.[35]

The men of the French Revolution were, in fact, far more likely to talk about women's duties than their rights. If they talked about women's "rights" at all, it was in some vague, unspecified way, and almost always in conjunction with a discussion of their "duties," which were anything but vague and unspecified. The writer Charles-Louis Rousseau, for instance, said: "Men! Give women their rights, but at the same time show them all their obligations. . . ."[36] Since a woman's "obligations" were to stay at home and be the good, submissive wife and mother eulogized by eighteenth-century moralists and philosophers, such duties were clearly inconsistent and incompatible with the kind of equal rights envisaged by Condorcet and others like him.

Two of the most comprehensive rejections of women's demands for political participation and equal rights were delivered, interestingly enough, in the name of education, and they were presented by two of the best-known figures of the Revolution: Charles-Maurice Talleyrand and Honoré-Gabriel Mirabeau.

Talleyrand presented his *Rapport sur l'instruction publique* in 1791. He begins by explaining that although men have been declared free and equal by law, they can only be made truly so by education. But what of women? "One cannot separate the questions relative to their education from an examination of their political rights," says Talleyrand. "If women are recognized to have the same rights as men," he contends, then "it is necessary to give them the same rights as men, [and] it is necessary to give them the same means of using them." But if, conversely, women were created uniquely for "domestic happiness and the duties of the home," then, says Talleyrand, "They must be formed early to fulfill this destiny."

Talleyrand admits that, in the abstract, the denial of equal rights for women "appears difficult to explain": one half of the population is excluded by the other from any participation in the government of their own nation, and even property owners are without representation or influence. There is, however, he says, "an order of ideas in which the question changes and is easily resolved."

Talleyrand's enlightening method of viewing what at first appears to be an injustice is, in fact, the philosophy of the Greatest Good for the Greatest Number. Everything that is contrary to this end is, he says, "an error"; anything that contributes to it is "a truth." It follows, therefore, according to Talleyrand, that if the exclusion of women from public employment increases the happiness of both sexes, then it is a "law that all societies must recognize and consecrate."

To Talleyrand, it is "incontestable" that it is in the best interest of women "not to aspire to the exercise of political rights and functions." This is nothing more than the "will of nature": by giving women "delicate constitutions . . . peaceful inclinations . . . [and] the numerous duties of maternity," "Nature," he explains, had indicated that women were destined for domesticity, and the harmony of society rests on this division of powers. France must remain faithful to this natural order, says Talleyrand:

Let us not invoke principles inapplicable to this question. Do not make rivals of the companions of our life: leave, leave existing in the world a union that no interest, no rivalry can break. Believe that the good of all demands it of you.

Lest the females remain still unconvinced, Talleyrand launches into a eulogy of their "fine lot in life." They are destined to live "far from the tumult of affairs," he says, enjoying in solitude the raptures of motherhood from which public cares could only distract them. Talleyrand's plan will assure them "the power of love," which other passions could only weaken, and is this not, he asks, to think of the happiness of their life? If women seek the same glory as men, they will, he warns, lose the right to distribute the crown of victory.

Talleyrand does admit that some women have reigned as queens with brilliance. "But what are a few exceptions?" he asks; they must not, he says, be allowed to "derange the general plan of nature." If some women happen to have the intelligence and talent that would enable them to enter the masculine world, Talleyrand insists that "they must be the sacrifice to the happiness of the great number." To allow them to have their way, he says, would be to destroy all women merely to have "in one century a few more men."

Talleyrand therefore declares that there is no need to search for a solution to a problem that is already sufficiently resolved. Women must be raised not to aspire to rights that the constitution refuses them, but to know and to appreciate their duties. In this way, he says, "they will find not chimerical hopes, but real goods under the reign of liberty and equality." The education envisaged by Talleyrand for women is therefore less a development of their minds as a formation of their characters, training them to be model eighteenth-century wives and mothers. In the end, Talleyrand explains that he has sought the "principles" of their education "in their rights, their rights in their destiny, and their destiny in their happiness."[37]

In the same spirit is Mirabeau's *Travail sur l'éducation publique*, which first appeared in 1791. As with Talleyrand, Mirabeau's ideas on the status of women are primarily based on the philosophy of the Greatest Good, and on what he perceives as a natural division of labor in society. Profoundly influenced in this respect by the writings of Rousseau, Mirabeau explains that since "men and women play an entirely different role in nature, they cannot play the same role in the social state."

Like Talleyrand and so many others before him, Mirabeau seeks to justify the existing masculine hegemony by magnifying and distorting the differences between the sexes. Mirabeau explains that man's role in life is determined by what he calls his "robust constitution" and his active, energetic, hardy, and persevering character. Anything that requires "considerable force, distant journeys, courage, constance, and stubborn debates" is, says Mirabeau, man's exclusive appanage:

It is he who must labor, negotiate, travel, fight, plead his rights and those of his brothers . . . in the public assemblies, in a word, regulate all affairs. . . .

Both man's rights and his duties are, he explains, the natural result of his physical and mental composition and capabilities. In contrast, a woman has a "delicate constitution," which is "perfectly appropriate" for what Mirabeau considers her "principal destination": perpetuating and rearing the human species and gentling man's more brutal self with the irresistible power of her weakness. Woman can only find true happiness in the seclusion of the home, and it is therefore for her own good, explains Mirabeau, that she is relegated there:

To impose troublesome tasks on these frail organs, to charge these weak hands with heavy loads, is to outrage nature with the most base barbarity.

To snatch women away from the protecting innocence of domesticity and to thrust them into the public milieu, says Mirabeau, could only destroy their most touching characteristics (such as their modesty, their exquisite sensibility, and their touching humility). "It is to confound everything," protests Mirabeau:

It is, by wanting to flatter them with vain prerogatives, to make them lose sight of the real advantages with which they can embellish our existence; it is to degrade them for themselves and us; it is, in a word, under the pretext of associating them to the sovereignty, to make them lose all their *empire*.

Therefore, according to Mirabeau, women are denied equal rights for their own good. Woman was made to reign in the home, he explains, and nowhere else. If a woman is to be renowned at all, Mirabeau says, it must only be as a good *mère de famille*, and it is to this end that she must be brought up (and not as imagined by "some philosophers"). As a result, concludes Mirabeau, the Revolution need concern itself very little with the education of females, since they must never be called upon to exercise the political rights and duties of men.[38]

NOTES

1. *Procès verbal et protestations de l'assemblée de l'ordre le plus nombreux du royaume, les C...* [Cocus] (Paris: 1787), pp. 12–14.

2. *Nouvelle Assemblée des notables cocus du Royaume, en présence des Favoris de leurs épouses, apellés pour certifier du cocuage de chacun des membres composant ladite assemblée, 1er juillet* (Paris: Imprimerie de Sylphe, 1790). Curiously enough, the *Réponse des femmes de Paris au Cahier de l'ordre le plus nombreux du Royaume* can be found among a list of supposedly serious pamphlets in Elizabeth Ratz's "The Women's Rights Movement in the French Revolution," *Science and Society*, 16 (1951–52), p. 153.

3. *Délibérations et protestations de l'Assemblée des honnêtes citoyennes compromises dans le procès-verbal de celle de l'ordre le plus nombreux du Royaume* (n.p.: 1789), pp. 11, 19, 21–26.

4. *Les Demoiselles du Palais Royal aux Etats-généraux* (n.p.: 1789), p. 1. This was soon followed by the anonymous, *Ressource qui reste aux demoiselles du Palais Royale, en suite de la réponse des Etats-généraux à leur requête* (Paris: Imprimerie de Grange, 1789).

5. *Déclaration des droits des citoyennes du Palais Royal* (n.p., n.d.), pp. 1–2.

6. [Vaines, Jean de], *Lettres de la Comtesse de . . . au Chevalier de . . .* (n.p., 1789), p. 18.

7. *Très Humbles Remontrances des femmes françaises* (Imprimerie Galante, 1788), pp. 8–9. This satire is mistakenly quoted as a serious work by, among others, Edmée Charriér in his *L'Evolution intellectuelle féminine*, (Paris: Albert Mechelinck, 1931), p. 60, and L. C. Rosenfield in "The Rights of Women in the French Revolution," *Studies in Eighteenth-Century Culture*, 7 (1978), p. 118.

8. *Requête des femmes, pour leur admission aux Etats généraux, à Messieurs composant l'Assemblée des Notables* (n.p., n.d.), pp. 8, 9, 10. Elizabeth Ratz, "The Women's Rights Movement," p. 153, mistakenly lists this satire as serious, as does Jane Abray, "Feminism in the French Revolution," *The American Historical Review,* Vol. 80, No. 1, February 1975, p. 46, and Rosenfield, "The Rights of Women," p. 118.

9. *Cahier des représentations et doléances du Beau Sexe, au moment de la tenue des Etats généraux* (n.p., n.d.).

10. *Lettre de ces dames à M. Necker, suivie de doléances très graves, 4 mars 1789* (n.p., n.d.), pp. 1–5, 10.

11. *Protestation des Dames françoises, contre la tenue des Etats prétendus généraux convoqués à Versailles pour le 27 avril 1789* (n.p., n.d.), pp. 8, 9, 12, 15.

Ratz, "The Women's Rights Movement in the French Revolution," mistakenly lists this satire as serious.

12. *Requête des dames à l'Assemblée Nationale* (n.p., 1789), pp. 3, 10, 13, and 14. Among the historians misled by this satire are Rosenfield, "The Rights of Women," p. 118; Alphonse Aulard, "Le Féminisme pendent la Révolution française," *Revue bleue*, 4th ser., 9 (1898), p. 362; Ratz, "The Women's Rights Movement in the French Revolution," p. 153; and Leon Abensour, *La Femme et le féminisme avant la Révolution*, (Paris: E. Leroux, 1923), p. 440, although the latter does express reservations about it in another part of his work.

13. While it is true that Mary Wollstonecraft and others did complain (with considerable insight) that women's style of dress hampered both their movement and the scope of their activities, and a few isolated women during the Revolution did find it expedient to dress like men, the idea that there was some sort of conspiracy afoot to force women into britches was a fiction begun by the satires and embroidered by later reactionaries. It was far too trivial a detail to occupy the attention of those people truly engaged in combating the numerous and far more serious results of sexual inequality and discrimination, and it was, moreover, one facet of their existence that women could have altered themselves, if they had so desired. Yet the idea of women in pants generated such an intense emotional response (rather like unisex bathrooms in another age) that it was used with great success by the opponents of sexual equality.

14. *Avis aux dames* (n.p., n.d.), pp. 4, 9, and 15.

15. Louis-Félicité Robert, *Adresse aux femmes de Montauban* (n.p.: 1790) [Extrait du *Mercure Nationale*, Vol. 2, No. 6]; for similar ideas see Mme S.-F. Genlis, *Mémoires,* in *Edits de Madame la Comtesse de Genlis*, 10 vols. (Paris: Ladvocat, 1825).

16. Etta Palm, *Appel aux Françaises*.

17. [Prudhomme], *Révolutions de Paris*, Vol. 12, No. 143, 31 March–7 April 1792, pp. 21–24.

18. [Prudhomme], *Révolutions de Paris*, Vol. 12, No. 150, 19–26 May 1792, p. 358.

19. [Prudhomme], *Révolutions de Paris*, Vol. 14, no. 180, 15–22 December 1792, pp. 595–596.

20. F.-A. Aulard, *La Société des Jacobins, Recueil de Documents*, 6 vols. (Paris: Quantin, 1889–1897), Vol. 3, pp. 520–521, 1909, "Séance du lundi 23 avril 1792."

21. [Prudhomme], *Révolutions de Paris*, Vol. 15, No. 185, 19–26 January 1793, pp. 234–235.

22. [Prudhomme], *Révolutions de Paris*, Vol. 15, No. 189, 16–23 February 1793, p. 37.

23. Maximilien Robespierre, *Oeuvres complètes de Maximilien Robespierre*, 10 vols. (Paris: Aux bureaux de la Revue historique de la révolution française, 1910–1913), Vol. 8, p. 278; see also *La Rocambole des journaux*, No. 6, p. 102; and Aulard, *La Société des Jacobins*, Vol. 3, pp. 497–498.

24. [Prudhomme], *Révolutions de Paris*, Vol. 14, No. 124, 19–26 November 1791, p. 335.

25. [Prudhomme], *Révolutions de Paris*, Vol. 14, No. 127, 10–17 December 1791, pp. 497–498.

26. *Révolutions de Paris*, Vol. 7, No. 85, 19–21 February 1791, p. 338.

27. Charles-Louis Rousseau, *Essai sur l'éducation et l'existence civile et politique des femmes, dans la constitution française*, pp. 32–33.

28. [Prudhomme], "De la Régence," *Révolutions de Paris*, Vol. 7, No. 86, 26 February–5 March 1791, pp. 380–382.

29. Jean-Denis Lanjuinaus, "Projet de Constitution," *Archives parlementaires*, Vol. 63, p. 564.

30. [Prudhomme], *Révolutions de Paris*, Vol. 14, No. 124, 19–26 November 1791, p. 357.

31. [Prudhomme], *Révolutions de Paris,* Vol. 7, No. 83, 5–12 February 1791, pp. 230–231.

32. [Beuvin], *Actes des Apôtres*, Vol. 3, No. 82, p. 9.

33. [Prudhomme], *Révolutions de Paris*, Vol. 7, No. 83, p. 235.

34. The reference here is to the Council of Mâcon, mentioned by Gregory of Tours, where the church actually argued over the question of whether or not women had souls. Their decision was that they did. Camille Desmoulins, *Révolutions de France et de Brabant*, No. 14, 1 March 1790, p. 24.

35. *Le Journal des Droits de l'homme*, No. 14, Wednesday, 10 August 1791, pp. 1-4; No. 15, 11 August 1791, p. 6.

36. Charles-Louis Rousseau, *Essai sur l'éducation et l'existence civile et politique des femmes*, p. 7; see also the anonymous, *Adresse au beau sexe*.

37. Charles-Maurice Talleyrand-Périgord, *Rapport sur l'instruction publique, fait au nom du Comite de constitution, à l'assemblée Nationale, les 10, 11 et 19 septembre 1791* (Paris: Imprimerie Nationale, 1791), pp. 117–121, and 125. For an interesting analysis of Talleyrand's reputation as a notorious libertine and philanderer, see Andre Castelut, "Talleyrand et les Femmes," *Historia*, 413 (April 1981), pp. 52–61.

38. Honoré-Gabriel Mirabeau, *Travail sur l'éducation publique* (Paris: Imprimerie Nationale, 1791), pp. 35–39.

9

The Club des Citoyennes Républicaines Révolutionnaires and the Year II

> They accuse us, these counterrevolutionary women, of having oppressed the people
> [Chabot, *La Société des Jacobins, séance de lundi 16 septembre 1793*]

For the female sex, as for the French Revolution itself, 1793 was a decisive year. Tempers were short, tolerance was in scant supply, and suspicion and accusation were rife. Most people were too worried about finding enough to eat or simply staying alive to even think about such esoteric topics as sexual discrimination and equal rights. Yet it was in 1793 that a new women's club was formed which in the course of its career would bring the entire question of sexual equality virtually to its end in the Revolution. It was in a way ironic, for although some of the members of the society had, in the past, voiced support for women's rights, the club itself was exclusively devoted to defending the Revolution and furthering what it interpreted as the Revolutionary cause. It was not any expressed philosophy of sexual equality that brought these women down, but the unconscious application of that philosophy as articulated by their own political activity.

On 10 May 1793 a group of *citoyennes* appeared at the Commune of Paris to announce (as required by law) the intended formation of an exclusively feminine club, which was to be known as the "*Société des femmes républicaines révolutionnaires*"—the Society of Republican Revolutionary Women. Meeting in the big old library of the Jacobins in the rue Saint-Honoré, their declared objective was "to deliberate upon the means of frustrating the projects of the enemies of the Republic."[1]

Who were these women, and what were they like? The two most famous were, of course, Claire Lacombe, the actresss, and Pauline Léon, who supported her widowed mother and younger brothers and sisters by making chocolates. Others, such as Justine Tribaut and Monic Mercière, sold pastries and cakes, but most of the rest are known only by their names. That they were not of the lowest classes (as is often suggested) is shown by the fact that almost all had been taught to read and write.[2]

The women of the Society of Republican Revolutionaries are traditionally described in the words of their enemies, which are not at all flattering. The police inspector Dutard wrote that "the Revolutionary Republicans are all frightfully ugly," while the Girondin Garsas described them as "Medusa's heads."[3] By far the best-known portrait is the one left by Françoise-Nicolas Buzot in his *Mémories*. Buzot described them as "horrible jades" and "fallen women, picked up from the filth of Paris, whose effrontery was only equalled by their lewdness." According to Buzot, they were "monstrous females who had all the cruelty of the weakness and all the vices of their sex." The very sight of them, he said, struck one with "horror."[4] In the same spirit, the *Salut Public* described Lacombe as a "counterrevolutionary bacchante," and said that it was well known "that she is very fond of wine, and that she is no less fond of the table and the men."[5]

The majority of these allegations were, however, groundless. Claire Lacombe, whom Buzot described as an "aged sloven," was both young and beautiful, as attested by the reviews of her theatrical appearances in the provinces (both before and after her adventurous career in Paris). Another source stigmatized the women of the Society as so ugly that young men avoided them,[6] yet the young and virile *enragé* Théophile Leclerc enjoyed an affair first with Lacombe, and later with Pauline Léon, whom he ultimately married. And although Lacombe's and Léon's liaisons with Leclerc suggest that at least some of the Republican Revolutionaries violated eighteenth-century sexual mores, they were not prostitutes, as a number of both contemporary and later writers contended. In fact, a deputation from the Society appeared at different times before both the Jacobins and National Convention to demand that something be done about the number of prostitutes infecting Paris.[7]

Although very little is actually known about them, in all probability the majority of the members of the Society of Republican Revolutionary Women were nothing more or less than *mères de famille*. That is how they described themselves, and that is how they were initially described by others. At the patriotic *fête* of 23 June 1793 Jacques-Louis David publicly praised the Society, calling them "true republicans, *mères de famille*, who, by their example, give their children the first lessons of virtue."[8] At the festival of the Unity and Indivisibility of the Republic held in August, Marie-Jean Hérault-Séchelles rewarded some of the women for their fight against despotism, saying:

Let all the generous and martial virtues flow, with the maternal milk, into the depths of all the nurslings of France! The Representatives of the sovereign people offer you . . . the laurel, emblem of courage and victory: transmit it to your children.[9]

The *Règlement* of the Society, drawn up in July, stressed both morality and virtue, those two principles so dear to the hearts of almost all Revolutionaries.[10] Also significant are the contents of a speech delivered at the Society by the "*citoyennes*" of the Droits de l'homme section, on the occasion of their ceremonial donation of a copy of the Rights of Man. The address refers to the Republican Revolutionaries as "the wives of *sans-culottes*" and presents a surprisingly traditional social philosophy. It is true that the women begin by congratulating the Society for having "broken one of the links of the chains of the prejudices . . . [that] seclude women in the narrow sphere of their homes, making passive and isolated beings from half of the population." But, although the women insist that the Declaration of Rights applies to both men and women, the *duties* of the two sexes, we are told, are different: a man's duties are "public" and a woman's are "private." In words surprisingly similar to those of Prudhomme, the women announce that "nature itself" has shown a preference for men, giving them the "robust constitution" needed to act in the army, the senate, and public assemblies. This is the way both reason and social conventions wish it, and, say the women, "one must yield to it." According to the women, their duties are the private ones of wife and mother. Unlike Prudhomme, however, these women do not believe that those "gentle functions" must consume quite all of a female's time. There are still a few "spare moments," they say, and how better to use them than by meeting together in patriotic societies, for the purposes of surveillance and instruction? In other words, these women were not demanding a modification of traditional sex roles. They still conceived of themselves primarily as wives and mothers, but they did not believe that those two functions must prevent them from taking part in the political activity of their day.[11]

Despite this evidence, the women of the Society of Republican Revolutionaries have gone down in history as anything but good *mères de famille*. This is partially because the two women whose names are most often associated with the club, Lacombe and Léon, were, at the time, still unwed (in fact, their position of leadership in the club was probably, in part at least, a natural result of their single state, since it gave them more freedom and time to devote to the club's affairs). Nevertheless, a good portion of what was said about the women of the Society of Republican Revolutionaries must be considered as deliberately libelous, manufactured by their enemies to discredit them. Women in the eighteenth century were considered most vulnerable in two areas—their appearance and their sexual mores—and it was here that their enemies struck.

Although they were later attacked, when they were first formed the Revolutionary Republicans were almost universally acclaimed for their virtue and patriotic zeal. They made stirring speeches against aristocrats, merchants, and counterrevolutionaries, and the Jacobins, the Paris Commune, and the National Convention all loudly applauded them. They were initially fairly closely associated with the Jacobins, in whose *salle* they held their own meetings,[12] and when the père Duchesne was arrested, they marched to his support, shouting: "*Vive la Montagne, vive Marat, guillotine les Brissotins!*" They played an important part in the *journées* of 31 May–2 June, which overthrew the Girondins, and when Marat was assassinated, they suggested that an obelisk be raised in his memory (and themselves marched in the ceremony, solemnly bearing a bathtub). Yet after the death of Marat, the Society's allegiance began to waver away from the Jacobins in the direction of the *enragés*.

The Society had much in common with the *enragés*. Both Jacques Roux and Leclerc believed that women could and must play an important part in the Revolution and were therefore more accepting of politically active women than severe moralists like Robespierre. Furthermore, the political and economic ideas of the *enragés* well approximated those of the Society. The Revolutionary Republicans began demanding the implementation of the Constitution, and even went so far as to accuse the leaders of the Revolution of personal ambition and corruption. "Believe us, four years of misery have taught us enough to recognize ambition even beneath the mask of patriotism," they said in a petition presented to the National Convention at the end of August; "We no longer believe in the virtue of those men who are reduced to praising themselves, we need more than words to believe that ambition does not reign in your committees; organize the government according to the constitution." They even went further than this, however, and asked what was the point of declaring a law of suspects if the men who enforced it were themselves suspect? Not surprisingly, the president of the Convention refused to admit them to the bar.[13]

It was at about this time that the Society moved their meetings from the Jacobins to the big old church of Saint Eustache, standing on the edges of the Halles. It was in some ways a fateful move, for it brought the women of the Society into direct conflict with the women of the Halles. The women of the Halles, once so violently pro-Revolutionary, were becoming increasingly disillusioned with a movement that only drove up prices and made bread hard to find. They now expressed their violence by snatching the tricolor away from any women who happened to be wearing it, beating them up, and generally creating an uproar in the streets. The disturbance became so great that complaints were finally brought before the Commune and the Convention, which sought to alleviate the situation by decreeing that all women were *required* to wear the tricolor, under severe penalties. The affair of the cockade died down, but the memory lingered, and enmity festered.[14]

It was after the Society moved to Saint Eustache that Pierre-Joseph Roussel and an English friend decided to attend one of its meetings. The account of that session, recorded in Roussel's *Château des Tuileries*, is the only existing description of one of the Society's meetings (except for the one that would end in disaster in October). Its accuracy is questionable, since Roussel found the entire spectacle utterly "hilarious" and "ridiculous" (he says they practically smothered from trying not to laugh) and used it as a vehicle through which to satirize the entire movement for women's rights. Thus, he reproduces a long speech supposedly delivered to the Society by Olympe de Gouges, who (apart from the fact that her politics were diametrically opposed to those of the Society and she did not like to speak in public) was by that time in prison. According to Roussel, the topic of discussion for the meeting was "the utility of women in a republican government." The women contended that the female sex was capable of taking part in all areas of administration, an idea that Roussel found "very comic." Whether or not this was actually the topic of conversation is unknown; the Society never made any such demands in public. At any rate, Roussel's amusement gradually began to turn into disquiet, and he wondered of what excesses such women might be capable. His English friend reassured him: "Your nation possesses the remedy: the weapon of ridicule and persiflage, which it knows how to wield so well, will destroy these comic pretensions." The Englishman did venture to suggest, however, that perhaps women should be given a little more legal influence in government, and he expressed surprise that the Revolution had not done this. Roussel replied:

It is precisely that overthrow which prevents the true philosopher from introducing a new subject of discord, by presenting some project to give women consideration in the government. They are strong enough with their ascendency over us. Let us leave them with the *empire* of grace and beauty.

Roussel's description of this session does, however, supply one valuable piece of information: it was the practice of the officers of the Society to wear red liberty caps at their meetings.[15]

It was in September that the Jacobins began to move against the *enragés*. The first to be arrested was Jacques Roux. On the 15th of the month, Leclerc prudently abandoned the publication of his newspaper, and on the 16th the Jacobins moved against the women. The Jacobins decided to attack the Society of Revolutionary Republicans not because they were women, but because the Society's political and economic ideas were at variance with their own, and because the women's accusations of corruption in high places were making more than a few of them a little bit uncomfortable. It is perhaps not insignificant that of the men who were most instrumental in the downfall of the Society—Fabre d'Eglantine, Chabot, Basire, Desfieur—many would soon be implicated in the scandal over the Compagnie des Indes and eventually go to the guillotine.[16] What makes the case of the Society of Republican Revolutionaries interesting, however, is that although it was because of their political ideas that the Jacobins decided to eliminate them, it was on the basis of their sex that they attacked them.

The break between the two societies first came at the 16th of September meeting of the Jacobins. When the Republican Revolutionaries were denounced in the Commune and the Convention later in October, the political motives were never mentioned, but they played a large part in the September 16th confrontation. The Republican Revolutionaries were accused of supporting Leclerc, now in disgrace. Chabot also complained that Lacombe had accused them of "having oppressed the people," and others noted that she was calling for "the constitution, the whole constitution, and nothing but the constitution." One member said: "The woman you denounce is truly dangerous because she is very eloquent." Another speaker began to attribute all the troubles that Paris had suffered to the female sex. At about this time Lacombe herself appeared in the tribunes and demanded speech. This produced a loud uproar, as the tribunes began to cry: "*À bas l'intrigante! À bas la nouvelle Corday! Va-t-en, malheureuse, ou nous allons te mettre en piéces.*" She stood her ground, however, and when order was finally restored, the president chided her:

He observed that it was thus that she justified the denunciations made on her account, and that it was a veritable crime against patriotism to cause trouble or to prolong it in an assembly of men who need to deliberate coldly on the interests of the people.

It was then decided that Lacombe should be arrested immediately, and she was led off to the Committee of General Security. Her house was searched, but since nothing incriminating was found, she was released.[17]

Lacombe was free and the Society still intact, but both were subjected to increasingly virulent abuse. In early October a deputation of Republican Revolutionaries appeared before the Convention to protest the harsh treatment and calumny to which they had been subjected. Lacombe said that she had been compared to the Medicis, Queen Elizabeth, Marie Antoinette, and Charlotte Corday, to which she replied:

Without a doubt nature produced a monster who deprived us of "*l'Ami du peuple.*" But we, are we responsible for a crime? Was Corday from our Society? Oh! We are more generous than the men. Our sex has only produced one monster, while for years we have been betrayed and assassinated by the monsters without number that the masculine sex has produced.

Lacombe also reminded the Convention that their rights were "the rights of the people," and that if they were oppressed, they had the right to resist.[18]

The Jacobins made their final move against the women's Society at the end of the month of October. A rumor of unknown origins spread among the women of the Halles that the Society of Republican Revolutionaries wanted to force all women to wear red liberty caps. Remembering the affair of the cockade, the women of the Halles went on the rampage. They crowded into St. Eustache where a meeting of the Society was being held, started yelling "*À bas les Jacobins!*" and "*À bas la cocarde!*" and finally converged on the members of the Society, who were beaten and "indignantly outraged," until saved by members of the revolutionary committee of the section, the police, and a justice of the peace.[19]

The next day, a delegation of women supposedly from the Halles appeared before the Convention to ask that their sex not be forced to wear red liberty caps, and they ended their petition by saying:

Citizen legislators, you are scarcely ignorant that the misery of France was only introduced by the instrument of a woman [Corday]; we demand therefore the abolition of their club.

Although the members of the section's revolutionary committee, the police, and the justice of the peace (while not sympathetic to the Society), had all deposited at the Commune fairly accurate accounts of exactly what had happened the day before, a very different version was now laid before the members of the Convention. They were told that the Republican Revolutionaries (who are, incidentally, never mentioned exactly by name) had gone "running through the streets of Paris," wearing red liberty caps, trousers, and with pistols stuck in their belts, and that they had tried to force every woman that they happened to meet to adopt their costume (exactly how this could be done was not explained); the good women refused, however, telling them that they obeyed only men and not other women, and that they had no intention of assuming a costume reserved exclusively for men. Both versions of the affair agreed on one thing: the result was a brawl, and the Republican Revolutionaries were acknowledged to have gotten the worst of it.[20]

Fabre d'Eglantine then arose and said that not content to demand the cockade, the women were now causing trouble over the liberty cap. If things were not stopped, he said, one would soon see women marching off for bread complete with pistols and bandoleers, as if they were going to the trenches. It was obviously all an ingenious plot, he said, engineered by the counterrevolutionaries:

It is very clever of our enemies to attack women's greatest passion, their attire;

and, under this pretext, putting in their hands arms that they do not know how to use, but the troublemakers could use very well.

Fabre d'Eglantine then turned his denunciation more pointedly in the direction of the Society of Republican Revolutionary Women by, predictably enough, questioning their sexual mores:

I have well observed that these societies are not composed of *mères de famille*, of daughters who work for their parents, of sisters taking care of their younger brothers or sisters, but of a species of adventurers, of *chevalières errantes*, of emancipated girls and female grenadiers.

His speech was interrupted at this point by applause. He then proposed that the Committee of General Security prepare a report on the women's societies. He was informed, however, that this was already being done.

Accounts vary as to what happened next. Some say that the original female petitioners began to cry: "*A bas les bonnets rouges! A bas les sociétés de femmes!*" Others report that one of the petitioners asked to be allowed to speak. Being passed to the bar, she demanded the abolition of all women's clubs (in the original petition, it should be noted, the request is only for the dissolution of "their club").

The next day, 1 November, Amar presented to the National Convention the report on women's clubs prepared by the Committee of General Security, which Fabre d'Eglantine had been told was already being drawn up. This report was prepared by one of the most powerful organs of the Revolution, and it can be regarded as the Revolution's final and official answer to demands for equality between the sexes and rights for women. The report spent very little time in discussing the affair that had ostensibly provoked it. Nor was it even primarily concerned with the question of women's clubs. It was, instead, a thorough and careful denial of any and all assertions of sexual equality. The grounds for this denial were the familiar ones: the mental and physical incapacity of the female sex, the arguments of utility and the sexual division of labor, and the interests of morality combined with the exaltation of the female as mother.

The original contretemps had occurred over red liberty caps, and even the previous day's petitioners had only asked that they not be forced to wear the *bonnet rouge*, making no mention whatsoever of trousers. Once again, however, the emotional idea of women wearing pants was introduced. Amar informed the Convention that the entanglement had involved some "six thousand women," as counterrevolutionaries disguised beneath "the mask of exaggerated patriotism" had tried to force the good "*citoyennes*" of Paris to wear red bonnets and britches. As a result of this fracas, he said, the Committee of General Security had met to decide on the fate of all women's clubs of any denomination (not just of the Society of Republican Revolutionaries). Amar informed the Convention that the Committee had examined the question in relation to society, convention, and politics. He then delivered their report.

Amar began by asking if women should be allowed to exercise political rights and to participate in governmental affairs. In a series of rhetorical questions, he asked: Do women have the depth of knowledge, the self-sacrifice, the impassibility needed to govern? No, he answered. Do women have either the physical or moral strength needed to exercise political rights? "Universal opinion rejects this idea," he said.

Amar then asked whether women should be allowed to gather together in political associations. The purpose of political associations, he said, is to uncover enemy plots, to survey the conduct of both individuals and public officials, and to inspire patriotic zeal by their members' virtuous conduct and wise counsels. Again he asked, can women devote themselves to these functions? No, he said, to do so would require them to neglect the duties assigned to them "by nature." The harmony of society, he explained, rests on the sexual division of labor:

This social order is the result of the difference that exists between man and woman. Each sex is called to the type of occupation that is proper for it; its action is circumscribed within this circle from which it may not escape.

This, said Amar, is the "imperious law of nature."

Amar then launched into a eulogy of his own sex. According to Amar, man is strong, robust, energetic, audacious, and courageous. He braves all perils and endures all inclement weather. He is "exclusively destined" for

agriculture, commerce, sailing, travel, war, everything that requires strength, intelligence, capability . . . [and] the profound and serious meditations that need a great application of mind and extended study.

In contrast, a woman's character is perfectly suited to her functions, which are to bear and raise children and to take care of the house. "When they have fulfilled all their duties," said Amar, "they will have deserved well of the country."

Amar conceded that women should be allowed to go and *listen* to public discussions (so that they could understand the principles of liberty and teach them to their children), but they should not be allowed to take part in those discussions, "of which the passion is incompatible with the gentleness and moderation that form the charm of their sex," he said.

It was, said Amar, essentially a question of morality, and "without morals there is no republic." A woman's virtue and modesty cannot permit her to show herself in public, he said, and "do battle with men." The

Romans never allowed their women to appear outside the house—or so Amar told his countrymen—saying:

Do you want to see them, in the French Republic, coming to the bench, to the tribunes, to the political assemblies, like men, abandoning both the reticence that is the source of all the virtues of their sex, and the care of their families?

Besides, he added, "lofty concepts and serious meditations" are above them anyway. Furthermore, Amar warned, the participation of women in public affairs is dangerous. Uneducated and lacking moral firmness, he said, women are more exposed to "error and seduction," and their "organization" predisposes them to degrees of exaltation and passion that (in a contradiction, typical of the times, of his earlier statement that women must avoid political discussions because their natural gentleness is incompatible with passion) he said would be "disastrous" to the best interests of the State. "We therefore believe," Amar concluded, "and doubtless you will agree, that it is not possible for women to exercise political rights." He then advised the Convention to destroy all female associations, which he said "the aristocrats" were using to set the female sex against their men.

Amar's report was loudly applauded. Only one man ventured to say that "despite the inconveniences cited" he did not believe that they could justly deprive women of the right to peacefully assemble. There were murmurs, but he continued: "Unless you contend that women do not form part of the human species, can you deprive them of this right shared by all thinking beings?" Basire then took the floor, arguing that since they had declared the government revolutionary until the peace, they could do anything they wanted to do. "It is therefore uniquely a question of knowing if the women's societies are dangerous," he said, and experience had shown that. At his motion, the Convention then adopted the decree proposed by Amar, which read:

Clubs and popular societies of women, under whatever denomination they might be, are forbidden.[21]

As a result of this decree, not only the Society of Republican Revolutionaries, but all women's clubs (even the Ladies' Aid Societies) were banned. A few days later, a deputation of women from the now defunct Society appeared before the Convention, insisting that the Society had been composed almost entirely of *mères de famille*, and that they had been dissolved on the basis of a false report. They were interrupted almost immediately by loud voices calling for the order of the day; it passed unanimously, and amid applause and jeers the women retired.[22]

The journalist Prudhomme greeted the new law with heartfelt approval. Women would now be tolerated only as "silent and modest spectators," he wrote, and that was how it should be:

Citoyennes, be pure and hard-working girls, tender and chaste wives, wise mothers, and you will be good patriots. True patriotism consists of fulfilling one's duties, and only wanting those rights alloted to each according to his sex . . . and not in wearing a liberty cap and trousers, and carrying pike and pistol! Leave that to the men, born to protect you and to make you happy.

He also urged them to punish rigorously any further attempts to disorganize society by indecently confounding and intermingling the sexes.[23]

The year 1793 was destined to mark the virtual end of the movement for sexual equality and women's rights in the French Revolution. By the end of the year, all of the movement's principal advocates had been eliminated one way or another. The *philosophe* Concorcet had been outlawed with the Girondins and would soon die in prison. Etta Palm d'Aelders, feeling herself threatened, had prudently decided to withdraw to her native Holland. Théroigne de Méricourt had sided with the Girondins in their split with the Jacobins and was consequently set upon by a group of Jacobins in mid-May and whipped half to death. The incident overset her sanity, and she never recovered.[24] Olympe de Gouges had been arrested in July for suggesting that a popular referendum should be held to determine France's future form of government. She had also called Marat and Robespierre corrupt and ambitious "insects" with dictatorial aspirations.[25] Her trial was held on the first of November, and she went to the guillotine two days later.[26] The inauguration of the Reign of Terror sent two other noted female figures of the Revolution to their deaths at this time—Marie Antoinette on 16 October and Mme Roland on 8 November. Although neither had ever in any way, except perhaps by their own conduct, championed the cause of either sexual equality or women's rights (Mme Roland, in fact, was a devoted disciple of Rousseau), their names were added along with that of Corday to the list that could be used as a dire warning of what would happen to women if they did not stay in their "place."

At the end of November, a delegation of women (probably former Republican Revolutionaries) tried to appear before the Commune of Paris. Their arrival was greeted with a violent popular outburst in the tribunes, and Pierre Gaspard Chaumette took the floor to pronounce what was virtually the last word on female aspirations for equality.

Calling the women "viragos" and "degraded beings who want to violate the laws of nature," Chaumette demanded that they be excluded from the Commune. When one member began to object that the law permitted them to enter, Chaumette interrupted. The law, he said, requires that morality be respected:

What! Since when is it permitted for women to abjure their sex and make themselves men? Since when is it decent to see women abandon the pious cares of
their home, the cradle of their children, to come into the public place, the tribunes, the bar of the senate . . . to fulfill the duties that nature confided to men
alone?

To whom, if not to women, he asked, did nature assign domestic duties?
"Is it to us? Did she give us breasts to nurse our children?" No. According to Chaumette, nature said to man:

Be man! the race, the hunt, the plow, politics . . . behold your share. She said to
woman: Be woman!

In recompense, Chaumette promised, women were to become the
divinities of the domestic sanctuary. "Impudent women who want to
become men," he said to the petitioners, "is your share not good
enough?" Women already reign by their beauty, he told them, and they
must be content with that. Do not envy us, he cried, echoing one of the
most common male fears during the Revolution; do not try to compete
with us.

Chaumette then issued a warning to the entire female sex, to beware of
"the depths of the abyss into which a moment of error would plunge
you." He advised them to look at what had happened to Marie Antoinette, Mme Roland, and Olympe de Gouges: "All these immoral
beings have been destroyed beneath the avenging iron of the law . . . and
you want to imitate them!" he cried. Women will only be "interesting"
and "truly worthy of esteem," said Chauette, when they do what nature
wanted them to do. It is because men want women to be respected that
they force them to respect themselves, he explained: if a woman acts like
a man, declared Chaumette, then men consider themselves free to act
towards her in any way they see fit.

Frequently interrupted by loud applause and encouragement,
Chaumette continued. Under the corruption of the monarchy, he said,
"women were everything because the men were nothing." But now, he
told his fellow magistrates, they were creating a Republic, and a republic
must be virtuous:

As much as we venerate the *mère de famille* who puts her joy and glory in raising
and caring for her children, in sewing her husband's clothes and soothing his
fatigues by taking care of his domestic needs, then so much we must despise and
spit on the woman without shame who dons the masculine role and makes the
disgusting exchange of the charms given her by nature for a pike and a pair of
pants.

Chaumette ended by suggesting that they no longer even receive deputations of women. The motion passed unanimously.[27]

The *Salut Public*, a revolutionary journal, took up Chaumette's speech and expanded on it as "an example to women." Marie Antoinette was described as "a bad mother" and "a debauched wife." Olympe de Gouges, they said, had wanted to become a "statesman," and she was punished by the law "for having forgotten the virtues proper for her sex." The greatest ire was reserved for Mme Roland, however, who was said to have flattered herself as a "*bel esprit*" and reigned in despotic corruption over her salon. She was "proud" and "opinionated," and (even though she was a mother) she had "sacrificed nature, by wishing to rise above it." Her desire to be clever, said the journal, "led her to forget the virtues of her sex, and this slip, always dangerous, ended by causing her to perish on the scaffold." The female sex was considered well warned. They were told to be good, submissive wives and hard-working, stay-at-home mothers, and on no account to interfere in politics or public affairs.[28]

The Jacobins had achieved their objectives: there was no more talk about women's rights, and the members of the former Society of Republican Revolutionaries lay low.[29]

NOTES

1. *Moniteur*, 13 May 1793, Vol. 16, p. 362. The Society is also sometimes known as the "Club des Citoyennes Républicaines Révolutionnaires."

2. For Lacombe and Léon, see the brief biographies in Chapter 3.

3. Cerati, *Le Club des citoyennes républicaines révolutionnaires*, p. 30; Dessens, *Revendications des droits de la femme pendant la Révolution*, p. 157.

4. François-Nicolas Buzot, *Mémoires* (Paris: Henri Plon, 1866), p. 72.

5. *Salut Public*, 24 Septembre 1793.

6. Tuetey, *Répertoire général*, Vol. 9, No. 659.

7. *Moniteur*, xvii–699, 21 September 1793, No. 264; Aulard, *La Société des Jacobins*, Vol. 5, p. 404, Séance de vendredi, 13 septembre 1793.

8. Cerati, *Le Club des citoyennes républicaines révolutionnaires*, p. 92.

9. Marie-Jean Hérault-Séchelles, *Discours prononcé par Hérault-Séchelles, président de la Convention Nationale, le 10 auguste 1793, à la fête de l'unité et l'indivisibilité de la République française*, p. 15; see also the anonymous, *Détail des cérémonies qui doivent avoir lieu pour le Fédération du 10 août 1793, au Champ-de-mars, et sur l'autel de la patrie, sécret de la Convention Nationale qui en ordonne l'envoi aux Départments et aux Armées* (Imprimerie de Guilhemat).

10. The preamble begins with the words: "The Republican Revolutionary Women, convinced that without morality and without principles, there is no liberty . . .," while Article XII says that since the women only unite to encourage each other in virtue, bad morals will be considered a principal cause for exclusion from the club. The *Règlement* is reproduced in Cerati, *Le Club des citoyennes républicaines révolutionnaires*, p. 29; it can also be found translated in Darline G.

Levy, Harriet B. Applewhite, and Mary D. Johnson, eds., *Women in Revolutionary Paris 1789–1795* (Chicago, IL: University of Illinois Press, 1980), p. 161.

11. *Discours prononcé à la Société des Citoyennes Républicaines Révolutionnaires par les citoyennes de la section des Droits de l'Homme* (n.p., 1793), pp. 3–5.

12. They were not there by invitation, however; they had simply installed themselves and then informed the Jacobins after the fact. When a group of women had requested permission to use the Jacobins' salle in February, president Dubois-Crance had said: "If we permit these *citoyennes* to meet here, thirty thousand women could assemble and excite a movement in Paris disastrous to liberty." Aulard, *La Société des Jacobins*, Vol. 5, p. 37.

13. *Pétition des Citoyennes Républicaines Révolutionnaires lue à la Barre de la Convention Nationale* (Paris: Imprimerie de l'Egalité, n.d.), p. 2. See also Leclerc, *l'Ami de peuple*, No. 18, 30 August, year II. For the political and economic affinity between the society and the *enragés*, see R. B. Rose, *The Enragés: Socialists of the French Revolution* (Melbourne: 1965), as well as Cerati, *Le Club des citoyennes*.

14. For the affair of the cockades, see especially *Le Père Duchesne*, Vol. 9, No. 288, pp. 7–8; *Moniteur*, Vol. 17, pp. 717, 718, and 737; and Aulard, *La Société des Jacobins*.

15. Pierre-Joseph Roussel, *Le Château des Tuileries*, pp. 35–45. A surprising number of historians have taken Roussel's account of the session as completely factual, their suspicions not even being raised by the supposed presence of Olympe de Gouges. See, for instance, Abray, "Feminism in the French Revolution," p. 52. The Regulations of the Society also stated (Article X) that the president would wear the bonnet of liberty.

16. For the political intrigues and associations surrounding this affair, see Scott Lytle, "The Second Sex (1793)," *Journal of Modern History*, 27 (1955), pp. 14–26, as well as Cerati, *Le Club des citoyennes*.

17. The three Jacobins who were most instrumental in bringing about this confrontation were Chabot, Basire, and Desfieux. Aulard, *La Société des Jacobins*, Vol. 5, pp. 406–408; *Moniteur*, Vol. 18, pp. 694–696; for Claire Lacombe's version see *Rapport fait par la citoyenne Lacombe, à la Société des Républicaines Révolutionnaires de ce qui c'est passé le 16 septembre à la Société des Jacobins, concernant cella des Républicaines Révolutionnaires, séance à S. Eustache, et les dénonciations faites contre la citoyenne Lacombe personnellement* (n.p., 17 September 1793).

18. *Moniteur*, Vol. 18, p. 69.

19. *Moniteur*, Vol. 18, p. 285; "Procès-verbal de ce qui est arrivé aux citoyennes républicaines-révolutionnaires," *Révolutions de Paris*, Vol. 12, No. 215, 13–20 November 1793, pp. 207–210.

20. There are a number of accounts of this session: *Moniteur*, Vol. 18, p. 296; the *Archives parlementaires*, Vol. 78, pp. 20–35, reproduces many others. The story of the last days of the Society is a complicated one and needs to be followed carefully through the original sources. By far the best account in a secondary source is to be found in Cerati, *Le Club des Citoyennes*. Most other works contain major errors, with many historians even going so far as to believe the tale of the women running through the streets in pants and pistols. See, for instance, Aulard,

"Le Féminisme pendant la révolution," p. 366. Other historians who have written on the subject include Margaret George, "The 'World Historical Defeat' of the Républicaines Révolutionnaires," *Science and Society*, 40 (1976–77), pp. 410–437.

21. *Décret de la Convention Nationale, du 9e jour du 2e mois de l'an 2e de la République Française, une et indivisible*, Archives Nationales, AD I 91. My account of this session is derived mainly from the *Moniteur*, Vol. 18, p. 299. The account given in the *Journal des Débats et des Décrets* (Brumaire, year II, No. 407, p. 133) and reproduced in the *Archives parlementaires* (Vol. 81, p. 48) is shorter and differs at a few points in wording.

22. *Moniteur*, Vol. 18, p. 350.

23. [Prudhomme], *Révolutions de Paris*, Vol. 17, No. 213, 7 Brumaire, year II, p. 150. Prudhomme also published the standard account of the Halles disturbance, complete with pants and pistols, but a week later he published the Republican Revolutionaries' version of the affair, saying that he had had no intention of slandering them, and that he had always admired their "pure principles and the services which they had rendered to the Revolution." The article that appeared before, he said, had nothing to do with them, but "other women," masquerading under their name. [Prudhomme], *Révolutions de Paris*, Vol. 17, No. 215, 13–20 November 1793, p. 207.

24. This was a particulary cruel and common form of popular punishment used against women during the Revolution. It was crudely effective, since it combined the pain of the whip with the humiliation of public exposure.

25. Olympe's outpourings were often more passionate than prudent. She was fervently dedicated to her vision of the Revolution, but that vision did not include violence and bloodshed. A crowned tyrant and a citizen tyrant commit the same crimes, she once wrote, even if their ambitions are different. At another time she said: "The blood of even the guilty, shed with profusion and cruelty, eternally soils these revolutions . . . one passes rapidly from one system of government to another . . . the inhumanities endured . . . have altered the public spirit . . . and the majority of the inhabitants, if they dared to admit it, would desire the approach of the foreigner, for so much domestic barbarity has rendered that of the enemy bearable!" Olympe de Gouges, *Adresse au Don Quichotte du Nord* (Paris: Imprimerie Nationale, 1792); *La Fierté de l'innocence, ou le Silence du véritable patriotisme* (Paris: Imprimerie Nationale, 1792); *Correspondance de la Cour. Compte moral rendu et dernier mot à mes chers amis, par Olympe de Gouges, à la convention nationale et au peuple sur une dénouciation faite contre son civisme, aux Jacobins, par le sieur Bourdon* (n.p., 1792); *Les fantômes de l'opinion publique* (n.p., n.d.); and *Les Trois Urnes, ou le Salut de la patrie* (n.p., 1793).

26. *Moniteur*, Vol. 18, pp. 326 and 344.

27. *Journal de la Montagne*, No. 6, 29th day of the 2nd month of year II, pp. 43–44; see also *Moniteur*, Vol. 18, p. 450.

28. *Salut public*, in *Moniteur*, Vol. 18, p. 450.

29. Around the middle of November, Pauline Léon married Leclerc; he volunteered for the army, and she stayed at home and kept house. But in April of 1794 they were both arrested, along with Claire Lacombe. The Leclercs were finally released in August of that year, after the fall of Robespierre. Lacombe remained in jail for another year, until she, too, was finally released.

10

Women in the Aftermath
of Revolution

> There are no people who have more esteem for women, who are
> more inclined to render them homage [than the French]; yet there
> hardly exists any who fear their domination more.
>
> [Ségur, *Les Femmes*]

In 1789, the French Revolution had been welcomed by the champions of
sexual equality as the long-awaited liberator of the female sex. By 1793,
the magnitude of their mistake had become obvious. As Revolutionary
authority and power increased, so, too, did the exclusion of women from
active participation in government and society.

In 1793, the same year in which they were forbidden the right of assembly and deprived of the right to petition the Commune, women were also
formally excluded from the army. A surprising number of women had
initially volunteered for the French army and had distingished themselves
in combat; several had even been honored by the government. But by
1793 public sentiment had begun to turn against them. In January, the
Révolutions de Paris had carried an article condemning the practice of
admitting women to the army. "*Citoyennes!*" it said:

Leave us the sword and battles, your delicate fingers are made to hold the needle
and scatter flowers on the thorny path of life; for you, heroism consists in bearing
the burdens of the home and domestic pains; your task is not to massacre a cruel
enemy. . . .[1]

In response to this widespread and growing spirit of social conservatism, on 30 April the Convention adopted a decree that officially excluded women from military service.[2]

After 1793, the politically active woman disappeared as an individual, although women as a group continued to play an important part in the bread riots and *journées* that periodically rocked Paris. Their participation in the events of Prairial, in the year III, however, precipitated harsh reprisals. Women were officially and specifically ordered to return to their homes and to stay off the streets. They were also formally excluded from the Convention, and from that time on were allowed to watch from the tribunes only if accompanied by a male.[3] An obscure incident in the year III in which a widow by the name of Vincent deliberately broke some seals led to the passage of a law entitled: "Law declaring that no woman may be established guardian of seals."[4] Females found wearing pants on the streets of Paris were now hauled off to the Police courts,[5] while women who were known to have once frequented popular clubs and societies were barred from the military barracks.[6] The politically active female became the object first of rejection, then finally of scorn. By 1799, a new play entitled "*Les femmes politiques*" had appeared in the theaters and was being greeted with loud applause. The hardy reception accorded this comedy was, said one observer, "a critique of those women who occupied themselves with politics, and [shows] the disfavor cast on the personage of the knitters or those who attended the tribunes."[7]

The various constitutions that followed each other in such rapid succession all defined the French citizen as a male being, and the term "*citoyenne*" gradually fell into disuse.[8] Although they might be allowed no participation in the government, however, women were frequently reminded that they were still bound by its laws. In March 1794 the Committee of Public Safety addressed itself to the problem of the intractability of the female sex, some of whom, it complained,

. . . say that the law cannot affect them, because they did not swear the civil oath; it is this idea, which was maliciously suggested to them, that easily carries them to seditious mobs.[9]

By the year VII, the nation that had once passed a law requiring all women to wear the tricolor now decided that it should be reserved only for "French citizens." A special commission established to investigate the subject reported that in "the first transports of liberty" the women had been swept up by the general enthusiasm and wished to wear the tricolor along with their fathers and brothers. But now, suggested the commission, so that the wearing of the cockade would be more "respectable," women were to be forbidden it:

If we wish to restore to things their true worth, if we wish to make the wearing of the cockade a respectable institution, let us no longer confound the destiny of the two sexes. The influence of women is in the family; that is where they may, that is where they must, exercise the republican virtues.

Women were advised by the commission to turn their attention back to their own "frivolous" and "changing fashions," in order to delight men's eyes and better ornament the nation.[10]

The position of women in France in the years following 1793 was in many respects actually worse than it had been in the days prior to 1789. A number of the complaints and demands made by women at the beginning of the Revolution had focused on the deplorable education traditionally given to their sex, and there had been high hopes of seeing it improved. But instead of establishing schools to expand the education of women, the Revolution had simply destroyed the convents and parish classes that had once formed the female sex's sole source of instruction. With a woman's destiny confined to the home, most revolutionaries agreed with Mirabeau and Talleyrand that the home was the place where she should be raised, and where she should be taught to know and appreciate her duties. Lakanal's plan for education, first introduced in 1794, would have established primary schools for girls, but by late 1795 he was still appearing before the National Convention to defend this aspect of his proposal, and although his system finally did pass into law, it was never executed and was finally abrogated by the decree of 1 May 1802.[11] Subsequent laws on education never even mentioned girls. After Napoleon's rapprochement with the Catholic church, some nuns did reopen their schools, and private boarding schools were set up for the bourgeoisie, but it was not until after the Restoration that the question of public education for women was once more raised.[12] The idea of secondary schools for girls was never even discussed.

As life settled down under the Directory to some semblance of normalcy, the education of females once again became a favorite topic for discussion and scholarship. As in the days before the Revolution, however, the more famous educational theorists, such as Blanchard, Levallois, Mme Genlis, and Mme Campan, still wanted to raise girls only to be good *mères de famille*. Even those who envisioned something broader almost always carefully hastened to assure their readers that they had no intention of turning women into scholars, or *femmes savantes*, as they were derogatorily dubbed. The *Project for a law forbidding women to learn how to read*, by Sylvain Maréchal, might in reality have been only a bad joke (although several ladies took it seriously enough to write refutations) but the Society of Science and Art in the *departement* of Lot was totally serious when it offered a prize for the best essay on the question "What is the most appropriate form of education for women in order to create the happiness of men in society?" One of the essays submitted was by a Mme Bernier, who based her response on the premise that:

"[Women's] destiny is to create the domestic happiness of man; it is after this principle that their education must be directed."

Mme Bernier's work is typical of post-Revolutionary educational theory and clearly illustrates the negligible legacy of the more radical Revolutionary ideas on the subject. To the evident gratification of the Society, she wrote: "It is very important that from childhood the young girl well understand that she is inferior to the man. . . ." The female was to be told from the cradle that she was born to be dependent and submissive. Any philosophy that sought to compare the sexes and confound their destinies was, according to Mme Bernier, "a very great error," and, she added, it was "absurd" to raise a woman like a man. A girl must be reared solely for her destiny of wife, mother, and housekeeper. Every aspect of her education was to be made relative to this. "One must inculcate at each moment in the head of a young girl that she is destined to create the happiness of a man," explained Mme Bernier; any pretensions towards equality "must be completely destroyed." Although women should not be left completely ignorant, conceded the author (lest they bore their husbands), the female sex was nevertheless, she declared, completely incapable both mentally and physically of any real study. Females should be inspired with a taste for only the domestic pleasures, and a girl was constantly to be told:

You can only truly fulfill your duties by sacrificing your inclinations to those of a husband; know how to yield your temperament and character . . . your only profession is to please him. . . .

If women could be trained to make men happy at home, concluded Mme Bernier, then men would be able to go forth into the world and do their great deeds. She won the prize.[13]

The rigid moral code and sexual differentiation consecrated by the Revolution also augured ill for feminine demands for expanded economic and employment opportunities. Professions and trades remained rigidly closed to the female sex. When a woman petitioned to be allowed to hold a chair in drawing at the *école centrale* of Chartres, she was refused because, she was told, "the interest of society and public morality exclude women from all professorships."[14] It is true that women were hired as instructors in public primary schools, but their pay was officially established as at least ⅙ to ⅓ less than that of male teachers.[15]

In only one major respect did the Revolution improve the position of women: in an effort to destroy the aristocracy, the National Assembly in 1790 declared equal inheritance for all, abolishing all former rights of primogeniture or masculinity, first in feudal tenure, and finally in all property. Considering the nature of the marriage laws at the time, however, such a ruling could be said to have benefited the husbands of France almost as much as the daughters.

True, women were given the right to serve as witnesses in civil acts, but in most other ways a woman's civil existence remained the same. The Revolutionary law that had established a procedure to confirm paternity and had held the father responsible for the economic support of all children of his begetting was abrogated by the Napoleonic Code. Article 340 of the Code actually *forbade* any paternity suits, while Article 341 *required* a search for maternity, so that the mother and not the State would assume the burden of the child's upkeep.[16]

The equal divorce laws of 1792 were also of short duration. After the coup of Prairial in the year IV, the reaction to the liberality of these laws gained in strength and violence. Typical of the tone of this literature was an essay written by Louis de Bonald entitled *Du divorce*. Bonald's major objection to divorce was that it presupposed an equality between the husband and wife ("the power" and "the subject"), which, he said, would overthrow the order of nature and the stability of modern society. The purpose of marriage, wrote Bonald, was the production and preservation of man (he did not say the human species). In this, as in everything else, the man was the active power, the woman was only the medium or means ("she receives in order to transmit").

Like many misogynists, Bonald sought a moral justification for his attitudes. According to Bonald, the position of the father to his family was identical to that of God to men, and a woman therefore owed her husband the same obedience and submission due her Lord. Divorce was a revolt against this system, he said, because it "deposed" the husband, granted the wife a right of judgment that nature reserved for the male alone, and introduced a species of polyandry. Furthermore, he warned, since the female's entire existence was defined by the family, any law that granted her the ability to withdraw herself from it effectively removed her from her "natural place" and left her an outcast of society. In surprising kinship with Voltaire, Bonald was an outspoken advocate of polygamy, arguing that the ancient customs of repudiation and polygamy were far more in accord with reason and nature than the present French laws on divorce, for, unlike the equal divorce laws, the old ways simply reinforced the man's position of power, kept women reserved and obedient, and avoided the public scandal of a woman voluntarily escaping from her natural state of dependence. This same line of reasoning led Bonald to declare that, unlike the infamy of wifely infidelity, a man's adultery was "without consequence" and could "only affect the heart of the wife." Furthermore, he explained, "the woman must be submissive to her husband, and the husband love his wife: now, submission is always exclusive and for one alone, whereas love can be shared." The fact that experience had shown that divorces were most often sought by wives was not, contended Bonald, an indication that women were more unhappy in marriage than men, but a proof instead of their "natural weakness" and "passion." The divorce law of 1792, he decided, was the single greatest

cause of the demagoguery, impiety, and general degeneration of France
that had so quickly followed it. He then chided the legislators of France:

Could you think that the *pères de famile* . . . consented to give the domestic
power that they hold from nature into your hands, so that their wives and
children could take advantage of the law to have the power to rise against them,
to examine their actions, to drag them before courts, to have their despotism
declared there . . .?

No, he decided, the French people could not so far have forgotten
"nature, reason, and their dignity." In this aspect, if not in all others, a
devoted disciple of a rechristianized Rousseau, Bonald declaimed harshly
against the insidious philosophy of the infidel Condorcet and warned his
countrymen:

Beware of creating powers, where nature only put duties, by decreeing the civil
equality of people distinguished from each other by domestic inequality.[17]

In response to this type of oratory, a decree was passed by 1795 abro-
gating the earlier divorce laws. The new divorce law finally published in
the year XI was very different from that of 1792. The husband was given
the right to demand a divorce on the basis of his wife's adultery, but the
woman was only allowed to do the same if her husband maintained his
concubine in their common home. In either case, the children were usually left with the father. Neither spouse was allowed to marry their
accomplice in sin, while the woman was to be condemned to a house of
correction for a period of not less than three months and not more than
three years.[18]

In most other respects, the marriage laws of France remained the same
as they had been before the Revolution. The debates surrounding the
composition of that section of the new civil code relative to marriage
were far more likely to seek ways to extend the powers of the husband
and father than to curtail them. Marriage was regarded as the basis and
sustenance of society. As one legislator explained it:

Marriage prepares the government of the family and brings about the social
order; it establishes the primary degrees of subordination necessary for its formation. The father is the *chef* by his force; the mother, the mediator, by her gentleness and persuasion; the children are the subjects . . . behold the pattern of all
governments.[19]

Subordination was considered necessary for both familial harmony and
prosperity, and the makers of the new law code were determined not to
leave French homes in a state of "anarchy." The new code would recall
women to the obedience they "owed" to their husbands, explained the

legislator Siméon: "The *puissance maritale*," he said, "proclaims, extends, and promises a better order, happier marriages, and more unity and bliss in families."[20]

When Robert Pothier's definitive treatise on French marriage law was republished in 1813, it required very little editing to bring it up to date, for the authors of the civil code had used Pothier as their major source. If anything, the power of the husband was increased. It was legally stipulated that the wife owed her husband full obedience, and the man's power to chastise her when she failed in her "duty" was supported by the explanation that "it is certainly necessary that the *père de famille*, as the domestic magistrate, may with moderation join force to authority to make himself respected in his home." The wife who complained of excessive brutality was required to *prove* that her life was in danger. Article 333 repeated the ancient law that a man could physically seize his wife and force her to return to him, but Article 334 denied a wife any similar right to "militarily constrain" her husband to receive her, because, said the law, "the wife . . . has no power over her husband." A wife was given only one new freedom of action: she had no need to be authorized by her husband in order to enter an action for divorce.[21]

The authors of the civil code argued long and hard over which of the various French property laws granted the husband the most extensive control over his wife's property. It was clearly understood that economic dependence assured domestic subordination, and this was what they were determined to preserve. The old laws governing the paraphernal system were considered to have given the wife "excessive independence." Said the legislator Albisson: "It is liable to put the sceptre of the family in her hand by an overthrow of the laws of nature, the sacred base of the domestic hierarchy, which must always be maintained." Others, such as Honoré Duveyrier, objected to the idea of community property because, said he: "Strict equity wishes that the man alone receive the fruits of the labor of which the man alone has the fatigue and danger." All agreed that the wife must be deprived of any control over her own property that would give her, in the words of Duveyrier, "that independence which her own interest condemns, which nature refutes, and which the law of France refuses." There was also a general fear that a wife's continued interest in her own property would distract her attention from the narrow limits of the home, where it was increasingly insisted that it should be confined:

Any system that associates her with exterior speculations and interests deters her primitive destination, alters the innocence of her affections, the purity of her desires, the simplicity of her duties; raises her thoughts and actions to a false independence which nature refused her, and directs her towards frivolity, dissipation, disorder, and vice, contrary to that alliance of attributes by which she is sovereign and slave: that touching accord of beauty and weakness, *empire* and submission, on which reposes her happiness and ours.[22]

The laws that eventually resulted from all of this discussion allowed a combination of the various systems that had previously existed under written and customary law, but with the power of the man over his wife's paraphernal and personal property increased to an even greater degree.

Of all the demands for sexual equality that were voiced during the Revolution, those that sought political rights for women probably met with the most dismal failure of all. Not only did they arouse the least support, but they also provoked some of the most violent reactions of alarm and rebuttal. In this area, as in most others, the Revolution appears to have left the position of women worse than before, for the limited political power exercised by female fief holders and religious communities in the *Ancien Régime* was destroyed along with all other feudal privileges. What a few had exercised as a privilege was now denied to all as a right. The Revolutionary movement for political rights for women also rallied the least number of adherents in the years that were to follow. Beginning around 1796, the advocates of sexual equality (and their opponents) once again began to take to their pens. There were a number of pleas for improved education for women, a few suggestions for more equitable marriage laws and increased employment opportunities, but almost no support for political rights for women. It was an idea that had seemingly been discredited by the Revolution itself. Yet the feminine demands for political rights that had increased during the years of the Revolution had in truth left a definite effect, for the opponents of equality in the years following the Revolution spent far more time than ever before refuting this aspect of the women's movement.

Most denials of women's political rights were based on the supposed subordination of the female in marriage. Rousseau was a favorite source, and readers at the turn of the century were constantly invited to consider the sexes in the state of nature, where man was (according to a male by the name of Guiraudet) "the *chef*, the master, the king, and the sovereign of his family." In the natural state, wrote Guiraudet, women and children could only stand in awed and frightened admiration of men's strength and address; according to him, this was one of the immutable laws of nature. But society had given the female pretensions, complained Guiraudet. She had begun to claim her right to equality as if it had been denied her by the injustice of man, and she flattered herself that her moral and intellectual inferiority were not really natural but the result instead of the inferior education to which men condemned her. Such ideas, Guiraudet told his readers, were an "abomination," an attempted "usurpation," and a "trap." Women were advised to go ahead and make themselves pretty, and to rest assured that they were important to men. But: "woe unto you," he warned, "if you wish to rival [man] or emulate him." Women will never be able to equal men, said Guiraudet, and their unnatural influence or power could only lead to the degradation of the arts, the debasement of society, and the overthrow of nations; he needed only to point an awful finger at the Revolution.[23]

The same arguments appear in the works of Louis de Bonald and others. In his *Théorie du pouvoir politique*, Bonald developed his favorite description of man as *"pouvoir,"* and woman as *"sujet."* The political state, said Bonald, "must be considered as a grand family, of which the leader or *power* is the father." Once again, the defender of tradition foresaw woe for those who confounded the two: "What lessons the universe gives of the deplorable effects of the weakness of the *power* and the vanity of the *subject!*" The idea appears once again that women are really so deplorably inferior to men that they can only be harmed by exposure to the dangers and demands of equal rights. Bonald warned: "Beware lest the philosophers [Condorcet] establish the most cruel inequality in the condition of the sexes, by wishing to establish between them an equality of rights."[24] In his volume *Je Cherche le Bonheur*, Antoine Clesse was another who expressed surprise at the bizarre "whim" of some women who wanted to escape the position of subordination he believed was assigned to them by nature, and who wished to "reign otherwise than by their weakness and their charms." To these oddities he could only reply: "No!"[25]

Even most latter-day champions of the feminine cause, such as Charles-Guillaume Théremin and the Princess de Salm-Reifferschield-Dyck, stopped short of supporting political rights for women. In his *De la Condition des femmes dans les républiques*, Théremin actually presented a detailed argument as to why women should be denied political power. He began by criticizing the post-Revolutionary position of women in France. Théremin defined happiness as "nothing more than the free exercise of all our faculties," which, he said, was currently denied the female sex. Surveying the effects of the Revolution on the condition of women, Théremin noted:

There has been neither an extension in the education of women nor an extension in their sphere of activity. The ability to inherit equally with us and that of divorce are the principal points that they have gained until now from the liberty of men.

At the same time, he said, every head of every family had been given the rights of a Salic monarch:

Never have the authority and the rights of women been more restricted . . . we have almost always in our laws considered the woman as the wife of the man . . . we have almost never treated them as citizens.

In their effort to make France a model of the Roman Republic, Théremin accused the French of having also revived the harshness of Rome. He dismissed the whole idea as an exercise in pedantry: not only had the French sought to revive Rome entirely, as if it were all good, he said, but they had also sought to reproduce Rome as it was two thousand years ago, and not as it would have been today. "It is necessary to move with the times," he observed, "and to have the courage to form new institutions."

But Théremin's courage failed at the thought of admitting women to politics. In a startling about-face, he declared that women were intimately united to their husbands, and together the two formed only one will with identical interests: "Their suffrage in the first place would be unnecessary, because the individual to whom they are attached cannot be doubly represented," he wrote, "and there is no need to manifest twice the same will. The husband and wife are only one political person and can never be anything else. . . ." Although he had earlier declared that "every woman born in the State bears at birth a right parallel to that of the man," Théremin now denied her the right to vote. Nor could this exclusion be based solely on the effects of the marriage vow, for he denied this right to all women, saying:

Mothers and wives, note this, that when your sons and your husbands deliberate in the sovereign assemblies, it is for you as well as themselves that they deliberate, it is your interests like their own that they stipulate. . . .

In words that echoed those of the Committee of Public Safety, he also reminded women that although they had not, like their men, sworn to obey the laws of the land, they were nevertheless firmly bound by the oath of their fathers and husbands.

Since women could not be allowed to vote, it naturally followed that they could not hold public office, either. "Just as their husbands or their fathers vote for them," explained Théremin, "they also fulfill these functions for them." To those women who would ask why they could not be allowed to do all this for themselves, he responded: "Without a doubt it is not a usurpation on our part . . . they never have possessed or exercised these rights." But, he assured them, they already possessed the greatest honor possible for women—they were citizens of France.[26]

The embryonic movement during the Revolution in favor of political, civil, educational, and economic equality for women failed mainly because of its inherent incompatibility with the basic ideology of the French Revolution itself. The French Revolution in no way altered the traditional eighteenth-century conceptualization of the female sex. Woman was still perceived as an inherently inferior being, created uniquely for man's usage and distinctively differentiated from him in character, ability, and destiny. It was not until the nineteenth century and the inescapable confrontation with the changes associated with the industrial revolution that it brought that these ideas could begin to be successfully challenged. The increasing educational achievements, economic power, and independence of nineteenth- and twentieth-century women translated into irrefutable reality what in the eighteenth century could be ignored as theory. Furthermore, the lack of female economic independence not only reduced the Revolutionary movement for women's rights to the theoretical level, but it also effectively reduced the size of the movement itself. The women of the French Revolution remained almost entirely dependent on their men for subsistence, a circumstance that effectively circumscribed their activity. It is interesting to note that the *enragés* and later Babeuf (if not quite all of his followers) were about the only factions within the Revolution to express any sympathy at all for the question of women's rights. Both have been seen as precursors of the socialists of the nineteenth century, who would also associate their movement with that of the feminists.

In many ways, the French Revolution only reinforced the traditional conceptualization of the female. The intellectual and social influence gained by the women of the upper classes in the course of the eighteenth century had provoked a violent reaction, which merged with the cult of sentimentalism and its accompanying glorification of the female in the domestic setting—a tendency that became even more popular in the course of the Revolution itself. It was a movement that could boast the enthusiastic support of a number of different women. There were few greater enemies of sexual equality than Jean-Jacques Rousseau, yet he was revered and adored by women everywhere. They wept over the *Nouvelle Héloïse* and vowed eternal devotion to the principles enunciated in *Emile*. Rousseau might have told women (gracefully) that they were weak and stupid, but he also told them that they were beautiful, that they were the moral half of humanity, and that they were utterly necessary for men's happiness. Men like d'Alembert or Riballier might revile him for the "poison . . . the venom hidden beneath the brilliant surface of [his] magic style,"[27] but women like Mme de Staël wrote eulogies to him. The secret of Rousseau's success was that he glorified and aggrandized women in the only career open to them—that of wife and mother—and he promised them in return love, respect, and happiness. It might have been a more subtle form of belittlement and a new justification for exploitation disguised as sentimentalism, but it set the tone for much of the nineteenth century. It also joined forces with one aspect of the women's movement that had always been more a demand for an increase in respect for women than a push for greater equality. It would take a long time to realize that true respect without equality was impossible.

The truth was, the eighteenth-century movement in favor of women's rights was in most ways antipathetically averse to the basic ideology of the French Revolution, and it attracted few supporters. The dissaffection of the majority of the men can be readily attributed to the basic fear and hostility such a movement would inevitably inspire in the male sex, but the lack of feminine support at first appears less easily explained. Nevertheless, the women of the Revolution were as much a product of their society as the men, and they had been trained since birth to accept their subservient state as natural. They had learned long ago that it was much easier to win a man over with a smile and a simulation of helplessness than by direct argument. The education and upbringing that they received could have been expressly designed to enervate the mind and spirit, and most women probably doubted their ability to compete with men as much as they feared any system that would force them to try. They had had it incessantly hammered into them by the wisest men of their day that the female sex was inherently inferior and that their subordinate condition was necessary both for their own good and that of society. Even such a social maverick as Mary Wollstonecraft, who must surely have known herself to be far more brilliant than a great many males of her day, was still not so bold as to proclaim the equal intelligence of the sexes. She even prefaced her revolutionary suggestion that women ought to be admitted to government with the timid "I may excite laughter, by dropping a hint. . . ."[28] Ridicule is a powerful weapon to depress aspirations and pretensions, and the men of the eighteenth century used it unmercifully. The woman who ventured to challenge tradition could only hope to make herself a public laughingstock. Even among those who might privately have believed in the equality of the sexes, it is not surprising that there were few brave enough to admit it.

What stands out most conspicuously is the failure on the part of any of the women of the late eighteenth century who had earned a reputation for either talent or intelligence willingly to champion the cause of their own sex. A good example can be found in Mme Roland. When she was 20, Mme Roland had once written to a friend:

One could say that women, favored by nature in so many respects, made to embellish the universe, only need to be raised like men to astonish them and show the virtues which, till now, one believes appropriate for men. . . .

Nevertheless, before she was 30, Mme Roland was laughing whenever anyone mentioned the equality of the sexes and once told a male acquaintance:

I believe, I would not say as much as any woman, but as much as any man, in the superiority of your sex in all respects. . . . It is for you to make the laws in science. Govern the world, change the surface of the globe, be proud, terrible, and wise, all that without us and by all that you must dominate us.[29]

A number of these women, such as Mme de Staël (and George Sand after her), far from seeking the emancipation of their own sex, actually professed to despise them and sought, instead, to identify themselves with the dominant sex. This disaffection from the ranks was recognized and depreciated even at the time. Mme Pipelet, who began near the turn of the century to advocate the equality of the sexes, criticized this tendency among literary and artistic women and urged them instead to

. . . use [your talents] in the defense of women; do not seek as others have done to be an exception among your companions, to adopt, with the talents that the men have appropriated, the tastes and opinions that characterize them: seek rather to honor your sex and to honor yourself in it.[30]

Charles Fourier (who has been credited with the creation of the word feminism) was another who sought to motivate women by scorning them for their blind submission to men, which, he said, only served to persuade their oppressors that they were born for nothing better than slavery. He, too, criticized the learned women of his day, who, he said, "embraced the philosophical egotism" of the male sex. Having once escaped the pitiful lot of their own sex, he accused them, they then simply closed their eyes to the misery of those left behind.[31]

In fact, even to speak of a "movement" for equal rights for women during the French Revolution is itself misleading. There was no organized, coherent movement, as such. Those few, isolated individuals who advocated equal rights for women never united to press for their common cause. The Revolutionary "movement" for sexual equality can virtually be reduced to the *philosophe* Condorcet and a few almost unknown women living on the fringes of society. Although they loom large in retrospect, at the time of the French Revolution itself these few isolated voices were scarcely heard amongst the thunderous roar of those demanding that women be "put back in their place."

Ever since the days of Greece, and probably before, men have been complaining that the women of their age were escaping from the subordinate position assigned to them by nature and society. The truth is, of course, that women have never been—nor could they ever be—kept in their allotted position, yet each generation of males has felt that it was somehow failing its self-appointed task of protecting the patriarchy, and the result is typically a combination of hostility, fear, and panic, which becomes even more apparent in times of social change.

The idea of sexual equality promised to bring with it a transformation of society the magnitude of which could hardly even be imagined. It would have forced a reexamination and alteration of every individual's self-perception, male or female. The idea of sexual equality also brought with it the threat of competition between the sexes, and the resulting fear of rivalry reechoes constantly throughout the Revolutionary period. The men of the French Revolution betrayed a characteristic male fear of female dominance, which has been shown to originate in the memory of the dominant power once exercised by the mother, combined with a resentment of the current power of sexual attraction exercised by the female sex in general.[32] The Revolutionary reaffirmations of male domination betray less an air of self-conscious superiority as a fear of female insubordination.

To these characteristic fears must be added the fact that the men of the Revolution were disproportionately afraid of their Queen, whom they recognized as a far more forceful individual than the King. As a subordinate and in some ways alien segment of society, women have traditionally been the victims of stereotyping, and in the course of the Revolution the female sex as a whole came to be identified with Marie Antoinette, who herself was gradually distorted until her character and personality could support the entire burden of blame for the coming of the Revolution.

If women could be held responsible for the corruption and degradation of the *Ancien Régime*, they could also be blamed for the ultimate "failure" of the Revolution. As early as 1789, satirical pamphlets and inflammatory journals had portrayed the female sex as the inherent enemy of the Revolution; in a few years, the idea had become so widespread as to be virtually commonplace. In the 1791 article "De l'influence de la Révolution sur les femmes," the journal *Révolutions de Paris* had reported that in 1789 the women (who under the monarchy had "trifled with the sceptre like a rattle") had expected to be able to play with the nation as with one of their dolls. They had soon learned differently. Although the women of the people, said the journal, had shown themselves to be good *citoyennes*, the rest "had fled this imposing male spectacle." Even those women who had wished to associate themselves with the Revolution were disparaged as being attracted mainly by the bright colors of the cockade and the romantic image of the uniforms of the National Guard. And when they saw their salons deserted, reported the journal, even these women "raved beneath their breath against the liberty that had changed the respect of their adorers." The identification of the female sex as a species apart was so great that the journal could actually brand all women above those of the people as "aristocrats."[33]

Women were especially accused of consorting and sympathizing with the clergy. Amar ended his 1793 report to the National Convention with the observation that

. . . since the beginning of the Revolution the women, more slaves to nobiliary and religious prejudices than men, have been constantly in the hands of the priests and the enemies of the State, and the prime movers of the troubles that have shaken the Republic.[34]

It is more than likely that when Robespierre wrote that women must be denied political rights to prevent them being used subversively by factions, this was the faction he had in mind.[35] The records of the Committee of Public Safety reverberate with accusations that "it is the women with the priests who have fomented and sustained the war in the Vendée," while the women in particular were accused of pitilessly and brutally murdering their enemies.[36] The women of the Halles in Paris, also, came to be continuously accused of being counterrevolutionary and royalist in sentiment.[37]

How much of this was true is difficult to say. Women had always been known in France as the "devout sex," and it is likely that more women than men both resented the Revolution's attacks on the clergy and continued to practice their religion, even after the official dechristianization of the State.[38] As the ones responsible for feeding the family and stretching the food budget, it was the women who most felt the squeeze of inflation and high prices, and it was the women who had to spend long and often futile hours waiting in bread lines. With the almost total failure of the Revolutionary legislation on poor relief, death and disease were already common by 1794. With the coming of the war and failure of the harvests, the inevitable result was famine. The death toll in the years 1795–96 was enormous, and the death rate for women was much higher than that for men. It was also the women who had to nurse their starving children and bury their newborn babies when their own starved bodies failed to produce the milk needed to nourish them.[39] Furthermore, women were apparently far more likely than men to be revolted by, or at least unenthusiastic for, the riotous murder and bloodshed that also accompanied the Revolution. The personal journals of the period are full of accounts similar to one left by the Englishwoman Grace Elliott, who relates the story of the escape of the Marquis de Chansenets from the attack on the Tuileries in 1792. At one point the Marquis is given food and water by a poor female shopkeeper, who tells him

that he must not stay there, as she expected her husband home every instant, and she said that he was a Jacobin, and detested gentlemen . . . that her husband had been very busy all day murdering the Swiss soldiers and the King's friends, and that she would not at all wish him to fall into her husband's hands. . . .[40]

Even among those women who were originally enthusiastic for the Revolution, the growing realization that Frenchmen had deliberately and definitively avoided including women in all their fine talk about liberty and equality would obviously cool the ardor of at least a few.

If the men of the year II and their later admirers could blame women for what was seen as the "failure" of the Revolution, then the Royalists and reactionaries could also hold them responsible for its near-success. The participation of so many women in the Revolution both shocked and revolted their society, for women were expected to be gentle, and their bloody excesses would be remembered long after those of the men were almost forgotten as commonplace. The French Revolution would forever afterwards be associated in the popular imagination with fishwives and furies and the "knitters of ninety-three." Some would even go so far as to attribute all the horror and destruction of the Revolution to the female sex. In his *Mémoires*, Buzot wrote:

It appears, in the final analysis, when things are well examined, that the French armies fought, the Assembly of the Nation dishonored itself, the public fortune was destroyed, and the whole Republic was tainted with French blood, only by the intrigues of the most hideous jades of Paris.[41]

There was nothing new in this, of course. Men had always found some woman to blame for everything that seemed to have gone wrong in history, from the Peloponnesian War to the fall of the Roman Empire.

The participation of women in the French Revolution both frightened and bewildered the men of the day, for they simply did not know how to cope with the situation. The heroism and courage displayed by women in the Revolution became legendary, and more than one writer in the years that followed would credit the women of the Revolution with more fortitude than their men. There were certainly few men in 1793 who had the courage to voice the sentiments expressed by women such as Olympe de Gouges or Claire Lacombe. The men of the Revolution were baffled, and they reacted in the only way they seemed to know: equality before the guillotine was about the only equal right granted to women by the men of the Revolution.

There is a story of a conversation that once took place between the widow of the *philosophe* Condorcet and the then General Bonaparte (renowned for his tendency to regard women as beings created only for recreation and reproduction). "I do not like women who meddle in politics," announced the General. "You are of course right, General," responded the widow tactfully; "But in a country where one cuts off their heads, it is certainly natural that they have the desire to know why."[42] The story well illustrates the point that, however little it may have intended to do so, the Revolution forced the women of France to become interested in politics. The women who took part in the *journées* of the Revolution were thinking about bread, not women's rights. If asked, they would probably have defined their sex role in much the same terms as the philosophers and legislators of their day, without realizing that by their very action they were challenging the validity of that stereotype. Yet the women of the Revolution unquestionably saw themselves as *citoyennes*, and although the word eventually might have fallen into disuse, the memory lingered.

The ideology of sexual equality had existed long before the Revolution, and although the Revolution itself had added little new to it, it nevertheless had a profound effect upon the movement, which was then still in its embryonic form. To begin with, it provided the movement (which would in only a few short years come to be known as feminism) with a vocabulary and phraseology, which would enable later generations of women to associate their cause with the increasingly popular one of freedom and humanity. It also encouraged the movement in a negative way, for by codifying and standardizing French law, the Revolution and the Napoleonic period that followed it could be said to have deteriorated the position of women in French society. It also made their classification as second-class citizens all the more obvious. In the *Ancien Régime*, women had been excluded from politics and government by custom; after the Revolution, they were eliminated by law. At the same time, the new philosophy of equality and liberty could only serve to expose this continued discrimination against women as the hypocrisy and prejudice that it was. And by singling women out and specifically excluding them, the new order managed to achieve what nothing else had ever done: it helped women to recognize themselves as a separate, and subjected, class in society. In the year VIII, Salm-Reifferschield-Dyck wrote: "It is especially since the revolution that this inconsistency has become more perceptible and that women, following the precedent of the men, have studied more their true essence and have acted in consequence."[43]

It has been said that the "feminists of the French Revolution" failed in their objective because their politics were at fault.[44] Condorcet and Théroigne were Girondins, Olympe de Gouges has been classified (however unjustly) as a Royalist, Claire Lacombe and Pauline Léon and their Society became *enragés*, while Etta Palm has been dismissed as a Dutch spy. Yet if Robespierre and the men of the year II are exalted as the purest expression of the Revolution, then their failure to associate any of the "feminists" of the day with their cause must be seen as an indictment not of these women and their supporters, but of the French Revolution itself.

NOTES

1. *Révolutions de Paris*, Vol. 15, No. 183, 5–12 January 1793, p. 120.
2. *Moniteur*, 2 May 1793, xvi–270; this law also sought to reduce the number of camp followers. In this latter respect it was enforced with difficulty. See complaints in *Moniteur,* 24 frimaire, year II, Vol. 18, p. 655; Aulard, *Recueil des Actes du Comité de Salut Public*, Vol. 9, pp. 331, 361, 398, 775; Vol. II, pp. 91, 258, etc. For secondary sources on the subject of women in the military, see Susan Conner, "Les Femmes Militaires: Women in the French Army, 1792–

1815," *Proceedings of the Consortium on Revolutionary Europe, 1982* (1983), pp. 290–302; Raoul Brice, *La Femme et les Armées de la Révolution et de l'Empire (1792–1815)*, (Paris: Edition moderne, n.d.); or Leon Schwab, "Les femmes aux Armées," *la Révolution dans les Vosges*, 6 (1912–13), pp. 109–115.

3. *Moniteur*, 29 May 1795, Vol. 24, p. 515.

4. Archives Nationales, AD II 48.

5. F.-A. Aulard, *Paris pendant la réaction Thermidorienne, et sous le Directorire: Recueil de documents* (5 vols.; Paris: Quantyin, 1902), Vol. 3, p. 548; Vol. 4, p. 624.

6. Such women, derogatorily dubbed "*tricoteuses*," were said to be provoking sedition. Ibid., Vol. 5, pp. 421, 433–434.

7. Ibid., Vol. 5, p. 739.

8. The National Assembly's 22 December 1789 decree divided the populace into "active" citizens—those paying a certain tax—and "passive citizens," i.e., women, foreigners, domestics, and poorer males.

9. Aulard, *Recueil des Actes du Comité de Salut Public*, Vol. 12, p. 271. When the National Assembly took the oath in 1790, both male and female spectators joined in. Elsewhere, the practice was sporadic: some places sometimes allowed women to take the oath, others did not. In general, mothers had more of a right to take the oath than childless women, but in time the consensus was that women had no need to take the oath at all, for their men had already sworn it for them.

10. Baron Felix Bonnaire, *Corps Législatif. Conseil des Cinq-Cents. Rapport fait par Bonnaire au nom d'une commission spéciale sur la Cocarde Nationale* (Paris: Imprimerie Nationale, year VII), p. 7.

11. See *Moniteur*, xxii–515; xxvi–321.

12. The legislation relative to the education of girls during the Revolution has been exhaustively covered. See, for instance, J. Balde, *Napoléon et l'éducation des filles*; Octave Gréard, *L'Enseignement secondaire des jeunes filles* (Paris: Delalain frères, 1883); or Louis Chabaud, *Les Précurseurs du féminisme, Mesdames de Maintenon, de Genlis, et Campan, leur role dans l'éducation chrétienne de la femme* (Paris: Plon, 1901).

13. Mme Bernier, *Quel est pour les femmes le genre d'éducation le plus propre à faire le bonheur des hommes en société?* (Paris: Imprimerie de Bossange, Masson et Besson, year XI), pp. 3, 4, 11, 12, 35.

14. *Moniteur*, xxvviii–270; 259.

15. *Moniteur*, xii–516; Baron Felix Bonnaire, *Corps législatif. Conseil des Cinq-Cents, Nouvelle Rédaction et réunion de tois projets de résolution sur l'instruction publique* (Paris: Imprimerie Nationale, year VII), p. 12.

16. Branca, *Women in Europe since 1750*.

17. L.-G. Bonald, *Du divorce, considéré au XIXe siècle, relativement à l'Etat Domestique* (Paris: le Clere, 1801), pp. 116, 128, 158, and 192.

18. *Loi relative au Divorce. Du 30 ventôse l'an XI de la République.* AD II 33, Archives Nationales.

19. J. Girard, Archives Nationales, AN II 33.

20. Archives Nationales, AD II 38.

21. Pothier, *Traité du contrat de mariage*, pp. 68, 311–313.

22. Archives Nationales, AD II 38.

23. T. Guiraudet, *De la Famille considérée comme l'élément des sociétés* (Paris: Desenne, 1797), pp. 27 and 43.

24. This work contains a spirited attack on Condorcet's advocacy of sexual equality in his *Esquisse d'un tableau historique*. Bonald takes Rousseau as his god and gospel and declares that "the 'prejudice' of the superiority of the man in the family will be maintained as long as the family itself." Louis de Bonald, *Théorie du Pouvoir politique et religieux dans la société civile démontrée par le raisonnement et par l'histoire* (Paris: Le Clére, 1848), Vol. 2, pp. 71, 99, and 462.

25. Antoine Clesse, *Je cherche le Bonheur, ou le célibat, le mariage et le divorce* (Paris: Moutardier, year X), pp. 199–200.

26. Charles-Guillaume Théremin, *De la Condition des femmes dans les républiques* (Paris: Laran, year VII), pp. 11, 31, 32, 37, 58, 60, and 61.

27. Riballier, *L'Education physique et morale des femmes, avec une notice de celles qui se sont distinguées dans les différentes carrières* (Paris: les frères Estienne, 1779), p. 23.

28. Wollstonecraft, *A Vindication of the Rights of Women*, p. 335.

29. Dessens, *Les Revendications*, p. 44.

30. Salm-Reifferschield-Dyck, *Rapport sur un ouvrage du C^{en} Théremin*, pp. 15–16.

31. Charles Fourier, *Théorie des quatre mouvements et des destinées générales*, in *Oeuvres complètes de Charles Fourier* (Paris: aux Bureau de la phalange, 1841), Vol. 1, pp. 221–222.

32. H. R. Hays, *The Dangerous Sex: The Myth of Feminine Evil* (New York: G. P. Putnam's Sons, 1964).

33. *Révolutions de Paris*, Vol. 7, No. 83, 5–12 February 1791, p. 229.

34. *Archives Parlementaires*, Vol. 81, p. 48.

35. Robespierre described politically active women as "as sterile as vice"; he would relegate the sex to the social role of reestablishing morality. Maximilien Robespierre, *Pièces trouvées dans les papiers de Robespierre et complices*, Brumaire, year III), pp. 95–96.

36. Aulard, *Recueil des Actes du Comité de Salut Public*, Vol. 9, p. 332, Vol. 11, pp. 278–279, etc.

37. See, for instance, Aulard, *Paris pendant la Réaction Thermidorienne*, Vol. 3, p. 41; Vol. 2, p. 566, etc., and [Hebert] *Le Père Duchesne* (Paris: Edhis, 1969), Vol. 9, No. 288), p. 78.

38. Olwen Hufton, in her article "Women without Men," notes the "particular role of village spinsters during the Revolution in sheltering refractory priests, organizing clandestine masses, taking risks in holding communal recitations of the rosary . . .," p. 368. See also Hufton, "Women in Revolution," for the reemergence of religious fervor after 1792.

39. See Olwen Hufton, "Women in Revolution."

40. Grace Dalrymple Elliott, *Journal of My Life During the French Revolution* (The Rodale Press, 1959), pp. 47–48. See also Roger Dupuy, "Les femmes et la contre Révolution dans l'ouest," *Bulletin d'histoire économique et sociale de la Révolution Française* (1980), pp. 61–70.

41. François-Nicholas Buzot, *Mémoires* (Paris: Henri Plon, 1866), p. 72; see

also F. L. Pelletier-St. Jullien, *Le Démérite des femmes, poème* (Paris: Debray, year XI).

42. Dessens, *Les Revendications*, p. 104.

43. Constance Salm-Reifferscheild-Dyck, *Rapport sur un ouvrage du C^en Théremin, intitulé: de la condition des femmes dans une République, par Constance D. T. Pipelet* (Paris: Imprimerie de Gillé, year VIII), p. 5.

44. One of the more recent writers to make this statement was Abray, "Feminism in the French Revolution," p. 61, but it can be found in the works of many earlier writers on the subject.

Bibliography

A. PRIMARY SOURCES

1. Printed Documents

Aulard, A. *Paris pendant la Réaction Thermidorienne et sous le Directoire: Recueil de Documents*, 5 vols. Paris: Quantin, 1902.

————. *Paris sous le Consulat: Recueil de Documents*, 4 vols. Paris: Quantin, 1909.

————. *Paris sous le Premier Empire: Recueil de Documents*, 3 vols. Paris: Barbier, 1923.

————. *Recueil des Actes de Comité de Salut Public*, 28 vols. Paris: Imprimerie Nationale, 1893–1964.

————. *La Société des Jacobins. Recueil de Documents*, 6 vols. Paris: Quantin, 1889–1897.

Brette, Armaud. *Recueil de documents relatifs à la convocation des Etats Généraux de 1789.*

Caron, Pierre. *Paris pendant la Terreur. Rapports des agents secrets du Ministère de l'Intérieur*, 4 vols. Paris: 1910–1958.

————. *Rapports des agents du Ministre de l'Intérieur dans les Départements (1793–an 2)*, 2 vols. Paris: Imprimerie Nationale, 1951.

Chassin, C.H.-L. *Les Elections et les Cahiers de Paris en 1789*, 4 vols. Paris: Quantin, 1888.

Debidour, A. *Recueil des Actes du Directoire Exécutif*, 4 vols. Paris: Imprimerie Nationale, 1817.

Douarche. *Les Tribunaux civils pendant la Révolution.*

Grimm and F. D. Diderot. *Correspondance littéraire, philosophique et critique*, 15 vols. Paris: 1877–1881.

Guillaume, M. J. (ed.). *Procès-verbaux du comité de l'instruction publique de l'Assemblée législative*. Paris: 1889.

————. *Procès-verbaux du Comité d'instruction publique de la Convention Nationale*. Paris: Imprimerie Nationale, 1801.

Lacroix, Sigismond. *Actes de la Commune de Paris pendant la Révolution*. Paris: DuPalais, 1921.

Lacombe, Paul. *La Bibliograhie Parisienne*. Paris: Chez P. Rouquette, 1887.

Tourneax, *Le Répertoire des sources imprimées de l'histoire de Paris*. Paris: 1890–1913.

Tuetey, Alexdre. *Répertoire général des sources manuscrites de l'Histoire de Paris pendant la Révolution française*. 11 vols. Paris: 1890–1914.

2. Journals

[Peltier]. *Actes des Apôtres*.

[Leclerc]. *L'Ami du peuple*.

[Marat]. *L'Ami du peuple, ou le publiciste parisien*.

La Bouche de fer.

[Beaumont, Mme de]. *Le Bulletin*.

[Desmoulins, Camille]. *Courrier de France et de Brabant*.

Courrier de l'hymen, Journal des dames.

Journal d'instruction sociale, par les citoyens Condorcet, Sieyès et Duhamel.

Journal de la montagne.

Le Journal de la Société de 1789, devenue *Mémoires de la Société de 1789*.

Le Journal de Paris.

Journal des débates de la Société des Amis de la Constitution séanté aux Jacobins à Paris.

Le Journal des Droits de l'Homme.

Journal Encyclopédique.

La Gazette des Halles.

Le Mercure National.

Le Mot à l'oreille ou le Don Quichotte des Dames, Nouveau Journal Républicain.

[Verte-Allure, Mme de]. *L'Observateur féminin*, devenue *l'Etoile du matin ou les Petits Mots de Mme de Verte-Allure, ex-religieuse*.

[Martel]. *L'Orateur de peuple*.

[Hébert, Jacques-René]. *Le Père Duchesne*.

Réimpression de l'Ancien Moniteur. Paris: Plon-Frères, 1847.

[Desmoulins, C.]. *Révolutions de France et de Brabant*.

[Prudhomme]. *Révolutions de Paris*.

Le Tocsin de Richard sans-peur.

Le Véritable Ami de la Reine, ou Journal des Dames, par une société de citoyennes.

[Mercier, Louis-Sebastien]. *Tableau de Paris*.

3. Printed Books, Memoirs, and Pamphlets

a. *Works whose author is known*

[Agier, P. J.]. *Du mariage dans ses rapports avec la religion et avec les lois nouvelles de France*. 2 vols. Paris:Imprimerie Librairie Chrétienne, year IX.

Agrippa, Henricus Cornelius. *De la précellence du sexe féminin*. Translated by Gueudenville. 3 vols. Leiden: 1726.

Albisson. *Opinion sur le projet de loi concernant le contrat de mariage et les droits respectifs des époux, séance du 19 pluviose*, year XII.

Alembert, Jean Le Rond d'. "Lettre à J. J. Rousseau, citoyen de Genève, sur les Spectacles," in *Oeuvres complètes d'Alembert*. Paris: A. Belin, 1822.

[Alkan, M.]. *Les Femmes compositrices d'imprimérie sous la Révolution Française en 1794, par un ancien typographe*. Paris: Dentu, 1862.

Amiard, Vve. *Petit Saint-Cyr national, fondé par la Société de bienfaisance pour l'éducation des pauvres demoiselles, sans distinction de naissance*. Paris: Imprimerie de Pougin, n.d.

————. *Plan d'un hospice d'éducation, pour les jeunes demoiselles dénuées de fortune, sous la protection de la nation, et approuvé par l'Assemblée Nationale*. N.p., n.d.

Antraigues, Emmanuel-Louis-Henri de Launay, Comte d'. *Observations sur le divorce*. Paris: Imprimerie Nationale, 1789.

Archambault, Mlle. *Dissertation sur la question: Lequel de l'homme ou de la femme est plus capable de constance? Ou la Cause des Dames*. Paris: Pissot et J. Bullot, 1750.

Argenson, Réne-Louis de Voyer, Marquis d'. *Considérations sur le gouvernement ancien et présent de la France*. Amsterdam: 1784.

Artaize, Chevalier de Feucher d'. *Lettre à Mme d**** [Gacon-Dufour], *auteur du Mémoire pour le sexe féminin contre le sexe masculin*. Paris: Chez tous les Marchands de Nouveautés, 1788.

————. *Nouvelles Réflexions d'un jeune homme, ou Suite à l'Essai sur la dégradation de l'homme en société*. Paris: Royez, 1787.

————. *Réflexions d'un jeune homme. Dégradation de l'homme en société, ou Essai sur la decadence du goût des arts et des sciences*. Paris: Chez Royez, 1786.

————. *Prisme moral, ou Quelques pensées sur divers sujets*. Paris: Migneret, 1809.

Bachelier. *Mémoire sur l'education des filles, presenté aux Etats Généraux*. Paris: 1789.

Bar. *Motifs des dispositions du titre III du livre premier du code civil, sur les droits des époux, présentés au nom du comité de législation*.

[Baret]. *Requête des filles de Paris à l'Assemblée Nationale*. Paris: Balanchon, 1789.

Bernier, Mme née Villers. *Discours qui a concouru à l'Institut national de France, sur cette question: Quelles doivent être, dans une République bien constituée, l'étendue et les limits du pére de famille?* Paris: E. Charles, year IX.

————. *Quel est pour les femmes le genre d'éducation le plus propre à faire le bonheur des hommes en société?* Paris: Imprimerie de Bossange, Masson et Besson, year XI.

Blanchard, Jean-Baptiste, l'abbé. *L'Ecole des Moeurs ou Réflexions morales et historiques sur les maximes de la Sagesse*. 3 vols. Lyon: J. M. Bruyset, 1782.

————. *Préceptes pour l'éducation des deux sexes à l'usage des familles Chrétiennes*. 2 vols. Lyon: Bruyset ainé, 1803.

[Boissel, Françoise]. *Le Catéchisme du genre humain*. N.p., 1789.

Bonald, Louis de. *Du divorce, considéré au XIXe siècle, relativement à l'Etat Domestique*. Paris: Le Clère, 1801.

_____. *Théorie du pouvoir politique et religieux dans la société civile démontrée par le raisonnement et par l'histoire*. Paris: A. Le Clère, 1848.

Bonnaire, Baron Felix. *Corps législatif. Consiel des Cinq-Cents. Nouvelle Rédaction et réunion de tois projets de résolution sur l'instruction publique*. Paris: Imprimerie Nationale, year VII.

_____. *Corps législatif. Conseil des Cinq-Cents. Rapport fait par Bonnaire au nom d'une commission speciale sur la Cocarde Nationale*. Paris: Imprimerie Nationale, year VII.

Bonneville, N. *Le Nouveau Code conjugal, Etabli sur les bases de la constitution, et d'après les principes et les considérations de la loi déjà faite et sanctionnée, qui a préparé et ordonné ce nouveau code*. Paris: Imprimerie du cercle social, 1792.

Booser, Mlle. *Triomphe de la saine philosophie, ou de la vraie politique des femmes*. Paris: Debrai, n.d.

Bouchotte, M. *Dernières Observations sur l'accord de la Raison, et de la Religion, pour le rétablissement du divorce, l'anéantissement des Séparations entre époux, et la réformation des loix relatives à l'Adultère*. Paris: Imprimerie Nationale, 1791.

_____. *Observations sur l'accord de la Raison et de la Religion pour le rétablissement du Divorce, l'anéantissement des séparations etre époux, et la réformation des loix relatives à l'adultère*. Paris: Imprimerie Nationale, 1790.

Bouchu, René Victor. *Les femmes*. Chaumont: Cousot, 1812.

Boudier de Villement, Pierre Joseph. *L'Ami des femmes, ou Morale du sexe*. Paris: Royez, 1788.

_____. *Conseils aux femmes*. Paris: Gustave Sandré, 1852.

[Butot]. *Cours de morale fondé sur la nature de l'homme*. London: 1789.

Buzot. *Mémoires*. Paris: Henri Plan, 1866.

Caffiaux, Don Philippe-Joseph. *Défenses du beau sexe, ou Mémoires historiques, philosophiques et critiques pour servir d'apologie aux femmes*. 3 vols. Amsterdam: 1753.

[Cailly]. *Les Griefs et plaintes des femmes mal mariées*. Paris: Boulard, 1789.

Campan, Mme. *De l'Education*. Paris: Baudouin frères, 1824.

Caradeuc de la Chalotais, Louis-René. *Essai d'éducation nationale ou plan d'études pour la jeunesse*. N.p., 1763.

Carrion-Nisas. *Discours prononcé contre le projet de loi, titre X, livre III du Code Civil, sur le Contrat de Mariage et les droits respectifs des époux*, séance du 19 pluviôse, year XII [1804].

Catalani, Vincenzo. *L'Ami du beau sexe, ou Nouvelles Réflexions sur l'influence des Femmes dans la société, et sur leur éducation*. 3 vols. Bourg nella Bressa: Janinet, year XIII [1805].

Cerfvol (de). *La Gamologie, ou de l'Education des jeunes filles destinées au marriage*. Paris: 1772.

Chabot, Francois. *Projet d'acte constitutif des Français*. Paris: Imprimerie Nationale, n.d.

Chamcenetz, Louis-Pierre, Quentin de Richebourg. *Petit Traité de l'amour des femmes pour les sots*. À Bagatelle, 1788.

Chanterolle, Mlle de. *À messieurs les auteurs de l'"Esprit des journaux."* Paris: Chez les Libraires associés, 1778.

———. *Aspect philosophique.* Paris. P.-D. Pierres, 1777.

Charron. *Pétition à l'Assemblée Nationale, par Montaigne, Charron, Montesquieu et Voltaire; suivie d'un consultation en Pologne et en Suisse.* Paris: Desenne, 1791.

Choderlos de Laclos, Pierre-Amboise-François. *Dangerous Connections, or Letters Collected in a Society and Published.* 4 vols. London: T. Hookham, 1784.

———. *De l'Education des femmes.* Paris: A. Messein, 1903.

———. *La Galerie des dames françoises.* London, 1790.

———. *Troisième Essai sur l'éducation des femmes.* Paris: 1783.

[Clapies, Charles]. *Paradoxe sur les femmes, où l'on tâche de prouver qu'elles ne sont pas de l'espèce humaine.* Cracow, 1766.

[Clement, Mme]. *Les Femmes vengées de la sottise d'un philosophe ou Réponse au projet de loi de M S*** M***.* Paris: Imprimerie de Biant, 1801.

Clesse, Antoine. *Je cherche le bonheur, ou le Célibat, le mariage et la divorce.* Paris: Moutardier, year X.

Coicy, Mme. *Demande des femmes aux Etats Généraux, par l'auteur des femmes comme il convient de les voir.* N.p., n.d.

———. *Les Femmes comme il convient de les voir.* 2 vols. London and Paris: Bacot, 1785.

Condorcet, Jean-Antoine-Nicolas de Caritat, Marquis de. *Avis d'un père proscrit à sa fille.* N.p., n.d.

———. *Oeuvres complètes de Condorcet.* 21 vols. Paris: 1804.

Courtenai de la Fosse Ronde, Mme. Sophie-Remi. *l'Argument des pauvres aux Etats Généraux.* N.p., n.d.

Damours. *Lettres de milady *** sur l'influence que les femmes pourraient avoir dans l'éducation des hommes.* 2 vols. Paris: 1784.

Danton, George-Jacques. *Oeuvres de Danton*, recueillies et annotées par A. Vermorel. Paris: F. Cournol. 1866.

[Delanaup]. *Satire contre les femmes et les chimères qui les ont perverties, par Ch. D***.* Paris: Mongie, Colnet, Debray, year XII.

Dell'Acqua. *Essai sur la supériorité intellectuelle de la femme.* Berlin: 1798.

Desmarest. *Premiers Eléments de l'Instruction Républicaine par la citoyenne Desmarest.* Paris: year II.

Desmoulins, Camille. *Oeuvres de Camille Desoulins.* 2 vols. Paris: Charpentier, 1874.

Diderot, Denis, and d'Alembert, Jean (Editors). *Encyclopédie et dictionnaire raisonné des sciences, des arts, et des métiers, par une société de gens de lettres.* Paris: 1751–1780.

Diderot, Denis. *Oeuvres complètes.* Paris: Le Club française du livre, 1971.

Dinouart, Abbé Joseph-Antoine Toissant. *Le Triomphe du sexe, ouvrage dans lequel on démontre que les femmes sont en tout égales aux hommes.* Amsterdam: I. Racon, 1749.

"Duchêne." *Cinquième Lettre bougrement patriotique de la mère Duchêne où elle félicite les dames françoises sur leur amour pour leur patrie.* Paris: Guilhemat, n.d.

———. *Septième Lettre bougrement patriotique de la Mère Duchêne sur le décret portant égalité des droits aux successions ab intestat.* Paris: Guilhemat, n.d.

Dupont de Nemours, Pierre-Samuel. *Sur les institutions religieuses dans l'intérieur des familles, avec un essai de traduction nouvelle de l'oraison dominicale.* N.p., n.d.

————. *Vues sur l'éducation nationale.* Paris: Chez du Pont, year II.

Du-Puis, Vital. *Tableau du mariage, ou Conseils aux filles et aux garçons.* Toulous: Imprimerie de J.-M. Baume, n.d.

Duveyrier, Honoré. *Rapport fait par Honoré Duveyrier, Tribun, au nom de la section de législation, sur le projet de loi concernant les contrats de mariage et les droits respectifs des époux,* séance du 19 pluviôse, year XII.

Elbée, L.-A. *Asyle toujours ouvert aux plus infortunées et aux plus à plaindre des jeunes filles qui veulent toujours être honnêtes et verteuses.* Paris: Imprimerie de L. Jorry, 1789.

————. *Plan d'un chapitre noble de Femmes, qui seroit en même temps une maison d'éducation pour les jeunes personnes faites pour jouer le plus grand rôle dans la Société, afin d'y rétablir les bonnes moeurs autant qu'il est possible.* Paris: Chez Planche, 1789.

————. *La Véritable Ressource que l'on peut tirer du rouge en faveur des pauvres femmes et veuves d'officiers.* N.p., n.d.

Fauchet, Claude, l'abbé. *La Religion nationale.* Paris: Bailly, 1789.

[Fauqueux, A.]. *Des femmes et de leurs differents charactères.* Paris: Delaunay, 1817.

Fénelon, François de Salignac de la Mothe, Archevêque de Cambrai. *De l'Education et des devoirs des filles.* Paris: Vve Hérissant, 1776.

[Ferrières, Ch-Elie]. *La Femme et les voeux.* Paris: Poincot, 1788.

[Fevre du Grand-Vaux]. *Lettre à Mme la comtesse de * * * sur l'éducation des jeunes demoiselles.* Paris: 1789.

Fourier, Charles. *Théorie des quatre mouvements et des destinées générales* in *Oeuvres complètes de Charles Fourier,* Vol. 1. Paris: Aux bureau de la phalange, 1841.

Fumelh, Mme de. *Deuxième discours à la nation française.* Paris: Chez Lacloye, 1789.

————. *Discours à la nation française.* Paris: n.p., 1789.

Gacon-Dufour, Marie Armande Jeanne d'Humières. *Contre le projet de loi de S* * * M* * * [Sylvain Maréchal] portant défense d'apprendre à lire aux femmes, par une femme qui ne se pique pas d'être femme de lettres.* Paris: Ouvrier, year IX.

————. *De la nécessité de l'instruction pour les femmes.* Paris: F. Buisson, year XIII.

————. *Les Dangers de la coquetterie.* Paris: Buisson, 1788.

————. *Mémoire pour le sexe féminin contre le sexe masculin.* Paris: Royez, 1787.

Galiani, Ferdinando, l'abbé. *Dialogue sur les femmes.* Paris: Gustave Sandré, 1852.

Genlis, S.-F., Mme de. *Adèle et Théodore, ou Lettres sur l'éducation, contenant tous les principes relatifs aux trois différente plans d'éducation des princes, des jeunes personnes et des hommes.* Paris: M. Lambert et F. J. Baudoiun, 1782.

_____. *Discours sur la suppression des convents de religieuses et sur l'éducation publique des femmes*. Paris: Onfroy, 1790.

_____. *L'Epouse impertinent par air, suivie du Mari corrupteur et de la Femme philosophe*. Paris: Maradau, 1804.

_____. *De l'Influence des femmes sur la littérature française, comme protectrices des lettres et comme auteurs, ou précis de l'histoire des femmes françaises les plus célèbres*. Paris: Maradan, 1811.

_____. *Mémoirs inédits de Madame la Comtesse de Genlis*. 10 vols. Paris: Ladvocat, 1825.

Girard, J. *Considérations sur le mariage et sur le divorce*. Paris: Imprimerie de Deltufo de Everat, 1797.

Gossin. *Motions sur l'article XII du titre 9 du nouveau projet sur l'ordre judicares*. N.p., n.d.

Gouges, Marie dite Olympe de. *Action héroique d'une Françoise, ou la France sauvée par les femmes*. Paris: Guillaume junior, n.d.

_____. *Adresse au Don Quichotte du Nord*. Paris: Imprimerie nationale, 1792.

_____. *Adresse au roi. Adresse à la reine. Adresse au prince de Condé. Observation à M. Duveyrier sur sa fameuse ambassade*. N.p., n.d.

_____. *Adresse aux represéntans de la nation. Mémoire pour Madame de Gouges, contre la Comédie Françoise*. N.p., n.d.

_____. *Avis pressant à la convention, par une vrai républicaine*. N.p., n.d.

_____. *Avis pressant, ou Réponse à mes calomniateurs*. N.p., n.d.

_____. *Le Bonheur primitif de l'homme, ou les Rêveries patriotiques*. Paris: Royer, 1789.

_____. *Le Bon Sens François, ou l'Apologie des vrais Nobles, dédiées aux Jacobins*. N.p., n.d.

_____. *Les Comédiens démasqués, ou Mme de Gouges ruinée par la Comédie-françoise, pour sa faire jouer*. Paris: Imprimerie de la Comédie-françoise, 1790.

_____. *Correspondance de la Cour, Compte moral rendu et dernier mot à mes chers amis, par Olympe de Gouges, à la convention nationale et au peuple sur une dénonciation faite contre son civisme, aux Jacobins, par le sieur Bourdon*. N.p., n.d.

_____. *Le Cri du sage, par une femme*. N.p., n.d.

_____. *Départ de Necker et de Mme de Gouges, ou les Adieux de Mme de Gouges aux François et à M Necker*. Paris: 1790.

_____. *Dialogue allégorique entre la France et la Vérité. Dédié aux Etats Généraux*. N.p., n.d.

_____. *Discours de l'aveugle aux François*. N.p., n.d.

_____. *Droits de la femme. À la Reine*. N.p., n.d.

_____. *L'Esprit françois, ou Problème à résoudre sur le labyrinthe des divers complots*. Paris: Vve Duchesne, 1792.

_____. *Les Fantômes de l'opinion publique*. N.p., n.d.

_____. *La Fierté de l'innocence, ou le Silence du véritable patriotisme*. Paris: Imprimerie nationale, 1792.

_____. *Lettre à Mgr le duc d'Orléans, premier prince du sang*. N.p., n.d.

_____. *Lettre au peuple*. Paris: Maradan, 1788.

_____. *Lettre aux littérateurs français*. N.p., n.d.

_____. *Lettre aux représantants de la nation*. Paris: Imprimerie de L. Jorry, n.d.

_____. *Lettres à la Reine, aux généraux de l'armée, aux amis de la constitution et aux Françaises citoyennes. Description de la fête du 3 juin*. Paris: Imprimerie de la Société typographique, n.d.

_____. *Mes voeux sont replis, ou le Don patriotique*. N.p., n.d.

_____. *L'Ordre national, ou le Comte d'Artois inspiré par Mentor, Dédié aux Etats généraux*. N.p., 1789.

_____. *Pacte national, par Mme de Gouges, adressé à l'Assemblée nationale*. Paris: Imprimerie de la Société typographique, 1792.

_____. *Philosophe corrigé*. N.p., 1788.

_____. *Pour sauver la patrie, il faut respecter les trois ordres, c'est le seul moyen de conciliation qui nous reste*. N.p., n.d.

_____. *Le Prince philosophe*. N.p. n.d.

_____. *Projet sur la formation d'un tribunal populaire et suprême en matière criminelle, présenté par Mme de Gouges, le 26 mai 1790, à l'Assemblée Nationale*. Paris, Imprimerie du "Patriote françois," n.d.

_____. *Remarques patriotiques*. Paris: 1789.

_____. *Repentir de Mme de Gouges* [5 September 1791].

_____. *Réponse à la justification de Maximilien Robespierre, adressée à Jérôme Pétion, par Olympe de Gouges. Pronostic sur Maximilien Robespierre*. N.p., n.d.

_____. *Réponse au champion américain ou Colon très-aisé à connaître*. N.p., n.d.

_____. *Séance royale. Motion de Mgr le duc d'Orléans, ou les Songes patriotiques*. N.p., 1789.

_____. *Sera-t-il roi, ou ne le sera-t-il pas?* N.p., n.d.

_____. *Testament politique d'Olympe de Gouges* [4 June 1793].

_____. *Le Tombeau de Mirabeau*. N.p., n.d.

Grafigny, Mme de. *Lettres Péruviennes*. Paris: Duchesne, 1752.

Gouber de Groubentall. *Discours sur l'autorité paternelle et le devoir filial, considérés d'après la Nature, la civilisation et le Pacte social*. Paris: Chez l'auteur, 1791.

Guiraudet, T. *De la Famille considérée comme l'élément des sociétés*. Paris: Desenne, 1797.

Guyomar, Pierre. *Le Partisan de l'égalité politique entre les individus ou problème très-important de l'égalité en droits de l'inégalité en fait*. Paris: Imprimerie nationale, n.d.

Hamilton, Elizabeth. *Lettres sur les principes élémentaires d'éducation*. Paris: Demonville, 1804.

Helvetius. "De l'Esprit," in *Oeuvres complètes*, 1774.

Hennet, Albert-Joseph-Ulpien. *Du divorce*. Paris: Desenne, 1789.

Hérault-Séchelles. *Discours prononcé par Hérault-Séchelles, président de la Convention Nationale le 10 août 1793, à la fête de l'unité et l'indivisibilité de la République française*, year II,

Holbach, Paul-Henri-Dietrch, Baron d'. *Système social, ou principes naturels de la morale et de la politique*. Paris: Niogret, 1822.

"Jodin, Mlle." *Vues législatives pour les femmes, adressées à l'assemblée nationale*. N.p., 1790.

Lacombe, Claire. *Rapport fait par la citoyenne Lacombe, à la société des républicaines révolutionnaires, de ce qui c'est passé le 16 septembre à la Société des Jacobins, concernant celle des républicaines révolutionnaires, séance à S. Eustache, et les dénonciations faites contre la citoyenne Lacombe personnellement.* 17 September 1793.

Lambert, Ann Thérese. *Avis d'une mère à son fils, et à sa fille.* Paris: Chez Etienne Ganeau, 1734.

————. *Réflexions nouvelles sur les femmes.* London: Chez J. P. Coderc, 1730.

Laugier, E.-M. *Tyrannie que les hommes ont exercée dans presque tous les temps et pays contre les femmes.* Paris: Cul-de-sac Saint-Dominique, 1788.

"Launay, Florentine de." *Etrennes aux grisettes; requête présentée à M. Silvain Bailly, maire de Paris. Par Florentine de Launay, Contre les marchandes de Modes, Couturières, Lingéres et autres Grisettes commerçantes sur le pays de Paris. Ec.* N.p., 1790.

Lebrun, Ponce-Denis Ecouchard. *Aux Belles qui veulent devenir poètes,* in *Oeuvres.* Paris: Lemoine, 1827.

LeGouve, Gabriel. *Le Mérite des femmes, poème.* Paris: Didot, 1801.

Le Masson le Golft, Mlle Marie. *Lettres relatives à l'éducation.* Paris: Buisson, 1788.

[Lemontey, Pierre Edouard]. *Récit exact de ce qui c'est passé à la séance de la Société des Observateurs de la Femme, le mardi 2 novembre 1802, par l'auteur de Raison, Folie, etc.* Paris: Deterville, year XI.

Le Noble, Pierre. *Projet de loi pour les mariages présenté à l'assemblée nationale.* Paris: Garnéry, year II.

Leprince de Beaumont. *Magasin des jeunes dames ou instruction des jeunes dames qui entrent dans le monde.* 4 vols. Paris: J. F. Bassompierre, 1772.

Levallois, J. P. Alphonse. *Hommage au beau sexe ou Discours sur les femmes.* Mortagne: Marre-Roguin, 1813.

Lezay-Marnezia, Claude-François-Adrien. *Plan de lecture pour une jeune dame.* Paris: Prault, 1784.

Ligne, Charles-Joseph, Prince de. "Réflexions sur les femmes," in *Mes écarts ou ma Tête en Liberté.* Paris: E. Sansot et Cie, 1906.

Mabley, Gabriel Bonnot, Abbé de. *De la Législation, ou Principes des loix* in *Collection complète des oeuvres de l'abbé de Mabley,* Vol. 9. Paris: Imprimerie de C. Desbrières, year III.

Maintennon, Françoise d'Aubigné, Mme. *Conseils et instruction aux demoiselles pour leur conduite dans le monde.* Paris: Charpentier, 1857.

————. *Lettres et entretiens sur l'éducation des filles.* Paris: Charpentier, 1861.

Maistre, Joseph de. *Oeuvres complètes.* Genève: Slatkine Reprints, 1979.

Maréchal, Pierre-Sylvain. *Projet d'une loi portant défense d'apprendre à lire aux femmes.* Lille, Castiaux, 1841.

Marivaux, Pierre Carlet de Chamblain de. *La Nouvelle colonie ou la ligue des femmes.* Paris: Libraire Hatier, n.d.

Mirabeau. *Travail sur l'éducation publique.* Paris: Imprimerie Nationale, 1791.

Miremont, Anne d'Aubourg de la Bove, Comtesse de. *Traité de l'éducation des femmes.* 7 vols. Paris: P.-D. Pierres, 1779.

Moitte, Mme. *Suite de l'âme des Romaines dans les femmes françaises, par Mme Moitte, auteur du projet des dons offerts, par des femmes d'artistes célèbres, à l'Assemblée Nationale*. Paris: Imprimerie Knafren, n.d.

Montesquieu, Charles de Secondat, Baron de la Brede et de. *Oeuvres complètes de Montesquieu*. 3 vols. Paris: Librairie Hachette et C^le., 1874.

[Moulières, Raup-Baptestin de]. *Les Généreuses Françaises. Anecdote historique. Prompts effets du bon exemple. Nécessité de l'établissement d'une Caisse patriotique.* Paris: 1789.

Necker, Suzanne Curchod, Mme. *Mélanges extraits des manuscrits de Mme Necker*. 3 vols. Paris: C. Pougens, 1798.

————. *Réflexions sur le divorce*. Lausanne: Durand Ravanel, 1794.

"Orléans, S. A. S. Mgr. Louis-Philippe-Joseph d'." *Traité philosophique, théologique et politique de la loi du Divorce*. N.p., June 1789.

Oudot, C. F. *Essai sur les principes de la législation des mariages privés et solennels, du divorce et de l'adoption qui peuvent être déclarés à la suite de l'acte constitutionel*. Paris: Imprimerie Convention National, n.d.

Palm, Etta née d'Aelders. *Appel aux Françaises, sur la régénération des moeurs et nécesseté de l'influence des femmes dans un gouvernement libre*. Paris: Imprimerie du Cercle Social, 1791.

Pelletier-St. Julien, F. L. *Le Démérite des femmes, poème*. Paris: Debray, year XI.

Pierre Le Noble. *Projet de loi pour les mariages, présenté à l'assemblée nationale*. Paris: Garnery, year II.

Pothier, Robert. *Traité de la communauté, auquel on a joint un Traité de la puissance du mari sur la personne et les biens de la femme*. Paris: DeBure, 1770.

————. *Traité du contrat de mariage*. 2 vols. Paris: Letellier, 1813.

[Poullain de la Barre, François]. *De l'Egalité des deux sexes, discours physique et moral où l'on voit l'importance de se défaire des préjugés*. Paris: Chez Jean du Puis, 1673.

[Puisieux, Philippe Florent de]. *La Femme n'est pas inférieure à l'homme*. London: 1750.

Puisieux, Mme de, née Madeleine d'Arsant. *Conseils à une amie*. N.p., 1749.

Roland, Mme. *Comment l'éducation des femmes pourrait contribuer à rendre les hommes meilleurs*. Paris: 1777.

Ranto de Laborie. *Lettres sur l'éducation des femmes et sur leur caractère en général*. Saint Omer, 1757.

Re[s]tif de la Bretonne, Nicolas Edne. *L'Année des Dames Nationales ou Histoire, jour par jour, d'une femme de France*. Paris: Duchêne, 1791–1794.

————. *Les Contemporaires*. Paris: G. Charpentier et C^ic, 1884.

————. *La Femme infidèle, ou la Femme lettrée, ou la Femme monstre*. Paris: Maradan, 1788.

————. *Le Gynographe ou Idées de deux honnêtes femmes sur un projet de règlement pour mettre les femmes à leur place et opérer le bonheur des deux sexes*. N.p., n.d.

————. *Les Parisiennes, ou XL caractères généraux pris dans les moeurs actuelles, propres à servir à l'instruction des personnes du sexe*. 4 vols. Paris: Guillot, 1787.

————. *Le Paysan et la paysanne pervertis*. Paris: A. Dupret, 1888.

_____. *Le Thesmographe, ou Idées d'un honnête homme, sur un projet de règle-ment, proposé à toutes les Nations de l'Europe, pour opérer une Réforme générale des Loix.* Paris: Maradan, 1789.

Reyre, Abbé. *Ecole des jeunes demoiselles ou Lettres d'une mère vertueuse à sa fille avec les réponses.* 2 vols. Paris: Varin, 1786.

Riballier. *L'Education physique et morale des femmes, avec une notice de celles qui se sont distinguées dans les différentes carrières.* Paris: Les Frères Estienne, 1779.

Riccoboni, Marie-Jeanne Laboras de Mezieres, Mme. *L'Abeille,* in *Oeuvres com-plètes de Mme Riccoboni.* Vol. 1. Paris: Volland, 1786.

Rigal, Mme. *Discours prononcé par Mme Rigal dans une assemblée de femmes artistes et orfèvres, tenue le 20 septembre, pour délibérer sur une contribu-tion volontaire.* Paris, 1789.

Robert, Louise-Félicité Guinement de Keralio, dame. *Adresse aux femmes de Montauban.* N.p., 1790.

_____. *Extrait des délibérations de la Société fraternelle des deux sexes, séanté aux Jacobins . . . du 4 décembre de l'an III.* N.p., n.d.

Robert, Marie-Anne de Roumier, Mme de. *Voyage de Milord Céton dans les sept planètes ou le nouveau mentor.* 2 vols. Paris: rue Serpente, 1782–1787.

Robespierre, Maximilien. *Oeuvres complètes de Maximilien Robespierre.* Paris: Aux bureaux de la Revue historique de la Révolution Française, 1910–1913.

_____. *Pièces trouvées dans les papiers de Robespierre et complices.* Brumaire, year III.

Roland de la Platière, Marie-Jeanne Phlipon, dame. *Mémoires de Mme Roland.* Paris: Baudoin fils, 1820.

Rousseau, Charles-Louis. *Essai sur l'éducation et l'existence civile et politique des femmes, dans la constitution française.* Paris: Imprimerie de Girouard, n.d.

Rousseau, Jean-Jacques. *Oeuvres complètes de J.-J. Rousseau.* Paris: Chez P. Dupont, 1824.

Roussel, Pierre. *De la Femme, considérée au physique et au moral.* 2 vols. Paris: 1788–1789.

_____. *Système physique et moral de la femme ou Tableau philosophique de la constitution de l'état organique, du tempérament, des moeurs et des fonc-tions propres au sexe.* Paris: Vincent, 1775.

_____. *Le Château des Tuileries.* Paris: Lerouge, 1802.

Roux, Jacques. *Discours prononcé dans l'Eglise des cordeliers le 19 avril dernier, par J. Roux, qui vient d'être assasiné par dix-huit aristocrates.* Paris: Vᵛᵉ Petit, 1792.

Sade, Marquis de. *The Marquis de Sade: The Complete Justine, Philosophy in the Bedroom, and Other Writings.* Translated by Richard Seaver and Austryn Wainhouse. New York: Grove Press, 1965.

Saint-Just, Louis-Antoine. *Esprit de la révolution et de la constitution française.* N.p., 1791.

_____. *Fragments sur les institutions républicaines 1793–1794.* Paris: Techener, 1831.

Saint-Lambert, Jean Francois. *L'Analyse de l'homme et de la femme*. Vol. I, in *Oeuvres philosophiques de Saint-Lambert*. Paris: chez H. Agasse, year IX.

Saint-Pierre, Jacques-Henri-Bernardin de. *Discours sur cette question: Comment l'éducation des femmes pourrait contribuer à rendre les hommes meilleurs* in *Oeuvres complètes de Saint-Pierre*. Paris: Méquignon-Marvin, 1818.

————. *Etudes de la Nature*. Paris: P.-F. Didot le jeune, 1792.

————. *Paul et Virginie*. Paris: M. Ardant, 1855.

————. "Lettre à Mme Dupin sur les femmes," in Gaston Villeneurve-Guibert, ed., *Le Portefeuille de Mme Dupin*. Paris: Calmann Lévy, 1884.

Saint-Ursin, P.-J. Marie de. *L'Ami des femmes, ou Lettre d'un medecin, concernant l'influence de l'habillement des femmes sur leurs moeurs et leur santé*. Paris: Barba, 1805.

Salm-Reifferschield-Dyck, Constance-Marie de Théis, Mme Pipelet de Leury, then princesse de. *Epître aux femmes*. Paris: Desenne, 1797.

————. *Rapport sur un ouvrage du C^{en} Théremin, intitulé: De la condition des femmes dans une République, par Constance D. T. Pipelet*. Paris: Imprimerie de Gille, year VIII.

————. *Sur les femmes politiques* (1817) in *Oeuvres complètes*. Paris: Firmin-Didot frères, 1842.

Sédillez, M. L. E. *Du divorce et la répudiation. Opinion et projet de Décret*. 9 September 1792.

[Séguier, Ant.-Louis]. *Façon de voir d'une bonne vieille qui ne radote pas encore*. N.p., n.d.

Ségur, Vicomte Alexandre de. *Les Femmes: Leur condition, leurs moeurs et leur influence dans l'ordre social chez les différents peuples*. 3 vols. Paris: Treuttel & Wurtz, year XI.

Senac de Meilhan, Gabriel. *Du gouvernement, des moeurs et des conditions en France avant la Révolution avec le caractère des principaux personnages du règne de Louis XVI*. Hambourg: B. G. Hoffmann, 1795.

————. *Portraits et caractères des personnages distingués de la fin du XVIII siècle* Paris: J-G Dentu, 1813.

Siméon. *Discours sur le titre X du livre III du Code civil, intitulé: Du contrat de mariage et des droits respectifs des époux*, séance du 20 pluviôse, year XII.

Talleyrand, Charles-Maurice de. *Rapport sur l'instruction publique, fait au nom du Comité de constitution, à l'assemblée nationale*. Paris: Imprimerie Nationale, 1791.

Théremin, Charles-Guillaume. *De la Condition des femmes dans les républiques*. Paris: Laran, year VII.

Théroigne de Méricourt, Anne-Josèph Terwagne, dite. *Aux 48 Sections*. Paris: Imprimerie de F. Dufart, n.d.

————. *Les Confessions de Théroigne de Méricourt; extrait du procès-verbal inédit qui fut dressé à Koufstein*. P. Westhausser, 1892.

"Théroigne de Méricourt." *Théroigne de Méricourt, la jolie Liégeoise; correspondence publiée par le Vte de V... Y...*, 2 vols. [apocryphal; by Vte de Varicléry]. Paris: Allardin, 1836.

Thomas, Antoine-Léonard. *Essai sur le caractère, les moeurs et l'esprit des femmes dans les différents siècles* in *Oeuvres complètes de Thomas*. Vol. 4. Paris: Desessarts, year X.

Toselli, Benedetto. *Apologie des femmes ou Vérités qui font triompher le beau sexe*. Turin: Soffietti, 1798.

Turgot, Anne-R.-J. "Lettre à Mme de Grafigny sur les lettres Péruviennes" (1751), in *Oeuvres de M. Turgot*. Vol. 9. Paris: Delance, 1810.

[Vaines, Jean de]. *Lettres de la comtesse de . . . au chevalier de . . . .* N.p., n.d.

Villette, Charles-Michel, Marquis de. *Mes Cahiers*. Senlis, 1789.

Voltaire. *Oeuvres complètes de Voltaire*. Paris: Garnier frères, Libraires-Editeurs, 1883.

Williams, David. *Observations sur la dernière constitution de la France avec des vues pour la formation de la nouvelle constitution*. Paris: Imprimerie du Cercle Social, year II.

Wollstonecraft, Mary (Godwin). *A Vindication of the Rights of Women*, 3rd ed. London: J. Johnson, 1796.

b. *Works with no known author*

Adresse au beau sexe, relativement à la révolution présent, par M.L.C.D.V. N.p., 1790.

Adresse aux bonnes citoyennes, par la Société des Amis de la Constitution. Limoges: Imprimerie de la Société des Amis de la Constitution, n.d.

Adresse aux dames parisiennes. Le Voyage de Saint-Cloud, ou le Service du bout de l'an. Paris: Imprimerie de Jean Leguen, 1790.

Adresse des Dames de la Halle, à l'assemblée nationale, séance 27 août 1791. Paris: Imprimerie Nationale.

Arrêté des demoiselles du Palais-Royal conféderées pour le bien de leur chose publique. N.p., n.d.

L'Art de rendre les ménages heureux. Paris: Imprimerie de l'Assemblée Nationale, 1789.

Assemblée de tous les bâtards du royaume, avec leur demande à l'Assemblée Nationale. N.p., 1789.

Des avantages attachés à la clôture des femmes et des inconvéniens inséparables de leur liberté. Paris: chez A. Lanoe, 1816.

L'Avis aux dames. N.p., n.d.

Avis important d'une Dame des Halles, pour la diminution des vivres. Paris: Lacloye, n.d.

Avis intéressant concernant les jolies filles à marier ou de l'Abus des dots dans le mariage. Paris: Imprimerie de Momoro, 1789.

Cahier des doléances et réclamations des femmes, par Mme B... B.... N.p., 1789.

Cahier des plaintes et doléances des Dames de la Halle et des marchés de Paris, rédigé au grand salon des Porcherons, le premier dimanche de mai, pour être présenté à MM les Etats-Généraux. N.p., 1789.

Cahier des représentations et doléances du beau sexe au moment de la tenue des états généraux. N.p., n.d.

Cahier des plaintes et doléances des Dames de la Halle et des marches de Paris. N.p., 1789.

Cahiers des voeux et doléances de la communauté des Marchandes de Modes, Plumassières, Fleuristes de Paris. N.p., n.d.

C'est foutu, le commerce ne va pas. Paris: Imprimerie de la petite Rosalie au
    Palais Royal, 1790.
Compliment des Dames Poissardes à leurs frères du Tiers Etat. N.p., n.d.
*Les concitoyennes, ou Arrêté des Dames composant l'ordre de la vrae Noblesse de
    Brest en Bretagne, du samedi 24 janvier 1789.* N.p.
De l'influence des femmes dans l'ordre civil et politique. à Eleuthéropolis, 1789.
Declaration des droits des citoyennes du Palais-Royal. N.p., n.d.
*Déliberations et protestations de l'assemblée des honnêtes citoyennes compromises
    dans le procès-verbal de celle de l'order le plus nombreux du royaume.*
    N.p., 1789.
Les Demoiselles du Palais-Royal aux Etats-Généraux. N.p., 1789.
*Detail des cérémonies qui doivent avoir lieu pour le Fédération du 10 août 1793, au
    Champ-de-mars, et sur l'autel de la patrie, secret de la Convention
    Nationale qui en ordonne l'envoi aux Départements et aux Armées.*
    Imprimerie de Guilhemat.
*Discours prononcé à la société des Citoyennes Républicaines-Révolutionnaires par
    les citoyennes de la Section des Droits de l'homme.* N.p., 1793.
Le Divorce, par le meilleur ami des femmes, suivi d'une adresse au clergé. Paris:
    Chez Gueffier le jeune, 1790.
*Doléances particulières des Marchandes Bouquetières, Fleuristes Chapelières en
    Fleurs de la Ville et des Faubourgs de Paris.* N.p., n.d.
l'Enrolement des dames citoyennes pour faire la guerre aux ennemis des français.
    Paris: Imprimerie de L. Jorry, n.d.
La Femme patriote, ou le Gros Bons-Sens. N.p., n.d.
Les femmes françaises à la Convention Nationale. N.p., July 1795.
Les femmes françaises à la Nation. N.p., July 1795.
*Les Femmes, la toilette et le jardin des Tuileries; avec des anecdotes pour servir de
    préservatif aux étrangers.* Paris: Imprimerie Poulet, n.d.
Les Femmes telles qu'elles sont. Paris: Tiger, 1804.
Les Femmes, ou les aveux d'un vieillard. Paris: Au magasin des pièces de théâtre,
    year IX.
*Les Femmes traitées comme elles le méritent ou le beau-sexe à Long Champs, par
    Mme Louise de P***.* Paris: Chez Taignon, n.d.
Les Filles mariées dans la ci-devant province de Normandie, au corps législatif.
    N.p., n.d.
La Galerie des Etats Généraux. N.p., 1789.
*Grande Confédération des citoyennes actives jacobines, pour n'épouser aucun Aris-
    tocrate. Extrait des registres des Amis de la Constitution.* N.p., n.d.
*Grande et Horrible Conspiration des demoiselles du Palais-Royal, contre les droits
    de l'homme.* Imprimerie Girard, n.d.
*Hommage rendu aux dames françaises sur leur patriotisme pour accélérer la fête
    civique du 14 juillet 1790.* Paris: Imprimerie de Valleyre, n.d.
*Il est temps de donner aux époux qui ne peuvent vivre ensemble la liberté de former
    de nouveaux liens.* Paris: Imprimerie de Gueffier, n.d.
Invitation aux dames françaises. N.p., n.d.
Lettre de ces dames à M Necker suivie de Doléances très-graves. N.p., n.d.
*Lettres d'une citoyenne à son amie, sur les avantages que procurerait à la nation le
    patriotisme des dames.* Grenoble and Paris: Vve Lambert, 1789.
Liste des citoyennes, femmes ou filles d'Artistes, qui ont fait hommage de leur

bijoux à l'Assemblée Nationale, le lundi 7 septembre 1789, à titre de contribution volontaire destinée à l'acquittement de la Dette publique. Versailles: Imprimerie Royale, 1789.

Mémoire sur le divorce. N.p., n.d.

Motion des Dames à l'assemblée nationale, sur la sanction Royale. N.p., n.d.

Motions adressées à l'Assemblée Nationale en faveur du sexe. Paris: Imprimerie de la Vve Delaquette, 1789.

Nouvelle Assemblée des Notables cocus du Royaume, en présence des favoris de leurs épouses (1er juilet). Paris: Imprimerie de Sylphe, 1790.

Nouvelle Proclamation pour lever et enrôler dans toute l'étendue de la République 300,000 filles et femmes pour aller aux frontières. Paris: Imprimerie de P. Provost, n.d.

Observations sur le divorce. Paris: Imprimerie Nationale, 1790.

Offre généreuse des dames françaises du Tiers Etat ou moyen de Rétablir les finances en 24 heures. N.p., August 1789.

Opuscule sur les Maximes du nouveau droit française. Paris: Rousseau, year V.

Petit Commentaire sur le titre de la petite brochure: Petit traité de l'amour des femmes pour les sots. à Bagatelle, 1788.

Pétition des citoyennes de Nantes à la Convention Nationale. N.p., n.d.

Pétition des 2100 filles du Palais-Royal à l'Assemblée Nationale. Paris: Vve Macart, 1790.

Pétition des Citoyennes Républicaines Révolutionnaires lue à la Barre de la Convention Nationale. Paris: Imprimerie de l'Egalité, n.d.

Pétition des femmes du tiers état au Roi. N.p., 1 January 1789.

Pétition sur les effets des moeurs des épouses dissolues. Paris: Imprimerie du Lycee des Arts, n.d.

Procès-verbal et protestations de l'assemblée de l'ordre le plus nombreux du royaume, les C... [cocu]. Paris: 1787.

Protestation des dames françaises contra la tenue des Etats prétendus généraux, convoqués à Versailles pour le 27 avril 1789. N.p., n.d.

Quelques Principes. Paris: De l'imprimerie de Demonville, n.d.

Réclamation de toutes les Poissardes avec un petit mot à la Gloire de Notre Bonne Duchesse l'Orleans. Paris: P. Emsly, n.d.

Remontrances, plaintes et doléances des dames françaises, à l'occasion de l'assemblée des Etats Généraux, par M.L.P.P.D. St. L. N.p., 25 March 1789.

Réponse à M. de B***, auteur de la liste jaune des C. de Paris, par la Ctesse de R.***. N.p., n.d.

Réponse des femmes de Paris au cahier de l'ordre le plus nombreux du Royaume. Paris: 1789.

Requête des dames à l'Assemblée Nationale. N.p., n.d.

Requête des femmes, pour leur admission aux états généraux, à MM composant l'assemblée des notables. N.p., n.d.

Ressource qui reste aux demoiselles du Palais Royal, en suite de la réponse des Etats Généraux à leur requête. Paris: Imprimerie de Grange, 1789.

Second Procès-verbal de l'assemblée de l'ordre le plus nombreux du royaume, tenue à la plaine de Longs-Boyaux. à Concornibus, Imprimerie Kornemanique, 1789.

Du sort actuel des Femmes. Paris: Imprimerie du cercle social, 1792.

Tout le monde s'en fout, et moi, je chante. N.p., n.d.
Les Très Humbles Remontrances des femmes françaises. Imprimerie Galante, 1788.
Très Sérieuses Remontrances des filles du Palais-Royal et lieux circonvoisins à messieurs les nobles. Paris: 1788.
L'Unique remède aux maux de l'Etat, ou Mémoire adressé aux états généraux. N.p., 1789.
La Vieille Bonne Femme de 102 ans, soeur du curé de 97 ans à Messieurs les Etats Généraux. N.p., 1789.

B. SELECTED SECONDARY WORKS

1. Journals

Abray, Jane. Feminism in the French Revolution. *The American Historical Review*, 80, No. 1 (February 1975): 43–62.
Un Arrêté féministe du Comité de Salut Public en l'an III. *Révolution française*, 60 (1911): 266.
Ascoli, George. Essai sur l'histoire des idées féministes en France du XVIᵉ siècle à la Révolution. *Revue de synthèse historique*, 13 (1906): 25–57, 161–184.
Aulard, Alphonse. Féminisme pendant la Révolution française. *Revue bleue,* 4th ser., 9 (1898): 362–366.
Darrow, Margaret. Popular Concepts of Marital Choice in Eighteenth-Century France. *Journal of Social History*, 19, No. 2 (1986): 26–72.
Hufton, Olwen. Women and the Family Economy in Eighteenth-Century France. *French Historical Studies*, 9, No. 1 (Spring, 1975): 1–23.
_____. Women in Revolution, 1789–1796. *Past and Present*, 53 (1971): 90–108.
_____. Women without Men: Widows and Spinsters in Britain and France in the Eighteenth Century. *Journal of Family History*, (Winter, 1984): 355–376.
Humphreys, A. R. The Rights of Women in the Age of Reason. *Modern Language Review*, 41 (1946): 257–263.
Louges, Carolyn C. Noblesse, Domesticity and Social Reform: the Education of Girls by Fenelon and Saint-Cyr. *History of Education Quarterly*, 14, No. 1 (1974): 87–113.
McLaren, Argus. Some Secular Attitudes toward Sexual Behavior in France: 1760–1860. *French Historical Studies*, 8, No. 4 (1975): 604–625.
Phillips, Roderick. Women's Emancipation, the Family, and Social Change in Eighteenth-Century France. *Journal of Social History*, 12, No. 4 (Summer 1979): 553–568.
Punter, D. 1789: The Sex of Revolution. *Criticism*, 24 (Summer 1982): 201–217.
Shorter. Female Emancipation, Birth Control and Fertility in European History. *American Historical Review*, 78 (1973): 605–640.
Soboul, Albert. Sur l'Activité militante des femmes dans les sections parisiennes en l'an II. *Bulletin d'histoire économique et sociale de la Révolution Française* (1979): 15–26.

2. Books

Abensour, Leon. *La Femme et le féminisme avant la Révolution.* Paris: E. Leroux, 1923.

Angenot, Marc. *Les Champions des femmes: examen du discours sur la supériorité des femmes, 1400–1800.* Montréal: Presses de l'Université du Québec, 1977.

Beauvoir, Simone de. *Le Deuxième Sexe.* 2 vols. Paris: Gallimard, 1949.

Berkin, Carol, and Lovett, Clara, eds. *Women, War, and Revolution.* New York: Holmes and Meier, 1980.

Bloch, J. H., ed. *Women and Society in Eighteenth-Century France: Essays in Honor of John Stephenson Spink.* London: Athlone Press, 1979.

Bourdin, Isabelle. *Les Sociétés populaires à Paris pendant la Révolution.* Paris: Librairie du Recueil Sirey, 1937.

Bouvier, Jeanne. *Les Femmes pendant la Révolution.* Paris: E. Figuiere, 1931.

Branca, Patricia. *Women in Europe Since 1750.* New York: St. Martin's Press, 1978.

Bridenthal, R., and Koonz, C. *Becoming Visible: Women in European History.* Boston: Houghton Mifflin, 1977.

Cerati, Marie. *Le Club de citoyennes républicaines révolutionnaires.* Paris: Editions sociales, 1966.

Charrier, Edmée. *L'Evolution intellectuelle féminine.* Paris: Albert Mechelinck, 1931.

Dessens, Alfred. *Revendications des droits de la femme pendant la Révolution.* Toulouse: Imprimerie Ch. Marqués, 1905.

Duhet, Paul-Marie. *Les Femmes et la Révolution, 1789–1794.* Paris: Julliard, 1971.

Duray, A. *L'Instruction publique et la Révolution.* Paris: Hachette, 1882.

Fauchery, Pierre. *La Destinée féminine dans le roman européen du 18ᵉ siècle (1713–1807).* Paris: Colin, 1972.

Fritz, Paul, and Morton, Richard (eds.). *Women in the Eighteenth Century and Other Essays.* Toronto: Hakket, 1976.

Garaud, Marcel, and Szrumkiewicz, Romuald. *La Révolution française et la famille.* Paris: Presses universitaires de France, 1978.

Goncourt, Edmond de. *La Femme au dix-huitième siècle.* Paris: Charpentier, 1877.

Hays, H. R. *The Dangerous Sex: The Myth of Feminine Evil.* New York: G. P. Putnam's Sons, 1964.

Hoffmann, Paul. *La Femme dans le pensée des lumières.* Paris, 1977.

Hufton, Olwen. *The Poor of Eighteenth-Century France.* London: Oxford University Press, 1974.

Hughes, Peter, and Williams, David (eds.). *The Varied Pattern: Studies in the Eighteenth Century.* Toronto, 1971.

Hunt, David. *Parents and Children in History: The Psychology of Family Life in Early Modern France.* 1970.

Hyslop, Beatrice Fry. *French Nationalism in 1789 According to the General Cahiers.* New York: Columbia University Press, 1934.

———. *A Guide to the General Cahiers of 1789.* New York: Columbia University Press, 1936.

Jacob, Eva, ed. *Women and Society in Eighteenth-Century France*. London: Athlone, 1979.

Johnson, Douglas. *French Society and the Revolution*. New York: Cambridge University Press, 1976.

Joran, Théodore. *Les Féministes avant le féminisme*. Paris: Gabriel Beauchesne et fils, 1935.

Kaplow, Jeffrey. *The Names of Kings: The Parisian Laboring Poor in the Eighteenth Century*. New York: Basic Books, 1972.

Larcher, L. J., and Martin, P. J. *Les Femmes peintes par elles-même*. Brussels, 1858.

Lee, Vera. *The Reign of Women in Eighteenth-Century France*. Cambridge: Schenkman Publishing Co., 1975.

Lucas, C., and Lewis, G., eds. *Beyond the Terror*. Cambridge: Cambridge University Press, 1983.

Luppé, Alberte, Comte de. *Les Jeunes Filles dans l'aristocratie et la bourgeoisie à la fin du dix-huitième siècle*. Paris: Champion, 1924.

Martin, Olivier. *La Crise du mariage pendant la Révolution*. Paris: A. Rousseau, 1901.

Noiset, L. *Robespierre et les femmes*. Paris: Nilsson, 1932.

Outhwaite, R. B. *Marriage and Society: Studies in the Social History of Marriage*. London: Europa, 1981.

Proceedings of the Consortium on Revolutionary Europe, 1980, 1982, 1983.

Proceedings of the Annual Meetings of the Western Society for French History, 1980, 1982, 1984. Lawrence, KS: University of Kansas.

Reynier, G. *La Femme au XVIIe siècle*. Paris: 1933.

Rose, R. B. *The Enragés: Socialists of the French Revolution*. Melbourne: 1965.

Rude, George. *The Crowd in the French Revolution*. Oxford, 1967.

Segalen, Martine. *Mari et femme dans la société paysanne*. Paris: Flammarion, 1980.

Spencer, Samia, ed. *French Women and the Age of Enlightenment*. Bloomington, IN: Indiana University Press, 1984.

Sullerot, Evelyne. *Histoire de la presse féminine des origines à 1848*. Paris: A. Colin, 1966.

Traer, James F. *Marriage and the Family in Eighteenth-Century France*. Ithaca: Cornell University Press, 1980.

Turgéon, Charles. *Féminisme français*. 2 vols. Paris: L. Larose.

Index

About the Author

CANDICE E. PROCTOR has taught at the University of Idaho and at Midwestern State University. She spent a year in France collecting the material for this book, and currently lives in Australia.